Expert Reviews and Commentaries About *Three Key Years*:

"The national debate about supporting children in their first years of life would be far better informed if people who are concerned about that topic would read this book."

— JAMES J. HECKMAN, PH.D.
American economist and Nobel Laureate; Professor of economics, University of Chicago
Author of multiple reports, papers and books on early childhood brain development economic issues

"How should society respond to the science of early brain development? George Halvorson has written a compelling and passionate argument for the ways society should invest in the critical first three years.

His analysis ranges from families and parents to the educational system to technology and even the prison system — in each case bringing us back to the foundations and opportunities created by development in the early years of life for each child.

The challenges he presents are matched by the urgency of the need."

— ROSS A. THOMPSON, PH.D.
Distinguished Professor Laureate, University of California, Davis
National expert on Toxic Stress Syndrome Causation, Prevention and Treatment

"What happens during the first three years of life is the most important time in determining how our children's brains grow and develop.

This extraordinary book describes a few simple things parents can do during this time that can make a profound improvement throughout their child's life.

Should be required reading for all parents."

— DEAN ORNISH, M.D.
tive Medicine Research Institute
·sity of California, San Francisco"

D1004512

"Three Key Years *is a perspective changing book. It gives us an important new reality and understanding. Reading this book will have an impact on every child I come in contact with, directly and indirectly! Together we can change the lives of every child by using our own "inner-child" to TALK, READ, PLAY and SING.*

Three Key Years *should be required reading for every community leader, activist, organizer and community member. This will make a difference in the lives and livelihoods of your community.*

As a community developer, we look for impact and we look for value. Here it is. Read it! Enjoy!

What a great gift of Love!

Thank you for this book!"

— MICHAEL A. GOZE
CEO, The American Indian Community Development Corporation

"*In this extremely useful book, George Halvorson applied extraordinary knowledge and wisdom to ensuring that children gain the ability to develop and thrive towards and throughout adulthood.*

Three Key Years *teaches us that the very first years of life are the essential building blocks to a successful life.*

This is a must-read book for parents, family members, and anyone interested in securing productive, thoughtful, and happy future generations of Americans."

— RON POLLACK
Executive director, Families USA
Health Care Reform Activist and Community Leader

"We need to support our children in their development in the first years of life. We need to help every child. We also need to help every family.

Three Key Years gives us clear pathways we can use to help our communities and our families help our children.

I strongly recommend that people who are concerned about the future of our children in every community read this book."

— MARCUS BRIGHT PH.D.
Executive director, Education for a Better America
Education leader, National Action Network (NAN)

"George Halvorson has taken a deep and long standing awareness, concern and knowledge about health care disparities and health care inequity, and applied that knowledge to early brain development for children — one of the most pressing issues of our time.

He unlocks patterns and he identifies trends in data that we all need to understand and he makes concrete suggestions for solutions that, if enacted, will change the life trajectories of millions of American children."

— SUSAN TRUE
Director of education strategy and ventures, Kenneth Rainin Foundation
Former executive director, First 5 California, Santa Cruz County

"In an era of political gridlock and polarized education discourse, we spend most of our time explaining what we can't do ... and why.

In Three Key Years, *Halvorson suggests a compelling alternative: that we collectively focus our energies on functionally supporting children's development from the very beginning of their lives."*

— CONOR P. WILLIAMS, PH.D.
Senior researcher, Early Education Initiative, New America Foundation
Founder, Dual Language Learners National Work Group New America, Education Policy Program

"The experiences children have during their first few years profoundly impacts the way their brains form and develop with consequences that play out over future decades.

Each child has many possible futures. We can create the best ones with some extra early attention. Otherwise, we miss a big chance and we pay the consequences.

Compelling new evidence of this reality is emerging from neuroscience, child development, economics and other fields.

In this highly useful and functional book, George Halvorson offers practical blueprints for how we can, in our daily lives as parents, grandparents, and organizational leaders, create bright futures for the children we love."

— AARON J. SOJOURNER, PH.D.
Professor of economics, Carlson School of Management, University of Minnesota

"The goal of an affordable national health system begins with healthy people, which focuses each of us on the first three years of life.

Three Key Years *explains from an unexpected but very clear public health perspective why we need to make helping all children from all groups in those first years a national priority.*

It also explains why leaders from all groups should seize the opportunity to help their own group's children improve their success levels in life, by getting the right levels of brain stimulation and brain exercise in those first key years.

Anyone concerned about the future of our children in America should read and understand this book."

— SENATOR DAVID DURENBERGER
U.S. Senate (R/MN) 1978 to 1995
Chairman, National Institute of Health Policy (NIHP)

Three Key Years

by George C. Halvorson

Other Books by George C. Halvorson (partial list)

Epidemic of Care

Strong Medicine

Ending Racial, Ethnic and Cultural Disparities in American Health Care

Primal Pathways

Cusp of Chaos

The Art of InterGroupPeace

Health Care Will Not Reform Itself

Don't Let Health Care Bankrupt America

KP Inside

Peace In Our Time

ISBN 978-0-9964994-0-8

Dedication

This book is dedicated to all the children of America who did not get the key support needed by each child in those key months and years of their life — and it is dedicated to all of the people who are working to make sure that does not happen to the children who are being born now.

Every child we save is a child we save.

Let's save every child.

Acknowledgments

Thank you to Susan True, John August, Camille Maben, Dr. Ross Thompson, Dr. Nadine Burke-Harris, Ron Pollack, Ray Baxter, Jim Wunderman, Ann O'Leary, Jean Bradford, Linda Halvorson, Kelli Johnson, and Gina Halvorson for your thoughts, wisdom, guidance, direction, feedback, and support for this book. It is deeply appreciated.

This is a better book because of your input.

Contents

Each Child We Save Is a Child We Save

THREE KEY YEARS.

Too many people do not know that the first three years of life are the key and most important years when brains develop in our children.

Biologically, those are the years where we make the overwhelming majority of the neuron connections in our brains — and those are the years when each brain goes through the processes that will determine both the physical structure and infrastructure of the brain, and the key future capabilities of each brain.[1]

If we don't get those first three years right for each child, we handicap children for life — relative to the structure, function, and capability of each child's brain.

The basic biological truth is that we each build the basic strength levels of our brains in those first years of our lives. We all then build the wisdom and the knowledge base that we each have in our brains through multiple levels of learning processes that extend through our lifetimes.

But we build our wisdom, our judgment, and our personal knowledge in those later years on the physical footings, the functional foundation, and the basic underpinnings that we create for each brain in those first three key years of life.

Exercise is key.

Brains need exercise in those first years to develop at the best and highest levels.[2]

Brains that get direct exercise in those years actually are physically different than unexercised brains. The exercised brains are each clearly, directly, and individually strengthened by that exercise. It is an amazingly simple and direct process.

If we do not exercise each brain well in those years, the brains without exercise have fewer internal connections and those brains have fewer brain cells available to help us think. Physical exercise makes physical muscles bigger and stronger and — in a very similar process — mental exercise makes our brains grow bigger and stronger.

The cutoff for that process is not absolute, but an extremely important portion of our biological brain development process for each of us is overwhelmingly focused on those first three years.

If we miss those first key years of great brain plasticity and brain growth, we can still have some positive impact on our brain capacity after that point, but to a significantly smaller degree, and with significantly more difficulty than the opportunity that exists in those first years.

We can and should continue to improve each child's brain functioning after those first key years, but the process is both biologically and economically more costly and more difficult after that time.

Learning Does Not Begin at School

Brain science is on the cusp of a golden age. We now understand some key brain development issues for children in a way that we did not understand them before. People used to think that learning started for children when the children arrived at school.[3]

That was a completely wrong and totally inaccurate belief.

It could not be more wrong. That belief is dangerously and dysfunctionally wrong.

Learning starts at birth. Some learning starts just prior to birth, but the period of time immediately after birth is extremely important. The first three months of life are times when the baby's brains are structured in ways that affect long time emotional security and stability for each child. Children who feel secure and responded to in the first three months tend to have different interaction patterns as early as year one that sometimes last for many years.

The entire first year of life is an extremely important time of learning and brain development for each child. Children who have their brains exercised through adult interactions in that time period benefit significantly from those interactions.

Years two and three are extremely important, as well. Those are times of great biological connectivity for all babies and all children.

The process is the same for children from every group, ethnicity, race, and culture. Those first three years are biologically the times when all babies from all groups build key-capacity in their brains.[4]

Learning in those first key years strengthens brains in ways that create life long impact. Children who learn the most in those first years of life, and the children whose brains are exercised well and often in those first key years, have benefits from those first years that continue for their entire lives.

Children who get the least brain exercise in those early years far too often have challenges and difficulties that also continue for their entire lives.

Children with the least brain exercise in those first three years are less likely to read in school. Children whose brains are not exercised in those key areas are much more likely to have health problems, learning problems, and behavior problems.

Those children are much more likely to drop out of school — and those children are far more likely to end up in jail. The percentage of children who have very small vocabularies in kindergarten — who end up in jail — is a painful and shocking number.[4]

We Can Create Positive Life Trajectories In Those Key Years

We now know what that set of brain development problems, issues, and opportunities is for each child. We now know what can help create positive life trajectories for children based on those first three years of life.

We now also know what can create negative, dysfunctional, and damaging life trajectories for our children — life paths that are also a direct extension of the developmental support that is given or not given to each child in those first three key years of life.

We need to save children. All children. Now that we know about the importance of brain development processes in those first months and years, we owe it to all children to give each child the support in those first months and years that will make life better, and that will make thought processes stronger for each child.

The interactions that help children are not complicated. We need to talk, read, play, interact, and sing to our children at that time of high opportunity learning. We know that the children who have adults talking to them, interacting directly with them, and reading to them in those key months and years have many more neuron connections made in their brains.

We now know that very basic interactions with parents and with other caring adults have an almost magical ability to strengthen the basic biological connections happening in those key time periods in each child's brain.

Knowledge is power. We need all mothers, all fathers, and all families of newborn children to have the power of knowing the realities, the science, the biology, the basic types of possible brain exercise activities, and the very important consequences of either building — or not building — the brain connectivity levels for their babies and their infants, in those first years of life.[5]

We need all families, all parents and all communities to know the opportunities that exist to create emotional security in their children in the first three months of life, and we need all parents, families, and communities to understand the opportunities that exist to create learning-capacity strength and greater learning ability levels in their children in the first three years of life.

We very much need our governmental leaders, our group leaders, and our educational-system leaders to understand that set of issues — so we can make informed decisions at multiple levels in multiple settings to support strengthening the brains of all children in those key months and years, when those biological processes are happening for each child.

The Experience Is Specific to Each Child

This process happens one child at a time. It happens individually and it happens directly for each child.[6]

We need to help each child in that time of opportunity and need. Families and parents can provide that help and support directly to each child, and various other resources can also help in various intentional, functional, and strategic ways to provide the right level of help for each child.

Overall — collectively — our ethical responsibility to each child should require us to figure out how each child can be helped in those key first months and years now that we know that science and now that we know the consequences to each child of not providing that support at that time of opportunity and biological structuring for each child.

The early brain development process that happens for each child creates a very personal set of functional consequences for each child. Each brain develops in the same time frames and each brain develops in those time frames based on its own direct experience during that time.

It is a universal, biological process that affects every child. Every child faces the same biological realities in the same high opportunity time frames.

That same kind of basic physical development process happens in each child's brain. Biology dictates the process. The first three years of life are critical for each of us because that is when that very basic set of purely biological processes happen that give us many of the basic underpinnings that we use for the rest of our lives.

Every Child We Save Is a Child We Save

Because we now know that science to be true, we also now know that we can do important things that will create very real and almost immediate value for

every child. We need to do several crucial and valuable things for each child —
because lives are changed significantly when those key things are done for each
child in those first days and years of life.

That opportunity and functionality exists for each child. As a society, we
need to use that knowledge to help each child succeed, and we need to use that
knowledge to help each child thrive.

Each child we save is a child we save. Each child we save by helping the child
in those key years is individually, personally, and directly saved.

Let's save our children. We can achieve that goal. This book is intended to
provide a set of information about both brain science, and brain development
processes that can help each child to be saved.

The information we now know about those processes can be used to change
many lives in ways that we did not understand until we developed a better
understanding of the basic issues, and the basic and core science and biological
processes that relate to developing brains.

This book is an invitation to change lives. This book is intended to both
make people aware of those opportunities and to point to things we can do as
parents, families, educators, caregivers, and communities to help children lead
better lives.

Use this book and use its basic information in any way that can help make a
difference in the life of an individual child, or in the lives of numbers of children
in any and all of the groups and the communities who are part of your life.

You Can Help a Child Today

This is a very immediate and extremely current set of realities. Children are
being born every day. Each child who is born gives us the opportunity today to
do this process well.

This actually can be a very personal opportunity for you as a reader of this
book to make a difference in the life of a child. You can personally use this

knowledge to change lives. Teaching this information to a relevant parent or to a relevant family can change the life of a child forever.

If you personally teach this information to a parent at the right time who then changes parenting behavior because of this information, that child can literally benefit for life. The differences in life trajectories can be huge when parents have this knowledge. This is incredibly powerful information.

You can also personally identify a child who is in that time of opportunity and need, and you can personally take the time in some way to individually help or support the specific and direct interactions that will make a difference for that child.

Take that opportunity to change a life. Help save a child today. A child who you help to save today — either directly with your own interactions or indirectly by helping relevant people understand those issues — is a child whose life will be different, and whose life will be better because you helped make that difference in key and basic life-pathways a reality for that child.

Now is a good time to save a child. Wherever you are is a good place to make a difference in the life of a newborn child, an infant, a toddler, or a small child. The value you add for each child who has a different life trajectory because of what you did with that knowledge can be huge.

Simply reaching out and teaching those issues to one parent and directly sharing this information with one family in ways that help one newborn or one infant child with better support in those key areas, could change that child's entire life.

How many other things can you do today that will change an entire life and make that life better?

We Owe It to All of Us to Do This Well

Now that we know this science to be real and true, and now that we understand what those processes and key time frames that help each child actually are, we owe it to all of us to make a difference in children's lives.

Knowledge is strength. Deeply important and powerful knowledge creates a clear combination of opportunity, responsibility, and accountability for whoever holds that knowledge.

That particular body of knowledge needs to be both shared and used.

We need all parents to understand those opportunities and those risks for their children. We also need all families to understand those opportunities and those risks for the children in their family.

We need our community groups, schools, and our public officials to also all understand those issues, opportunities, and risks for the children who are relevant to them.

We need our government programs and our health care caregivers to all understand those sets of issues and to all help our children in those key years get the support each child needs.

When we all understand those sets of issues, we have the chance to be creative in multiple problem solving ways at multiple levels to create the support that each child needs. The time for creativity and innovation is now.

Our creativity as individuals and as groups has not been focused on those issues and those opportunities in the past. We need to focus our group and individual creativity on those issues now, and we need innovative people who understand this set of opportunities to figure out a variety of ways to have our children benefit from that knowledge.

When we actually understand a problem, and when we fully understand an opportunity, then we often can figure out a wide variety of creative, innovative, practical, operational and functional ways to take advantage of the opportunity.

Let's trigger group and individual creativity on this issue and let's have a thousand flowers bloom relative to making real improvements in children's lives as a result of that innovation and creativity.

Our children need us to be caring, responsible, accountable, and to be focused on helping each child in that key time of high opportunity and high need for each child.

Let's meet that high level of need. Now that we understand what can be done, let's do what needs to be done to do what needs to be done for every child.

Each child we save is a child we save. Lives matter. We can, in fact, change lives by helping our children in that window of wonderful biological opportunity that is a gift given to each child.

Three Key Years.

Let's not let them be wasted for anyone.

CHAPTER ONE

The Facts Are Painfully Clear and the Opportunities and Dangers Are Obvious

THE FUNCTIONAL REALITY for our early brain exercise impact is painfully clear. The best predictor for which children from all groups will end up in prison by age 18 is the number of words in each child's vocabulary at kindergarten.

Very young children with vocabularies that only contain hundreds of words are far more likely to go to jail than the children who enter kindergarten with thousands of words in their vocabularies. The learning process for each and every child starts at birth — and even the first year of life is a critically important year for each child.

New research shows us that we can see differences in the learning levels of children as early as 18 months — with some children already months behind other children at that age.[3]

We can predict with a very high level of accuracy by age three which children are going to be unable to read — and we know that the children who are reading impaired by the third grade are 40 percent more likely to get pregnant in their teen years, 60 percent more likely to drop out of school, and more than 70 percent more likely to end up in jail.[7]

That is not an insignificant or small-scale problem.

We know that we have more people in jail than any country in the world — two or three times more prisoners per capita than any western country — and we know that more than 60 percent of our prisoners either read poorly or can't read at all.[8-10]

We also know that 85 percent of the school age children who are currently in our juvenile justice system either read poorly or can't read at all.[11] Most of the children in the juvenile justice system today are labeled functionally illiterate by the people who study their literacy levels.

Children who have trouble reading are far more likely to have significant problems with other key areas of their lives. The correlation is obviously not 100 percent, but the data clearly tells us that the children who do not learn to read are far more likely to drop out of school, far more likely to be in trouble with the law, and far more likely to end up in jail.

We also know from relatively new and extremely important biological science that the basic ability levels that are needed to support reading in children happen in the first three years of life. Brain development starts at birth.[1]

We now know that brain exercise for infants and babies in those first years of life gives us stronger brains. Children whose brains are functionally exercised by direct interactions with adults in the first three years of life end up with brains that are better able to learn when each child reaches school.

That difference in learning readiness happens for children because those first three years are the major and most important years for physical brain growth and for brain structure development for each child.

Year one is extremely important. Measurements show us that children who do not get their brains exercised in the first year of life tend to fall behind other children in important ways by the time they are only 18 months old.[3]

Our brain biology is built on having the first three years of life — for every child — be the years when neuron connectivity levels in the brain are established that last a lifetime. If we exercise baby brains, then the neuron connectivity levels in the exercised brains are high. If we don't exercise brains at that point, a natural pruning process happens and we end up with fewer connections in the unexercised brains.

That exercising, building, and structuring process starts in each brain even before birth. Key parts of that process are most intense in our first three years of life. The impact of the brain structuring process begins immediately.

Good research now shows us that even the first weeks of life are relevant, and the first three months of life actually can be very important for the emotional structuring of each brain.

Studies have shown us that the children who are responded to most effectively in the first three months can have higher levels of emotional stability that can sometimes help those children for their entire lives.

Children who feel a sense of security, safety, and direct parental responsiveness in those very first weeks and months can end up with positive emotional grounding levels for their thought processes that can create affirming underpinnings for the child's emotional well being that can last for years.

The appendix to this book has an addendum that contains a description of the opportunities and the risks that exist in those first three months for each child.

The first three months are not as important, however, as the first three years. Every month is important during that three-year time frame for each child. Those first three years are, in their entirety, extremely important years for the biological brain growth processes for all children. Brains who are exercised in those initial three years of life tend to be both bigger and stronger brains.

We need everyone who is concerned about the future of children in this country to clearly recognize and understand the fact that the first three years for each child offer the biological opportunities to significantly support and build the strength of each brain.

Education Does Not Start at Kindergarten

People used to believe that education for each child starts at kindergarten. Those people were wrong. The brain of each child begins a frantic growth and education process as soon as each child is born.

Literally millions and millions of neuron connections are constantly being activated in the brains of 1-, 2-, and 3-year-old babies and infants, and those connections are activated for each child based on the direct and individual learning experiences that happen for each baby and for each child in those few and critical key years.[2]

Unfortunately, we don't have a shared awareness and a shared understanding as a country about either those processes or those time frames. We currently have some very inconsistent behaviors as a nation relative to the experiences of children in that time of opportunity.

We are not currently giving the same level of brain exercise and the same levels of brain growth interactions to all of our children. We actually have significant differences today in the experiences of individual children in our country.

Individual children from various groups in various settings across our society are functionally experiencing very different support levels and very different brain exercise levels in those first years.

We do not have a uniform approach that extends across all families, all groups, all settings, and all children relative to the brain exercises and the learning experiences that exist for each of the very young children in our country today.

Some parents and some families are giving their children extensive and consistent brain-building interactions and high levels of direct and individual support in those first key years today.

That is a very good thing for those children. Those children who do have extensive interactions with adults in those first key years tend to be doing very well on reading skills, on the various standardized tests that children take in grade school and high school, and even on the tests they take as entrance tests for college admissions.

The children who are receiving extensive and consistent brain connectivity exercise levels in those first years of life tend to find learning to be an easier process, and those children are doing consistently and sometimes remarkably well on all of the learning level measurements and tests that we use to track performance and ability for our children.

Unfortunately, that high level of learning activity, and those consistent levels of brain exercise experience are not true for all children in our country in those first key years of life for each child. Significant numbers of our children do not get that daily brain exercise, and too many of our children do not have the daily interactions with adults that build stronger brains.

Far too many of the children who have low and much less consistent levels of early brain exercise in those key years today end up with both lower test scores, and a functional inability to read in those early school years when reading is so important to every child as an anchor for their overall learning processes, and their life long academic opportunities.[12,13]

Far Too Many Children Are Not Getting Early Brain Exercise

The children who have low levels of adult one-to-one interactions of the kinds that exercise brains in those early months and years find themselves very quickly at a disadvantage.[2] It does not take a long time to see the differences between children who have different levels of immediate interaction that builds brains.

Those babies with those low levels of interactions are actually often at an almost immediate disadvantage, and many are literally falling significantly behind by 18 months. That difference between children in experience and learning ability is not a long-term societal problem that plays itself out over decades. Those differences in the initial month and year interactions that happen with children creates a very real problem that has immediate consequences in the first years of life for far too many children.

The infants with low levels in the first 18 months of the kinds of basic adult interactions that build their brain capacity tend to have fallen measurably behind other children by 18 months, and they tend to fall even farther behind by the time they get to kindergarten.

Children who fall far behind by kindergarten generally never catch up relative to those basic learning capabilities. Catching up to at least some degree is not impossible, but the reality is that children with very small vocabularies at age three tend not to be learning ready at age six. The children who fall the most behind at that point tend to never catch up with the children who know many more words at age three and four, and who are learning ready when they get to kindergarten.

That is not a good future for those children. We cannot give up on those children, and we clearly need to help the children who have fallen behind in every way we can. We also very clearly need to do the right things in those first months and first years for all children, so that fewer children fall behind and fewer children face those challenges.

We all need to understand as parents and as families and we all need to understand as a community and as a society exactly what we functionally need to do in the first year, the second year, and the third year for each child to keep children in every group and every setting from falling behind.

The task is doable. The goal of helping children from all groups not fall behind can be achieved. That aspiration to help all children and to close the learning gaps we see today is far from hopeless because we now know how to keep those learning gaps from happening.

We did not understand either that process or those gaps for many years. The new science of brain development teaches us now why those problems exist, and it also teaches us what we need to do to keep them from happening in the future.

The new science of raising our children tells us how to help each of our children. We now know that we can help all children if we take advantage of the science we now understand about the development of children's brains, and if we apply that science to every child.

Keeping children from falling behind, actually, is not complex or difficult. The tools that build brains in babies and infants are basic and they are easy to understand and use.

We now know that baby brains grow stronger when adults talk, read, sing, play and interact directly with each baby. We now know that those basic and seemingly simple interactions between adults and children actually have huge power to strengthen brains.

Those very basic brain-strengthening tools that can close those learning gaps that create problems in so many settings today can be used for children across all groups and all settings. We can talk, read, play and sing in any setting.

The child raising tools that can achieve those gap-closing and brain strengthening goals are relatively simple and they are possible to do almost anywhere. There are no mysteries about what those tools are or about how those processes work.

We now know exactly what kinds of interactions work effectively to exercise baby brains, and we know how to do those specific and explicit interactions for every child. We now know how to support those interactions with children that build strong brains in ways that can be used in almost all settings.[14,15]

Talk, Read, Play, Sing, and Interact to Build Brains

That knowledge is not rocket science, but it can help create rocket scientists. The tools that work to exercise the brains of babies, infants and children are literally to talk, read, play and sing in safe and caring ways to each child. Children's brains are strengthened and billions of neuron connections happen when adults talk, play, read and sing to their children.

That set of activities seems very simple, but those simple interactions can have profound and direct biology based impact on each child. The basic and key tools that work to exercise baby brains work in every setting and they can help children in all groups and settings do well in creating powerful and useful neuron connections in their brains.

One-to-one interactions for each child with a caring adult that involves and includes those basic functions can accomplish brain growth outcomes that can make lives significantly better for each child.

Talk, read, sing, and play can be done almost anywhere. The consequences for each child — both positive and negative — of having or not having those direct interactions with each child last for the entire lifetime of each child. Children who have caring and trusted adults interacting regularly with them, and using those approaches can benefit hugely from those interactions.

The brain exercise process that adds value for each child is almost too basic to believe as a tool with the power it has for each child. Those tools and that impact are independent of economic status, race, ethnicity or culture. It is basic and pure biological science that applies to every child.

Talking to the child, reading to the child, and direct individual interactions with the child from caring adults in those key months and years all serve to exercise each baby brain.

Each and all of those interactions between an adult and a child work to create and solidify extremely important and highly useful basic neuron connections in each child's brain. We need all mothers, fathers, families, and all communities to understand the value and the impact of those basic behaviors so we can build strong neuron connectivity in every brain.

Too Many Children Have No One Interacting with Them

Too many babies today are not getting the stimulation needed to strengthen their brains in those key periods of time.

Too many babies and too many infants have no one talking to them, no one interacting with them, and no one reading to them in ways that exercise their brains in those first years of life when basic and universal brain biology creates benefits at the highest levels from those interactions. Too many children in our country today have low levels of the kinds of adult interactions with them that serve to stimulate and reinforce the neuron connections that make each child's brain strong.

The children who do not have those direct and personal interactions in those first years tend to have very small vocabularies when they get to kindergarten, and they tend to have major problems learning to read.

The interactions with each child that make children "reading ready" and "learning ready" before they get to school do not need to be complex, but they do need to be consistent and they do need to involve direct interactions with each child.

This is a very personal and very individual process. It happens one at a time in the brain of each child. It is a direct, individual, and personal process that happens in those key months and years for each and every child.

Today, some children in our country are getting those levels of direct and individual brain building interactions at a high level. Some children are getting moderate but still very useful levels of positive sets of interactions.

And some children are getting very low levels of those brain-strengthening interactions in those key time frames.

We know from multiple studies that babies in a number of families actually do receive direct and positive interactions from one or more adults today, and the results are that those babies who have high levels of interactions benefit directly from those interactions.

Too many other babies have very low levels of needed interactions in those key months and years, and those children with low levels of interactions tend to fall fairly quickly behind the children who do get that support.[16,17]

Not Sharing That Information with Parents Is a Massive Public Health Failure

We should not blame the parents for those differences in interaction levels. Parents all want their children to do well. But we have not supported that desire by all parents to help their children do well with the actual knowledge base about brain exercise and about neuron connectivity levels that parents need to help their children do well.

We have actually done a terrible job as a country and as a society of sharing that science and teaching those opportunities to all parents.

The vast majority of parents in this country have not been taught that those opportunities exist or that those tools can help their children.

We have not taught that information to all parents in part because too many people in key roles in this country do not know that information. Some of the very best science about brain development is relatively new. Some of the most useful information about those issues and processes hasn't been shared widely with people outside of the research community.

Many educators who really need that information to close the learning gaps in their schools don't understand those lifetime learning processes at this point in time. Even many doctors are unaware of those new learnings about brain development.

We actually have too many relevant caregivers for children who don't know the newest research about brain development time frames or who do not understand how those brain strengthening processes work for the children they care for as patients.

The learning process for our relevant caregivers on those issues has gotten better in the immediate past, as the researchers in multiple settings have been increasingly sharing their learnings with the caregiver teams, and as the American Academy of Pediatrics has begun to make early learning a priority, but much of that sharing of knowledge on these issues, even with caregivers, is very recent.

So blaming parents for not knowing that information and for not acting accordingly would be very unfair. We clearly have not done a good job at any level in sharing that information with parents because too many of the people who should be sharing that information with parents don't know that information themselves.

Even though that is true, that does not excuse our failure as a society to make use of that information and to share it effectively with all relevant parties. It is very much true that the lack of information sharing with our parents, families, and communities about those issues and those opportunities for their children represents a very real and significant failure at a major public health level for the country.

We need to remedy that deficiency and we need to do it quickly because not sharing that needed information with parents is a very clear public health failure that has consequences for far too many children that are significant. Those consequences will continue to damage us as a country at multiple levels for a very long time because too many children will not get the support they need as long as ignorance on those issues exists.

We Are at Risk of Becoming Bi-Polar on Connectivity Levels

We are in danger of becoming a bipolar country on the basic issue of brain functioning. Learning gaps exist and they are widening in too many settings. Attempts to close those gaps have been painfully unsuccessful. That failure is creating intergroup anger in many settings and is not giving the children on the low end of the learning gap the support they need to do well in life.

Both the long-term and short-term consequences of our growing bi-polarity as a country in learning ability and capability can be and will be dysfunctional and damaging to us all at multiple levels.

The children who are blessed today with having a deluge of direct support for their brain connectivity and their brain strengthening functions from the people in their lives in their first years of life are clearly benefiting in significant ways from that support.

The children who are not blessed with sufficient support for their brain connectivity functions in those first years of life, however, tend to be suffering from that interaction deficit. Those children who do not have those sets of interactions at sufficient levels in those first years tend to be situationally handicapped, and those children can be functionally disadvantaged for their entire lives from that lack of interactions and support in that key time frame.[18,19]

The Biology Is the Same for All Races and Ethnicities

Those are not racial issues. Those are not ethnic issues. They are not economic issues. They are clearly and purely biological and physiological process and timing issues. They are highly functional, physically developmental, directly biological timing and directly biological process issues that happen at an individual level for each child.

The differences that exist in those connectivity levels in the brains of children after the age of four, and the learning gaps that result when the children are in school are not based on racial or ethnic groups of any kind. Those gaps that we see today result from the early brain connectivity stimulation that happened for each child from each group in those settings.

The basic physical biology realities and processes, and the basic functional brain development time frames are the same for all children from all groups — and the differences that seem to exist between groups today actually relate directly back to the differences in those interaction levels for each child.

We need to understand that basic biology and we need to understand those universal brain strengthening time frames in order to understand why we have significant learning differences in groups of children from age four on through school and through life.

All children from all groups grow and reinforce their basic brain connections in that same exact first three years of life time frame. The learning gaps that appear after that point are based on the way those specific processes affected each child in those specific time frames.

All children from all groups who have their brains exercised in those first key years build stronger brains. The children who do not get that exercise in those years do not have the growth in neuron connectivity that is created by that exercise.[18-20]

All Groups of People Have High Performers Whose Brains Get That Early Exercise

All groups of people clearly have people today whose brains — very obviously — got that needed exercise at a personal level when that exercise process was most valuable and most deeply needed for them as a child.

Every group of people has many high performing and highly intelligent people today. Every group of people has high achievers, and every group has highly talented learners and doers. That is true because there are people from every group who got the support they needed in those key years.

There are clearly people in every group who had people interacting with them, talking to them, and responding in very direct, supportive and personal ways to them in those key months and years.

And every group of people also has people with lower skill levels — people who face major life challenges and difficulties at multiple levels of functionality — who did not get that same level of brain exercise, and who did not have those same sets of interactions in those key years.

The causality linking difference between the high performers and the people from all groups who face challenges, is the early brain exercise and the early brain connection support levels that happened in those first key years for each child — not the ethnicity or the race of the child.

All children from all groups, who do not get that direct brain growth exercise in those first key years, have a negative and unfortunate biological consequence in their brains of not getting the exercise.

The biology is universal. Those children who have lower brain exercise levels in those first key years end up with fewer neuron connections in their brains. Those brains with lower levels of exercise in those first years have fewer neuron connections, and people with that low level of early support tend to face significant lifelong challenges as a functional result of that biological reality.

It is important for everyone to understand that brain-strengthening processes and issues for each child are biological and universal — not racial, ethnic or cultural. Children from all groups make great brain connections with the right support, and children from all groups do equally poorly with inadequate support.

To close the learning gaps and prevent them from happening, we need everyone to understand that the differences we see in school related abilities and in reading readiness levels in children are based on each child's personal and individual interactions with the adults in their lives in their very first months and years of life — not on each child's ethnicity, culture, or race.[21,22]

We Need to Eliminate and Prevent the Learning Gaps That Exist Today

We do clearly have measurable and deplorable learning gaps today for too many groups of children in our schools in this country where there are performance differences for children that create learning problems in our schools. The learning gaps for various children are real and they are significant in some settings.

Those learning gaps that exist in our schools today can appear to have racial underpinnings. That appearance is wrong. The issues that create the learning gaps we see in our schools today are not functionally caused by either race or ethnicity.

Those early learning issues in those settings do tend to have patterns that create confusing, misleading and erroneous links to race and ethnicity.

Some degree of racial underpinnings do appear to be there for the children on either side of the learning gaps we see in so many cities and school systems today. That apparent linkage seems to exist because there actually are some clear economic differences between groups in this country. The facts about the economic disparity levels between groups are clear and they have been longstanding. Those differences in economic status do tend to functionally influence some levels of behavior.

24

There are some economic status-related differences for groups in this country that do very clearly tend to influence different activity patterns and different child raising approaches — and child raising practices — in families. For functional and economic resource related reasons that do link to basic income levels, there are some differences in those levels of interactions with children that do appear to people who do not understand the actual processes involved to have some level of linkages to race and to ethnicity.[18]

People from all races and ethnic groups can and do perform at the highest levels on every test — but we currently see average performance levels for groups of people that vary significantly between some of the groups that are most relevant to us today.

We clearly see some patterns of economic variation in our country that show that Hispanic, African American, and Native American populations have both lower average income levels as groups of people, and we know from years of data that most of our minority populations have higher levels of unemployment than White Americans.

Those overall differences in the overall average group economic patterns are clear and those differences between group averages in several learning performance areas are undisputed.[9,16,22]

What we need people from all groups to know and understand is that the differences between the groups are patterns — and those patterns are not absolute determinants for any given person. The actual results for each child are based on the early childhood brain exercise experiences of each child, and they are not created by those other factors. That is proven by the fact that there clearly are already many exceptions to those patterns.

There are, in fact, millions of people in this country from all groups today who are exceptions to those overarching economic patterns in very positive ways.

Individual people from all groups have done well economically. Some of our wealthiest and most successful Americans come from our minority populations.

But the overall patterns that show lower income levels by group and that show higher unemployment levels by group are undisputed. The consequences of those economic situations for the groups of people who are disadvantaged can be problematic and painful to the people who are directly disadvantaged in each of those areas.

Families with More Money Tend to Focus More on Children

What primarily links those economic patterns and those economic challenges by group to the neuron connectivity issues for individual children, and to the learning readiness issues by group for our very small children is this basic and obvious logistical reality — mothers, fathers, and families who have more money tend to be able to spend more time and focus more attention and resources on their very young children.[16,17,22,23]

We know from several studies that groups of people who have more money, generally tend to spend more time and focus more attention on their very young children — and those sets of children benefit from that attention for all of the biological reasons, brain development reasons, and brain exercise reasons that are explained in some depth a number of times in this book.[24]

Those sets of children who get more attention in those years have higher average reading scores than groups of people whose children, on average, have fewer books read to them or have fewer hours of direct attention and direct interaction time with adults.

Those differences are real and significant.

Parents and families who have more money tend to be able to have many more children's books in their homes. Those families with more resources also tend to use basic day care settings where the children receive one-on-one attention of various kinds from day care caretakers for at least part of each day — including having the caregivers in the settings that are used by higher income people have books in their settings and day care staff who read regularly to their children.

By contrast, the lowest income mothers and families tend to have more challenging and crowded living settings, and low-income families tend to have less well-staffed, less well equipped, or even non-existent day care arrangements.

Many of the low-income mothers have multiple jobs and many low-income parents also have highly problematic and challenging transportation issues getting to and from their places of employment.

It can be extremely difficult for a low-income mother with two or more part-time jobs to find the time and the energy — either at the end or at the beginning of the day — to create the kind of interactions with her child in those first years of life that are needed to create and reinforce connected neurons for her child.

When the mother has low resources and when the mother of a child has a problematic, difficult, and challenging transportation reality — and when the mother is focused primarily and basically on having enough money to buy basic food to meet the direct, basic, and clearly immediate daily nutritional needs of her child — then it can be extremely difficult for that mother — or father — to spend time in those first key years with each child — helping with the neuron connectivity needs of each child in those crucial areas of interaction, activity, and brain exercise levels where the neuron connections are strengthened for each child.

We Have Done a Stunningly Poor Job of Teaching the Science of Early Neuron Connectivity to All Parents and Families

The whole process of getting the right support for our youngest children in all homes is exacerbated for millions of children and their parents, by the fact that we truly have done an extremely, stunningly, and dysfunctionally poor job as a society in teaching new mothers and new fathers about the biological issues and the functional realities of neuron connectivity that exist for each child.

Parents who don't know that information can't make fully informed decisions about their own parenting approaches, and tend not to ask their day care settings or their friends and families to be a resource for their children in those useful ways.

Having large numbers of parents who do not know the basic biological realities for brain building in the first years of life clearly does represent a massive public health communications failure for us as a country.

Far too many parents in this country today do not know that they can strengthen their child's brain and those parents are then, of course, less likely to do specific things in intentional ways that strengthen brains.

Many Parents Believe Brain Strength Is Permanently Set at Birth

Most parents currently believe that the brain strength of their child is permanently set for each child at birth. Far too many people believe today that the brain strength and the brain capabilities of their child are fixed and cannot be changed once the child has been born.

That inability for anyone to improve brain strength in a child is clearly not true for all of the reasons that are described at length in this book, but that sense that brain strength for each child is set at birth, and then fixed for life does tend to be a very widely held belief on that particular issue.

Because that is the common belief for many people, far too many of the parents who believe that to be true do not do a number of the specific things that actually can and do help their child build a stronger brain in those key years.

Far too many people do not understand the opportunity to improve brain strength that exists for their child, and far too many people do not understand the basic tools and activities that are available to do that work for their child.

Almost all people understand now that doing physical exercise creates physical strength — but almost no one now knows that exercising the brains of children in those key growth years actually creates and enhances brain strength for those children.

28

Parents Want Their Children to Do Well

Experiments and observations have both shown that when parents learn that science, parenting approaches and parenting behaviors tend to change in ways that benefit the children. The First Five Commission for Children and Families has seen positive responses, even from basic advertising campaigns, that simply raised those issues.

All parents love their children and all parents want their children to do well. When parents learn about both brain development opportunities and literacy, that knowledge, all by itself, can and does often create new behaviors and different, more focused child interaction approaches for the parents who understand those issues.

The biological and functional reality is that children from all races and from all ethnic groups do well when their brain exercise needs are met. The public health policy reality we face is that we have done a very poor job of explaining that biological reality to parents from all groups in this country.

We need to do significantly better on that very basic public health accountability so that all parents in all settings can become part of the process that improves brain strength for their own children.

We Are All in Someone's Debt

If you are reading this book, we can say with some comfort and reasonable certainty that someone helped you directly in those key areas of your own life in those key first months and years after you were born.

People from all races and ethnic groups who are doing well in their careers and who are doing well in their life paths today can all look back at the fact that someone in our lives obviously met those direct interaction needs for each of us when we were in those first key years of our lives, and when we each needed those neurons in our own brains to be connected and to stay connected.

Those of us with those mental skills now would not be where we are today with those skills if those needs had not been met for each of us in those key years of our lives by one or more adults in our lives.

Those of us who have had success today — and that actually does include anyone who has the reading skill level necessary to read this book — should each express gratitude, if we still can, to the parents, the family members, family friends, neighbors, and to the childcare givers and the various baby sitters who met those needs for each of us in those key times when our own neurons were connecting, and when our own brains were in their biologically optimal times of growth.

If we had not each had that stimulation from someone at that time, we each would not be who we are today. I know, with gratitude, that if I had somehow personally been totally isolated from contact and isolated from those needed interactions, and if I had personally not been read to almost obsessively and talked to constantly and at length by my own parents and by my maternal grandmother, that it is entirely true and certain that I would be a very different person now with a very different set of skills and very different abilities today.

I am not a self-made man. The people who gave me that gift of those direct and caring interactions in those first key years of my life gave me the basic tools that I work with today.

We Should Each Pay Our Debt Personally to the Next Generation

I had to go through my own time of learning after that time. That is true for each and all of us. Learning is a continuing lifetime process. We should never stop learning, and our ability to learn extends across our entire lives.

Any wisdom or knowledge that I have acquired over the years of my life came from all of my various times, situations, experiences and processes of both teaching and learning — but the basic brain infrastructure that I have used to learn in all of those settings for all of those years to do that learning was a gift to me from those people who helped me directly in those very first years of my life.

30

We who succeed today in many parts of our life owe our success to someone who helped us in those years.

We each owe a debt. We each need to pay that debt forward to the next generation. We all owe it to the babies of today to make sure now that each child today gets the support levels that each child needs to develop at the level that is right for each child, and at the kinds of support levels that gave each of us the start that we each received in our own lives.

We each need to pay the direct and very real debt of our own development by helping others develop in the same ways.

Each Child We Save Is a Child We Save

Each child we save is a child we save. Each child we save by providing direct support to the child in those key years is a gift to society.

Each child we save is also a huge and direct gift to the child. We should give those gifts. We need each child to get the right level of support to enable each child to achieve real success and to have both a sense of personal security and a sense of personal inclusion that lasts for life.

We need to do this work one child at a time because our brains develop one at a time. We can't put chlorine or smart pills in the water to help people in groups become better thinkers. Each child goes through those years of development. Each child needs our help in those key years.

We need to figure out how to help each child — and we also need to figure out how to provide that help in ways that can help many children benefit from those levels of support during those key years for each child.

We all need to recognize that reality. Those first key years are extremely important years for each child. If we want our country to be strong going far forward into our future years as a nation, we need to deal with that opportunity in ways that make a real difference for the children who most need our support today.

We now need to collectively recognize the opportunity that is created by the fact that an extremely important time when we can functionally make real changes in the individual life trajectory for each and every child is in those immediate, high potential first three years for each and every child.

We also all need to recognize the functional reality that after those key years, the neuron connectivity process in each of us slows significantly. During those first three years, we can use, link, protect, and enhance tens of millions — even billions — of neuron connections relatively easily.

After that high opportunity neuron connectivity time, we can improve our functioning, and we can and do hugely improve our knowledge, our wisdom, and our full sets of talents, abilities and skills — but it is much harder after those key years to improve our basic brain capacity.

Toxic Stress Also Has Biological and Time-Related Links for Each Child

There is another extremely important reason why we collectively need to focus direct and focused attention on those initial years for each child.

The other hugely important biological factor that we need to understand relative to those first years of life for each child relates to the issue of toxic stress for children. Toxic stress damages baby and young child brains. Toxic stress damages children in important ways.[25]

Important new research shows that when children feel isolated and when very small children feel either threatened or unprotected, then there is a measurable buildup of damaging neurochemicals in each child's brain that can result in what the medical scientists and physicians call "toxic stress syndrome" for children.[26]

Children who suffer from toxic stress syndrome are significantly more likely to drop out of school, and those children who have toxic stress are more likely to have violence issues in school. There are some indicators that the toxic stress children may mature sexually at an earlier age — and girls with toxic stress syndrome are more likely to become pregnant at an earlier age.

A Caring Adult Can "Buffer" Against Toxic Stress

Extremely important and extremely useful research also shows us that toxic stress and the level of those toxic and damaging neurochemicals in children's brains can be "buffered" and significantly reduced in most children by as little as half an hour each day of direct and personal interaction with a loving and caring adult.[26,27]

Children need a caring and trusted adult in their lives. Each child has that need. Children need to feel secure and loved. Toxic stress chemicals literally build up in each child's brain in those first key years when that specific need is not met.

Those chemicals actually physically damage the brain. They change structure and functioning.

We now know how to prevent that damage. Researchers have done very powerful and important research on those issues. Those very damaging chemicals do not build up in the brain of a child if there is a caring and trusted adult who is consistently in each child's life.

It takes a relatively small amount of time with a caring and trusted adult each day to significantly neutralize those toxic stress chemicals in a child. The final chapter of this book points to some key research on that topic. Thirty minutes with a caring adult each day can have a major impact on defusing toxic stress chemicals for most children.

Studies have shown that a half-hour a day of direct support with a caring adult generally seems to create what the researches call a "buffer" for each child.

The solution for toxic stress development of having a half-hour of quiet adult interaction each day with each child is possible and doable for children in almost all situations. But most parents today don't even know that the toxic stress syndrome problem or risk exists, and almost no parents know now that something basic can and should be done to prevent and buffer toxic stress for their child.

Mothers who don't know today from other feedback and from other issues and teaching processes how important they each personally are to their children, should all know what a major impact each mother can make for her child by spending focused, loving, and caring time with her child in ways that actually create the needed buffer against those toxic stress neurochemicals for her child.

That information needs to be part of our improved public health awareness agenda. We need to do a much better job as a society teaching parents and the families of very young children about both neuron connectivity and brain strengthening issues and opportunities and about toxic stress prevention and toxic stress risk levels and potential danger.

We have not done a very good job of teaching that science and those issues to parents of young children, and significant numbers of children have been damaged and sometimes underdeveloped in important ways because those issues were not understood and not addressed.

Parents Appreciate Learning About Those Issues

The First 5 Commission For Children and Families for the State of California conducted a set of focus groups a year ago with new mothers and new fathers from settings across California. The author of this book chairs that commission.

The people who ran the groups could not find any parents at that point in time who knew explicitly about either the neuron connectivity opportunity for their children, or about the related support issues for those first years of life.

When the parents in those focus groups were told about the opportunity that actually exists to strengthen their children's brains, the results and the reactions from the parents were overwhelmingly positive. Parents were both eager and happy to learn about those opportunities.

Some of the parents — particularly in the father's focus groups — began talking about the competitive opportunity that might exist to make their children smarter than the children around them.

We know from several settings that when parents do learn about those issues, then parenting styles and parenting approaches do change for many parents. Knowledge about those issues has great power to inspire new ways of thinking about caring for children.

We clearly need to share the information about those issues and those opportunities with more parents. All parents love their children. All parents want their children to do well. The dreams of the parents that were expressed in those focus groups about their children's futures had an extremely consistent pattern of each parent wanting each child to succeed.

Too Many Parents Do Not Understand the Opportunities

Even though an extremely high percentage of parents and families across the country — from all economic and social groups — do not know about those particular sets of opportunities to strengthen their children's neuron connections and have no idea that the ability to increase their own child's brain capacity even exists, a number of families are providing high levels of support for their children in those time frames.

Some parents are doing many things right relative to developing their child's brain. Many parents today are clearly focusing extensive time and effort on their very young children. That behavior is creating benefit for those children.

We know that there are both cultural patterns and parental behavior patterns in some settings that have created extensive interaction opportunities and direct interaction experiences today for many children.

Some children now have families who focus extensive and very direct attention on the children. Some families have a rich supply of children's books in their homes and many families make reading time a key part of each child's day.

Those children who get that level of support are doing well in their school readiness.

Those homes tend not to know the most recent science on those issues, but they do tend to have a shared belief that their children's lives will be better with those levels of support. Those homes can still benefit from understanding the science and from reading the material in this book, because the interaction decisions with each child can be enhanced and improved when each parent has that additional level of guidance.

In a number of other homes, reading happens today with some regularity and significant levels of interactions with the children are a daily occurrence, but they are not happening at the same high levels as the highest interaction settings.

The children in those homes benefit from the current levels of interactions, and those children will benefit even more when the information in this book about the value of brain exercises is known and understood. Getting the public health communications agenda right will have a major positive impact on those families.

At the other end of that interaction continuum from the highest contact levels, some other children are not being read to at all. Those homes give us our highest opportunity levels.

In one survey of low-income families, more than 60 percent of the homes did not have one single children's book. The amount of reading time for children in those households was very low because the basic resource needed to read didn't exist in those homes.

Another important survey showed that higher income homes averaged more than a dozen books per child. That same survey encountered hundreds of lower income homes without a single children's book.[12]

As a result of those very different pathways for early childhood support, the gap in the reading readiness levels between some groups of children is wide and growing. The patterns are clear in both directions.[22,28]

More Than Half of Low-Income Homes Did Not Have a Single Children's Book

One important study showed that working and higher income mothers tended to read to their children, on average, more than 1,000 hours per child in the pre-kindergarten years.[13] That same study showed that the lower income mothers in the population that was studied only read, on average, to their children in those same pre-kindergarten years less than 30 hours per child.[28]

Those are averages. The lower-income mothers in that particular study were Medicaid eligible mothers. We know from basic research that there is a wide range of reading practices today for Medicaid mothers.

There are a number of Medicaid mothers who do read extensively, regularly, and well to their children. A major percentage of the Medicaid mothers who were studied, however, did not read to their children at all.

So those basic differences in the average numbers of hours read to children between those sets of people with different income levels are significant. Opportunities in biological brain connectivity levels and brain growth levels are clearly being lost for the children who are not having significant verbal interactions with adults, and who are not being read to by adults in those first key years.

We need all families and all communities to clearly understand this set of issues and their consequences. We also need to figure out various ways of having reading done for more children so that more children can achieve their potential, and not face the lifetime challenges that come from not being able to read.

We need books in all homes with children — and we need at least some people in all homes using those books with each child. We need all children who enter school to be ready to read when it is time for each child to actually read.

The vast majorities of people in our prisons today read poorly or don't read at all. Those prisoners were clearly not reading ready when the time to learn to read happened in their lives.

For the more than 60 percent of the people who are locked up in our prisons who either read poorly or who don't read at all, we need to recognize the fact that their personal path to prison too often leads directly back to being children who knew only hundreds of words at age three, and who knew only a few thousand words when they entered kindergarten.

The people who are in jail today do not tend to be the children who knew multiple thousands of words at that important point in their lives. They tend to be people who knew very few words and who subsequently did not learn to read and who were unable to do well in their schools. The percentages of high school drop outs from all groups who end up being imprisoned is a disproportionately high number, as this book describes in chapter seven.

A Majority of Births Are Now in Low-Income Families

That fact and those linkages are clear cause and good reason for us all to do the kinds of interventions we need to do now to change that sad and damaging path to the future for many more of our children.

We particularly need to do successful interactions for the children in the low-income homes where our research tells us the family tends to significantly lower amounts of time now talking to the children and even less time reading to the children.

Those prisoners who are in our jails today and who can't read now grew up in a time when less than 30 percent of our children were born to the low-income mothers who averaged significantly fewer reading hours for their children.

That percentage is changing significantly. The number of children who are born to low-income mothers in this country is actually increasing.

This year — across the entire country — for the first time ever, we will now have a majority — 51 percent of our total births — born to our Medicaid mothers.

By legal definition, the Medicaid mothers who made up more than half of the births in this country last year are low-income mothers.

The significance of those birth patterns creates a set of realities that we need to understand and respond to as communities and as a nation.

Knowledge Is Power and Knowledge Is Opportunity

The fact that most births in this country now are from our low-income mothers creates a huge opportunity for us to do a high value and high impact set of needed interventions.

That is a major reason why that public health agenda on this issue is so important. We need to start by having all parents — from all income levels and from all ethnic and racial groups — clearly understand the science, the reality, the functionality, the process, and the brain strengthening opportunity that exists for helping each child relative to those key issues in those key years.

Knowledge is power. We need all low-income mothers and all low-income fathers and their families to have that knowledge. We also need the relevant support groups for all families to understand the high value of exercising their children's brains in order to enhance and strengthen each child's neuron connections in those first key years of life.

We need everyone from all income levels to have that specific knowledge so that someone in each child's life can figure out ways to help each child.

All parents love their children. All parents want their children to do well. We need every parent to understand this science so that every parent can make informed decisions about the support that happens in those key months and years for their child.

It is functionally, ethically, and morally wrong for the people in leadership positions who now know and understand that science of brain strengthening for our very young children not to clearly inform each and every parent at every income level that those opportunities to help their child exist.

Talk/Read/Sing and Interact Directly with Each Child

We can succeed in doing this work if we make it a collective priority to do this work. We need to make strengthening brains a clear and well-supported public health priority — and we need all groups, and the leaders of all groups, to collectively commit to achieving that public health goal of strengthening neuron connectivity levels for each child born in America.

This effort can succeed because the interventions that work for each child to exercise each child's brain are actually pretty basic. Those are not impossible tasks to do.

We now know from all of the wonderful new research exactly what each child needs. We also now know how to meet those needs.

Interactions with an adult are vital. We now understand that all children need direct interactions with adults to build strong brains. Interactions are the key to brain development and interactions are actually possible to do.

One-to-one interactions with caring adults for each child anchor the basic functions that are needed for each child to build a strong brain.

One-to-one interactions between a child and an adult are the tools that make the brain development and the brain exercise process work. The tools that work involve the interactions described above. We need to talk, read, sing and play directly with each child.

Talking directly and often to the baby and infant has huge value and benefits for each child's brain. Talking, reading, singing, and directly interacting in various ways with each child is the key to success in exercising and building each child's brain.

We can succeed in this process because it doesn't take special equipment or a special setting to build the most important neuron connections for each child. It takes an adult who is spending time with each child and who is talking, reading, and interacting in very direct and caring ways with each child.

Every parent can fill that role. Parents are perfectly placed for most children to be their key interacting adult. Each parent can do that job and each parent can do it well.

Mothers tend to be the key support and first teacher for each child and that approach of having mothers in that role has great value at multiple levels. We need to support mothers in those roles and activities.

Fathers can also provide key levels of support and can do and create the full set of interaction levels with each child. Fathers can do that job just like mothers, to be the brain building and emotional support resources for each child.

Fathers and mothers can both do the extremely important work of being key supports for their child.

Other people in each family can fill that role as well. Families have always played a major role in raising children and we need to continue that approach today. We need families to be part of the team for each child whenever possible, and we need each family to understand and support the processes that strengthen the brains of the children they care for.

We need communities to understand and support those processes as well. It can be very useful and effective to have both a family and a village raise each child.

Read/talk/sing ought to be embedded in the overall parenting culture of America, and that approach should be embedded in the culture and belief system of each family and each community as well.

Families can be a key and high leverage resource that can help transform the life of each child. Families often have their basic family cultures and their shared family belief systems. Families who understand this science can choose to have family cultures, family behaviors, and family expectations that give each family successful children.

Those basic and very intentional interactions that provide value and benefit to each child should be understood and supported by all of the people relevant to each child.

All Languages Work to Exercise the Baby Brain

It doesn't make any difference what language is used with each child. Every language works to meet that neuron development need. The skill set and the mental exercise needed by each baby can be built with any language. The interactions with a loving adult that create emotional security for a child can also, obviously, be done in any language.

There is some good evidence that using multiple languages extensively with each child in those early years creates even stronger brains and much better language skills for the child later in life.

In some settings, the researchers have noted that dual language families chose intentionally only to speak to the children in one of the languages. That is very well intentioned as a behavior, but that decision to use only one language is sometimes not the best approach for the child. Talking only in one language is sometimes not the best approach for the child because all children in those key months and years benefit hugely from having many words directed at them, and the children will hear more words if both languages are used.

It doesn't make any difference in achieving the benefit of hearing language by a child what language is spoken. Large numbers of words spoken in any language directly to the child in focused ways create value for the child.

If some bilingual mothers currently speak fewer total words to their children because only one language is being used, then the most beneficial levels of brain exercise too often do not happen for that child. Fewer words are heard, and hearing fewer words is not the best process for a child.

But if bilingual mothers speak extensively to their children in both languages, then extensive speaking to the child in multiple languages can strengthen that child's brain, and the child can end up with higher skill levels in both languages.

It is an error to think that we need to use English as the only spoken language with each child. All languages build brains. Children in those key years benefit from having many words spoken to them regardless of the language.

We Need a Public Health Campaign to Teach That Science to Everyone

We clearly do need a well-supported public health communications campaign to get the most important levels of information about early childhood brain development out to all parents and to all families. We need "surround sound" on those key concepts and issues.

We need community groups, religious groups, and social groups to teach that science to all new parents. We need news media who understands those issues and who both explains them clearly, and writes important stories about the programs and tools that work to help children do well in those areas.

At one very basic level, we need all parents and all groups to know that children who can read are much less likely to drop out of school.

The functional consequence of helping each child build neuron connections in those years to the point where the children who are helped do not drop out of school is a huge and direct gift to each child. It is hard to find a more valuable gift for a parent or family to give a child.

A Million Dollar Gift to Each Child

The difference in average life income for the people who graduate from high school or college, and the average life income for the people who drop out of school and who work for the minimum wage or who are unemployed, is more than $1 million per child.

That means that parents and families who read, talk, and sing to their children in those first key years are giving their children the gift of $1 million in real money when their children do not drop out of school.

That also means that as we go forward as a country to compete with the rest of the world and as we help each child achieve those basic learning capabilities, we will have a stronger work force — with more people holding down jobs and more people paying taxes.

We will also have many fewer people who are locked up in prison, who are causing us to spend billions of tax dollars on their prison expenses, and who are largely destined for a renewed life of crime when they are released from prison.

We can change lives. We can save lives one at a time by creating the support each child needs to succeed at the time that support is needed by each child.

Economists from highly credible settings who have studied those issues show a positive return on investment that has almost no equal in any of the uses of our money as a country.[21,28-30]

Economists who look at the return on investment that we receive as a society by spending money to help young children build neuron connectivity strength in those key years ranges from a return of $6 to $9 for every dollar spent on the children. Those issues are discussed later in this book.

Nobel Prize winning Economist James Heckman has written with particular clarity and eloquence on those issues.

The sheer economic value of helping all children to be able to learn to read by helping with the brain development of each child in those three key years is massive.

Now that we understand this set of issues and now that we clearly see this opportunity for both children and our society, we owe it to us all — and we owe it directly to every child — to get this work done for each child and to get it done right. We have an ethical obligation on behalf of every child to help every child, and we have a societal obligation to give ourselves a better collective future by helping every child.

44

Neuron Connections Are the Key

We need to begin by understanding the biology. And we need to understand the relevant time frames for that biology.

This set of problems isn't about ethnicity or culture or race. It is about getting neurons to connect with one another in each child, and it is about the need and the opportunity to strengthen the connections that exist in each child's brain.[31]

Neuron connections are the key. Those first three key years of life are the years when those neuron connections happen, and those are the key years when those critically important connections are reinforced in the most effective way for each child.

Let's help every child strengthen those connections.

Three key years.

Let's not let them go to waste for any child.

CHAPTER TWO

The Biology of the Brain

WE HAVE HUGE brains.

People have massive brains. Our brains have billions of cells and even more billons of connections between the cells that create the functionality for our brain and our thought processes.

The heads of babies are disproportionately much larger than the rest of babies bodies — and that size difference make a clear statement about us and about what defines us, supports us, and keeps us alive from generation to generation. We are not the biggest or fastest or fiercest beings on the planet. We are, however, the smartest. We think to survive — and the better we think, the better our chances of survival tend to be.

Our large brains give us the tool we use to think.

Even though our brains are disproportionately large compared to the rest of the body at birth, we obviously are not born with all of our brain functioning in place. Our brains go through a clearly defined process and time of learning to function and to create the infrastructure and the lifelong internal neuron connectivity linkages that end up making each of us who we are.[9]

Our brains are actually developing and learning even before we are born. Some fascinating studies of brain activity show that newborn infant brains react differently when a very small baby hears a language that is different than the language that the baby heard through the walls of the mother's womb prior to birth.[32]

The language building parts of our brains are particularly amazing and worth understanding as an example of how the process works. The language learning process for each of us begins very early in our lives and goes through very clear stages.

All babies can hear all sounds in all languages at birth. Our brains can discern every sound when our brains are first born.[15,33-35]

Then — in a pruning process — we actually lose the ability to hear many sounds if we don't actually hear those sounds in our own life in those first years.

Every baby can hear all sounds from all languages in the first year of life. All babies have full sets of those sound discernment connections at birth. All children can hear all sounds from every language in that first year of life.

The reality is that not all languages use all sounds. So many babies don't hear some sounds in those first years. When that happens, those connections in our brain that allow us to hear those sounds disappear — literally pruned out.

Many of the sound detection neuron connections in our brain that don't get used in that time frame simply melt away. We lose them if we don't use them. Those connections that let us hear every sound are literally "pruned" at and eliminated from our brain if they are not used. Neuroscientists call that process neuron connection pruning.

Japanese children who do not hear the "R" and "L" sounds that are used in our language, but that are not used in their language, actually can never hear those "R" and "L" sounds later in life because those neuron connections are permanently gone from their brains for life.[32]

"Use It or Lose It" Is the Pattern

That basic "use it or lose it" process happens for multiple areas of our brain. We all start life with a massive brain capability with billions of neuron connections and then we each keep the neuron connections for life that are reinforced for each of us by being used in those first years of our lives when the pruning process in our brain is most extreme.

The first three years of our lives are the most important and highest impact years for the basic biological processes that build and structure our brains. Those are the years when our brains are shaped, formed, and even organized based on the exercise and the interactions that happen for each brain.

That pruning process is needed because it organizes the brain and creates more efficient brain functions. It creates pathways rather than just having a forest of connections and we use those pathways to think.

To build strong brains, we each need our brains to be stimulated and to be exercised during those key years. Babies and infants need the right stimulation in those key years so that the richest and most effective sets of neuron connections are retained in each baby brain and not pruned out of each baby brain.[34,35]

Those key years are when we need to stimulate and exercise every single baby brain if we want strong brains for life. The process is entirely biological. The biology of brain development actually has its peak levels in those first years of life.

Every input into our brain through our various senses in our first years of life actually exercises our brain. In practical and functional terms, what that tells us is that we need to have the right set of interactions with each child in that key time frame to build each child's brain. Interaction is the key factor that builds brains.

Every interaction with a baby and infant in those key years has an impact on the growth and the development of each brain. External input for each baby and each infant in those key years causes neuron connections in the baby and infant brain to be used, strengthened, and retained.

Retention of those neuron connections in each brain tends to be for life. The infrastructure we each build in our brain in those key years serves us forever.

Brains with More Connections Are Stronger Brains

When it comes to neurons and neuron connections in our brains, more is better.[1]

Brains with more neuron connections are stronger brains. Neurons connections solidify their existence in our brains when each infant and each baby receives stimulus through what the baby sees and through what the baby hears. Those connections in each brain are heavily strengthened by repeated use.

Repetition is a very powerful factor for building brains. Repetition of input in key areas creates brain connections that last for life.

Those connections that build the infrastructure for our brain in those key years give each of us capabilities that extend through our entire lives.

The Best Connectivity Strengthening Time for Each Brain Is Relatively Brief

That neuron connectivity strengthening process in our brains happens at its most intense and most beneficial levels in the first three years of life — and then the ability of external input to strengthen that aspect of our brain drops off significantly.

We can still have a positive impact on those components of our brain after that time — but it is significantly harder and the input that we receive after those first years does not align as well with that initial very best and highest opportunity time for intense brain structuring.

After those first years, the brain for each of us moves from building its basic biological infrastructure to actually using its basic infrastructure to think and to learn. The brain then goes through key learning processes to learn self-regulation, logical and abstract thought, basic components of memory, and other thinking skills. Those are all key areas of brain development.

Thinking and Learning Are Also Extremely Important

Thinking and learning are both extremely important processes for each of us. We all need to think and we all need to learn. Our lives are influenced heavily at multiple levels by what we learn and by what we think.

We are also heavily influenced by the thoughts and the facts that other people share with us in various teaching processes.

After the key neuron connections are made in our brain, we acquire information about the world around us that utilizes those neuron connections. Our subsequent learning processes and our information gathering experiences generally continue for each of us for our entire lives — and those information acquisition processes tend to function in the basic brain capacity that we each create in those first key years.

Learning for each of us can be much more difficult in later years — beginning at age four and five — if we have not built strong neuron connections in our brain in those first key years of biological development.

Studies show that children at 18 months who did not get the needed level of external input from adults in their world before that time can already have fallen behind in learning capabilities by that very early age.[2,3]

Some additional brain connectivity can also happen after those first years. Our brains don't become static or frozen. We can strengthen our neuron connectivity after those first years. The pace of brain strengthening slows, but it doesn't stop entirely. We should not give up on any children who did not get solid levels of brain exercise in those three key years because progress can be made with intensive support for each child.

That process is more difficult, but it can have a positive impact.

Adolescence Tends to Be Another Brain Capacity Opportunity

There is actually another major opportunity for new connections and for selective new brain growth that happens for each person at adolescence. Our brains tend to go through another set of structural and chemical changes at that point in our lives. That is another time when we can strengthen the capabilities of each child's brain.[36,37]

Those brain changes that happen at adolescence are nicely timed to deal with the physical fact and the functional reality that we each become able to make new babies at that time of our lives.

The limbic system part of the brain has a significant growth spurt during those adolescent years. All cultures tend to have a focus on specific learning processes for boys and girls at that point in our lives. It is not coincidental that there tend to be ceremonies and processes in many cultures that reflect the change from childhood to adulthood for each child at that point in our lives.

In the cultures where those "coming of age" ceremonies and celebrations happen, they tend to be aligned and roughly coincide with that second spurt of brain development and with adolescence.

Those particular years tend to be important periods of time for our intellectual life, our emotional life, and for our alignment with our cultures and our communities.

Those adolescent years are not, however, the primary years for foundational brain structuring and for neuron connectivity strengthening.

The first three years of our life are, clearly, the most important years by a large measure for the physical development and the physical structuring of our brains. Those first few years are the key years that determine how our neurons connect and those are the years that determine which connectivity levels will be strengthened and retained in our brains for our use throughout our lives.

Neurons Help Us Think

Those neurons and their connections are very important to us.

The neuron cells of our brains do the work of helping us think. The connectivity links and basic paths between those neurons give us the tools and the physical infrastructure and context that we use to think and do the things that our brain directs our body to do.

Those neuron connections could not be much more important to us. Our brains are more effective when we have more connections in place. Scientists have shown us the impact of having ample arrays of connections in each brain and the consequences of having fewer connections in place.

When we have a rich and robust array of those connections, then our brains are stronger and our brains function at higher levels.[1]

Learning Does Not Start at Kindergarten

We used to think that learning started in children at kindergarten times or even later for each child. We were wrong. Very wrong. We now know that learning actually starts at birth — even slightly before birth — and that extremely important learning that builds our brains runs at high levels through our first years of life.

We now know that building the learning capability for each child happens long before kindergarten and is most intense during those first years of brain development for each of us. We also now know that our neuron connectivity levels in each brain have actually begun to diminish significantly by our kindergarten years.

That piece of science has stunned many people. Relatively few peoples knew that "pruning" even existed as part of our brain biology and development.

Pruning is a powerful, necessary, but sometimes grim process. Neuroscientists can measure the impact of the pruning process on our brains.

The reality is — for all of us — that pruning happens. Unused connections get pruned. The connections in our brain that are pruned are lost forever. Our brain needs to go through that process to become more efficient and to create the connectivity pathways that help us think.

We do not prune or lose the brain connections that we functionally use. Connections in our brains that actually do get used by each of us in those key time frames tend to be reinforced, strengthened, and functionally preserved in our brains instead of lost to us.

So doing the things that we can do to keep important connections from being pruned in very young children is the right thing to do if we want our children to have stronger and bigger brains.

We Are Physically Weak in Our Earliest Years

We are physically entirely helpless in our earliest years. We could not be much more helpless than we are as infants. Unlike baby deer, we can't spring to our baby feet almost immediately after birth and sprint into the forest if we need to flee. We don't flee well in those first years.

In fact, we can't flee at all. We barely learn to crawl in our earliest months and years. We are functionally inert. But we are mentally on fire. We have massive levels of intellect related neuron connectivity reinforcing activity going on in our baby brains.

Those times of almost complete physical inability and extreme weakness are actually the times when we each build our own mental strength infrastructure at its highest level and rate of growth.

Brains Before Brawn

We begin to build physical strength in those earliest years and we can each continue to maintain or even build our physical strength in various ways for our entire lives. But we build our basic mental infrastructure strength in our first months and years of life. The years of major physical weakness for each of us are key years for making our brain strong.

As we become better informed and as we acquire learning, knowledge, judgment, and wisdom in various ways, we use the brain structure that we built in those first years to guide the actions of our physical body. As we each build our brain capability, we build our physical ability in a parallel and appropriately timed process.

Our Bodies Are Weakest When Our Intellect Is Least Developed

Our physical bodies give us the tools we need physically to interact functionally with the world around us and to make what we learn in our basic learning processes the guidance that each of us uses to interact in various physical and mental ways with the world we live in us.

In those earliest years of our lives — when we have no learning and no judgment — we also have bodies that are weak enough to keep us out of trouble. Our weak bodies and our inability to move quickly or well help make our bad or non-existent judgment in those early years less relevant.

That entire process and that set of linkages and alignments makes great logistical sense when we look at it as an entire process.

As we grow older, we go through significant times of learning — both about the world around us and about the people around us. All of that subsequent learning is done in the context of the brain infrastructure that we build and support in our first years of life.

We Need Direct Interactions with People to Build Each Baby's Brain

We need to understand the basic processes that can build strong brains in those first key years. Too many people do not know what those processes and opportunities are. That lack of knowledge about those opportunities is almost criminal — because that knowledge is basic, simple, easy to share, and because it is almost impossible to forget once we understand what that science is and once we each understand how relevant that science is to each of us.

We need everyone to understand the basic process so that we can do the things we need to do to help all children.

We can, in fact, help all children.

Interactions are the key. Babies need interactions with adults to build baby brains.

To build each baby's brain and to strengthen those neuron connections in those first years of life for each child, our infants and babies need direct and caring interactions with other people.

Interactions are golden. Interactions are the only sure process for exercising brains. Direct interactions with adults create the sparks that light up each baby's brain. When babies interact with adults through play and through adults talking to the child, then brain growth and brain strengthening happen for that baby.

Children with No Interactions Have Fewer Neuron Connections

Children who have no one interacting with them at that point do not have the basic neuron connection strengthening experiences that makes brains strong. The brains that do not have adults interacting with children in those times when neuron connections are happening end up with many fewer neuron connections in their brains. Those children fall behind other children — and that falling behind process can happen with painful speed.

The first year of life is extremely important for each child relative to the biology of each brain. The second and third years are major brain structuring years as well.

The process that builds connections in those key years is direct, consistent, and it is extremely important to each child's brain development.

Interactions with adults are key for each child.

We know that when you electronically scan a baby's brain, the parts of the brain that literally light up to show growth and active neuron linkages are the parts that light up when each baby is interacting with another person — not just with a pure external stimulus.[38]

Too Much Television Can Cause Reading Readiness to Deteriorate

That was important science to uncover. Interacting directly and personally with other people is the key factor for each child that triggers those connections. Some people thought that watching television might make people smarter. Brain scans and reading readiness tests both now show that isn't true. Babies who watch TV are often entertained by the TV, but their brains do not grow from TV watching. Brains build and retain connections in babies only when the babies interact directly with other people.

We now know that babies need those direct, one-to-one interactions with real people to strengthen and retain the neuron linkages that make brains strong. We also know that television viewing as a sole source of sensory input can even cause some very young brains to lose ground on their learning readiness levels.[39]

56

We Lose the Language Connections If We Don't Use Them

We have a much higher level of ability to both hear and learn other languages early in our lives and we tend to lose that ability as we age. Early neuron connections make it easy for most very young people to learn other languages. Those connections are much weaker in most people later in our lives.

People are not all identical and some people do continue to have great language learning proficiency later in life, but for most of us that language learning proficiency peaks at a very early age. A number of excellent research papers and books have focused on those issues.[40-42]

That is actually a very good argument for us speaking to young children in multiple languages when that possibility to speak in multiple languages exists. Speaking is a major neuron connectivity trigger. Children need to be spoken to in order to strengthen neuron connections.

Speaking directly to a child is a wonderful, essential, and very basic neuron connectivity-building tool. A key point for us all to recognize and remember is that any language can achieve those goals.

The Language Does Not Need to Be English to Solidify Brain Connections

We have seen some settings and situations where bilingual mothers in this country have chosen to speak to their children only in English to help their children be better at learning English. Helping children in this country do well in English can be a good thing. However — it is also very true that approach can unintentionally be a bad thing for a child. It can be a bad thing if speaking only in English reduces the total time spent speaking to each child.

It can be bad for a child if that approach of speaking only English reduces the total verbal interactions with adults that are experienced by the child. It would be far better to speak extensively in both languages or just speak extensively in the language that isn't English. Children's brains need many and frequent verbal interactions to grow — and any language that is spoken to the child does that job of triggering growth.

For brain growth it is more important for a child to be spoken to in any language than it is for the child to hear a specific language.

Hearing Multiple Languages Can Strengthen Language-Related Brain Capacity

Hearing multiple languages can be very beneficial for children because basic language skills can improve in each language and because increased verbal interactions for the child with the mother or with other family members creates brain strength for each child regardless of the language used for the interactions. Brain capacity grows even more when multiple languages are heard.

Sadly, brain capacity shrinks in areas that extend beyond language skills when the total amount of direct verbal interaction with a child is reduced significantly in order to focus on only having direct spoken interactions happen in one language.

Hearing music in those early years of brain development also tends to have an impact on the neuron linkages in the brain. Simple background music seems to have less positive impact on children's neuron capabilities then focused music and music that involves some level of interaction with the child.

Stronger connections and higher musical ability levels seem to be triggered by music that directly involves the child or music that involves the parent rather than music that is simply part of the background environment in a general and non-focused way.

We learn by doing. Our brains are set up to learn things by doing things. We learn to do conversations by conversing. We learn music by being musical. Our brains have great capacity for being strengthened and structured by what we actually do in those key years. We need to help children do the things in their lives that take advantage of that almost overwhelming plasticity and massive and time-linked connectivity opportunity for each child's brain.[43]

Toxic Stress Can Create Brain Related Problems

There is another key reason why we need to provide specific levels of support to each of our children in those first key years of life.

That other key reason is toxic stress.

What we did not understand well until fairly recently is that those key years are also the time when each child is at great risk for having toxic stress chemicals build up in each brain in ways that damage each brain. The first chapter of this book pointed out that those first years are also the high-risk time for toxic stress syndrome for each child.

That toxic stress syndrome is another clearly biological reality that can have a lifetime negative impact on each child.[25,43]

The children who get little attention, who feel isolated, or who are treated with negative or even abusive interactions actually have different levels of brain structuring built by being in a stressful environment. The brain of a child facing those kinds of negative experiences generates neurochemicals that can do damage to thought processes and trigger very different sets of behaviors, reactions, and thought processes for each affected child.

The children who are either neglected or abused end up with different behavior patterns that include being more aggressive and easier to anger than a child who hasn't faced toxic stress.

Those toxic stress levels in a child's brain can be prevented and even offset by the child having direct daily interactions with a caring adult.

The children who feel that there is a safe and caring adult in their world build different brain chemicals than a child who doesn't have that sense of safety and security.

Studies have shown that having more than half an hour each day of safe time with a caring adult can actually defuse and serve as a buffer against those damaging neurochemicals.

When very young children are isolated, ignored, or feel threatened, stress chemicals build in each child's brain. Those chemicals, over time, change both brain functioning and behavior patterns. It creates toxic stress syndrome for children when those neurochemicals are present in the brain of a child for extended periods of time.

Children with toxic stress syndrome tend to experience personality changes. Those children are more likely to have issues with physical violence and those children are more likely to become pregnant. They are more likely to drop out of school.

The children who suffer from toxic stress are damaged — and we now know that damage does not need to happen. It can be prevented. We know how to prevent it.

Direct interactions with a caring adult also prevent toxic stress. Studies have proven that to be true.

We need to make very sure that each and every child receives direct interaction with a caring adult every day at a level that eliminates the negative brain chemical buildup that creates toxic stress syndrome.[44]

The fact that the same kinds of basic daily interaction with an adult that build strong brains can also prevent and defuse toxic stress makes creating needed parenting process simpler than it would be if we needed separate parenting strategies to achieve each goal.

It is a very good thing for our children that the time spent reading, talking, and singing to each child can also create that needed direct interaction buffer time to defuse those destructive neurochemicals for each child.

That time spent talking and reading to each child can directly help each child increase his or her vocabularies and that same process can build needed connections that enhance reading skills for a child at the same time that it buffers toxic stress for that child.

60

Children do better in life — feel less stress — and interact better with other children and other people if the children feel safe, protected and loved, and if the children have direct interactions with adults the children trust.

Children need to feel cared for in order for the toxic stress levels to be buffered and in order for the learning process to have its maximum impact. Brain development processes are strengthened when a child feels loved and protected.

85% of the Children in the Juvenile Justice System Read Poorly

We need to help all of our children relative to each of each issues, risks, and opportunities.

Currently, we have record numbers of children in the juvenile justice system. The functional reality is that 85 percent of those children in the juvenile justice system today either read poorly or can't read at all.[11]

We could cut the number of children in the juvenile justice system and we could reduce the number of children who go to jail significantly — by half or more — by doing the right things to help each child build neurons in those first key years of life when neurons strengthen their connections and by also doing the right things for each child to help the child avoid toxic stress syndrome in those same years.

Thirty Minutes a Day Strengthens Brains and Buffers Stress

Science tells us that only half an hour of intervention for each child each day with a trusted adult can be enough to create a buffer against toxic stress for most children.[44] Thirty minutes can build a buffer that reduces the level of those damaging neurochemicals to non-toxic levels.

We also know that reading to each child for a half-hour each day both builds neuron connectivity and improves the vocabularies of children.

The children who have higher vocabularies at age three and age five are much more likely to learn to read and much more likely to avoid being dropouts or going to jail. We now know that those simple and direct interactions by an adult with each child every day in those years of highest opportunity have the ability to change lives in very positive ways for each child.

Children Need Adults Who Interact with Them

The key to success for each child is to interact directly with each child. That biological process is the same for every child. Interactions are key for brain strengthening. Interactions with trusted and caring adults are the essential child support tool that each child needs. Children need adults who interact with them and children need to feel safe in those interactions.

A wide variety of basic and achievable interactions can have a positive impact on the brain strength for each child. The interaction with each child can be talking, reading, singing, or playing in a wide variety of ways. Direct interactions with an adult are golden for brain development for each child and the look of interactions can damage brain development in each child.

Those same interactions with an adult that build strong brains can also be golden for the emotional security of each child as well.

The interactions with each child should be daily and they should be frequent when possible. But even infrequent interactions can make a positive difference. Every positive interaction can reinforce and strengthen the neuron connections that become permanent parts of the children's brains.

So even infrequent, but positive, interactions with a child are far better than no interactions for a child.

Isolation Can Be Poisonous

Isolation is bad for brain growth and structuring.

Isolation has poisonous impact on children. Children who are isolated end up with severe emotional limitations and their brains even show up on scans as being significantly smaller brains.[45,46] We need to eliminate isolation and we need to encourage and create regular and positive interactions if we want to build the best futures for each of our children.

The science is now much more clearly understood. The biology is well known. The time frames are also much more clearly understood. We now understand those aspects of biological brain development better than they have ever been understood.

The opportunities that are created by those processes for each child are extremely clear. The negative impact on children of not reinforcing and not retaining the right level and set of neuron connections in those early years is also painfully clear.

We need to address those negative impacts and we need to take advantage of those opportunities in ways that work for the well being of each child.

That is the next chapter of this book.

We understand the biology. Now we need to understand how to get the full benefit of the opportunities that the biology creates for each child.

CHAPTER THREE

We Do Need to Save Each Child

EVERY CHILD WE save is a child we save.

Each child has his or her own life path and that path begins for each and every child with those first three years of life. Every single child who has a better and more reinforcing first three years is a child who has a much better chance of having a better life.

Each child who does not get that needed support in those key years is a child who is highly likely to face major challenges and significant difficulties at multiple levels — through absolutely no fault or blame for the child.

To use a card game analogy for our brain functions, we each need to play the cards we are dealt for our brain capacity — but the dealing process for the brain capacity for each of us doesn't happen at birth. The dealing process for each of us happens in those first years of life when hundreds of millions of neuron connections either happen or do not happen in each brain.

Those first key years of life are the years where the neuron connections in our brains are either used and retained, or when neuron connections are not used, and are doomed to be pruned from each child's brain.[1,2,6,34,40,44]

Those first three years are key years for each and every child for brain development and growth. We need to help every child in every group and every setting build a strong brain in that period of time.

We can't abandon the children who do not get full brain exercise and support in those first key years. We also need to assist, protect, care for, and help the children who don't get the neuron connectivity support and reinforcement that was needed by each child in their first years of life.

We Can't Give Up on the Children Who Didn't Get Enough Early Support

We very much need to do what we can to help those children who don't get enough early support for their brain building process to succeed in their lives. We should not give up on those children. Improvement is still possible and that should be our goal.

We need to help those children who fall behind in those years catch up to the extent that catching up can be done after those first key years. We also need to help those children who fall behind find pathways and approaches to life that can create good lives for each child.

We may need, for example, to find some ways of employing people who don't have the capacity to learn to read.

Some progress on brain issues can be made after those first key years. That progress should happen for each child when it can be done. At least 10 percent of the children who fall far behind in their third grade reading skills can, with support, catch up with other readers. We need to provide the right levels of support for those children who have fallen behind.

The truth is that we cannot and should not abandon those children who fall behind. But, the truth also is that we should work very hard to have as few children in the status of falling behind as we possibly can.

We need a future where very few children find themselves in that sad situation of falling behind so badly that reading is an unattainable achievement.

Major portions of our intellectual development happen after those first years. Our brains develop their self-regulatory functionalities and competencies. Logical and abstract thinking are both learned after that time. Memory skills and memory capacity building happens after that time.

We develop both judgment and wisdom after that time, and that is true for all of us regardless of what our brain strengthening experiences were in those first years.

We Need a Public Health Campaign to Build Strong Brains

Those first years are, however, extremely important.

Those consequences from those first years of brain exercise and activity for each child — both positive and negative impacts — last for entire lives. We all should be aware of that reality and we all should support doing what needs to be done to keep the negative impacts from happening for each child.

We need a public health campaign for us all that helps create both universal awareness and shared support from all of us for all children in those first three years.

We need to make sure that every new mother and every new father in America knows this basic biological science about the impact of those key months and years for their child.

We need to look at what we can do collectively to help all children and we need to focus our public policy thinking on improving both parenting support and parenting education processes for those first key years in the context of helping every child succeed for life.

This is the right time for all of us to recognize the extremely important reality that we can make a huge difference for our children and that we can make that huge difference one child at a time.

We Can Help Each Child One at a Time

In addition to the public health approach that helps all children, we also should be making specific commitments to those goals of helping children in those first key years as parents, as families, and as community groups. We need groups of people to set goals to help children in their groups and communities one at a time. Every group and community should be part of that process. We need to help children from all groups collectively and individually, in each setting where we have children.

We need people in various groups to understand that even though it can be challenging to help all children in society or even in a setting simultaneously, we actually can help individual children in each family and we can help individual children in each group with focused efforts today.

The reality of functional brain development in each brain means that we can do that extremely important support process for children one child at a time.

This process of early brain development clearly happens individually for each child — one child at a time. Groups of people can, therefore, also help children now, one at a time, in a wide variety of ways that make sense and create real benefits for each child who is being helped and who can be logistically supported by each group.

Families in various settings can decide to make a family-based commitment to that process and those objectives.

A family might not be able to change the lives of all children in a community, but a family can decide to focus on children in each family and can succeed in changing the life of one child at a time in the context of each family by making sure each child in their family gets those key levels of support in those key years.

We Need to Help One Child at a Time with Direct, One-to-One Support

One child at a time is a key point and a key opportunity for us all to understand.

Brain growth is a very personal and very direct experience. Each brain has its own growth experience.

Each child needs the support of adults in those first three years to build strong levels of neuron connectivity in their brains. If we do not provide support to each child, then those very best and most effective developmental opportunities are lost forever for the child who doesn't get the support. Forever is a long time. That is a painful reality we all need to understand.

We also all need to understand that the support given to each child in those golden years doesn't need to be complicated. That basic package of support doesn't need to be high tech or complex. It doesn't need to involve multiple people and it doesn't need to trigger extensive external processes. That direct support for child brain development for each child can exist for each child at a very basic and direct level for each child. In fact, because each brain has its own path to growth and development, that support can and must exist and happen one child at a time.

The key to that brain strengthening process for each child isn't positive wishes, good intentions, and either wishful thinking or magical thinking. The key to building strong brains for each child is to figure out how to create and achieve basic one-on-one interactions by one or more adults with each child we help, one at a time.

The key to success for a child is for each child to have someone who talks to the child and to have someone who interacts directly with the child in those basic ways that lead to building better-connected brains for each child.

Interactions are the key. People need to figure out how to be sure that basic and direct interactions happen for each child. A wide range of interactions by an adult with the child can all be positive interactions that have a beneficial input for the child. Each child needs consistent access to those direct interactions with adults in order to strengthen the child's brain.

Talking, reading, and interacting in positive ways with each baby all work to help children in those years build strong brains.

Simple talking — and very basic reading — and simply asking questions to each child and setting up even the most basic verbal interactions directly and consistently with each child can all build the brain strength in our children that our children need to succeed.

Talk/Read/Sing and Interact Directly with Each Child

Knowledge is power.

We need the people who are responsible for raising each child in each setting to understand which interactions with children fill the role and perform the function of building strong brains.

A number of programs are being created in various settings to encourage parents and families to do the right set of things for each child.

Those programs all tend to focus on the specific sets of interactions that can be used to create the best outcomes for each child.

Read/Talk/Sing is a label for one set of interactions that is being used in several settings to help make brains strong for children. Some settings label the child support approach "Talk, Read, Play, and Sing."

The basic package of interactions that is being set up in each of those settings is basically the same for all of those kinds of programs. The people who advocate for those approaches and who are implementing them in various settings, all know that children need and benefit from direct adult interaction. The advocates know that the interaction with each child can be done in several basic ways that can all add benefit for the child.

Talk, Read, Sing and Play kinds of programs are all intended to teach parents how to interact with their children in useful and easy to do ways. Those programs encourage very basic interactions with each child and aim to set those basic interactions up in ways that can be pleasant and reinforcing for both children and the adults involved.

The Interactions Can Be Beneficial for Adults and Children

Those direct and basic interactions can have a huge positive impact on children. Children in those first years who have adults talking to them, reading to them, and singing to them in a context of adults interacting directly with each child, benefit significantly and immediately from those encounters.

It seems too simple to be true, but those basic and simple interactions with a child can change the child's life. That entire interaction experience can be

70

pleasant and enriching for both the children and for the adults who are doing the interactions.

All of those interactions can be fun and entertaining for both adults and children as well as enriching. They are essential for the child — because the consequences of not having those interactions is so negative and dire — and they can be very pleasant for the child because children find both comfort and joy from having those interactions with adults the children care for and trust.

All Children Need Basic Interactions

The key point for us all to remember is that all of our children need those basic levels of interactive stimulation with a caring and trusted adult in those first years. Children need basic levels of interaction with an adult — with a caring and trusted adult — in those first years in order to strengthen brains and to avoid toxic stress levels.[26]

Children very much need the sense of protection, the security, and a sense of safety in their lives that prevents toxic stress syndrome. That sense of safety for a child can only come for a child from direct interaction with another safe, loving, and caring human being.

We need at least one trusted adult for each child for those first years of life in order to give our children both growth opportunities and a sense of security and safety.

Each Child Needs at Least One Trusted Adult

That trusted adult in most settings for most children tends to be the mother. Mothers are naturally and functionally in that role for most children. Mothers tend to love and be bonded with their children and mothers tend to have both attachment and loyalty to each child. Children, of course, tend to love and be bonded to their mothers.

For a wide range of logistical, functional, and emotional reasons, the bulk of the most successful developmental and security-inducing situations for babies throughout human history have involved children and their mothers. We need to encourage and support mothers in those interactions with each child whenever we can help and support mothers in those functions and those roles.

We should not, however, assume that only mothers can meet those needs for our children.

Fathers Can Fill That Key Need as Well

Having the mother in that key role isn't functionally essential as the only interaction agent that can meet those needs for each child, however. Fathers can do that work as well and fathers can do all of those functions extremely well.

Many fathers read, talk, interact, sing, and care for their children and many children benefit in major ways when their fathers are in their lives in those key and direct ways.

Grandparents, aunts and uncles, and other relevant adults in the family or the community can also do those functions for children. All of those adult interactions support levels are good for children. The children benefit in each case from that support given to the child by one or more caring adults in their world.

Some experts believe that children have even higher levels of personal security and development when there are clearly two or three supportive adults in each child's life.

Day Cares Can Be Key to the Process

High percentages of children spend major parts of their day in various day care centers and baby-sitting situations. Cities and communities make various levels of day care available to parents for their children.

We need those day care sites to all be helping each child with those key sets of issues.

We need day care settings where the caregivers read to each child and interact in ways that strengthen brain development for each child. Our homes and families are the first teachers for most children and our day care settings are the second set of teachers.

We need to make those resources part of the support process for each child.

We need the institutional group day cares, the family-centered in-home day cares, and the family and community based babysitting approaches to each understand those basic sets of child development issues and to be part of the process.

What our children each need in those first key years is someone who cares about them who is performing all of the key brain exercise functions directly in a trusted way for each child.

Isolation Can Be Poison

A worst-case situation for a child can be for the child to be abused or even isolated. Isolation creates its own negative consequences.

A number of horror stories have resulted from orphanages in other countries that put their very young children in isolated white cribs and in confined and sterile settings in some very resource poor environments.[31] The goal and intent of those orphanages was not to damage those children, but the damage that was done by those levels of isolation for each child lasted for the entire lives of those children.

We need to do the exact opposite of those isolated orphan experiences. We need loving, direct, interactive experiences for each child and we need those loving, interactive experiences to start at birth.

Those first years are key.

Once those neuron connections happen — and once that sense of stress relevant security and functional stability is created for each child — then the future pathway for each child can be channeled to be the right path for each child and there is a high likelihood that the path that is created will last a lifetime.

The key for us as a society — and as parents, family members, and caregivers — is to focus on creating that path in a functional way for each child in those prime biological critical years. The key is to figure out for each child a "just-in-time" set of interactions and a set of situation-relevant support approaches that meets each child's needs for that level of security and the needed levels of growth in those key years of each child's life.

Children Who Miss That Opportunity Often Do Not Do Well

We need to be very honest with ourselves about that point and that process.

Children who miss that high leverage opportunity generally do not do well. There are scans of baby brains that show significantly smaller brains by age three for the children who are in isolated situations and whose brains do not get the exercise that is needed to have their brains grow.

Those smaller brains for those children are not smaller because of ethnicity, culture, or race. They are smaller because there was a direct and personal brain exercise deficit and a clear interaction deficit for each of those children that did not cause their brains to grow and well as the brains grew for the children who had more support in those key years.

We need each child to get the support each child needs. That can come from family, community, or even our official educational system extended to its farthest and most enlightened ends. The key point we need to focus on is how to be sure that someone on the relevant continuum of family and community that exists for each child meets the needs that exist for each child.

We Can Succeed Because We Know How To Succeed

We can succeed in doing this work because the basic needs for each child are not complex and because we know with some level of expertise exactly what those basic needs are.

We have that wisdom and we have that science. We have that skill set. We are capable of doing that work. We can do those specific functions. We

74

can create those interactions. Each child needs those basic and simple direct interactions. Each child needs to have someone talking, asking questions, explaining things, and having a shared interaction with the child about the world.

We need each child born in this country to have someone who can have those basic interactions with the child. The consequences of our failure to provide that support to each child who is not supported are both painful and real. The children with no interactions do not do well.

We need to address those issues for each child. The experience that is absolutely relevant to each child is the experience that happens directly for each child.

Each child we save is a child we save. Let's save each child.

CHAPTER FOUR

Parents Are the First Teachers and the Primary Level of Support, Protection, Safety, and Growth for Each Child

WE NEED TO help mothers and fathers do what needs to be done to support every child during those first key months and years of life.

The first level of support that exists in the real world for almost every child is the child's family — with the mother for each child usually in the direct center of the safety net and serving as the primary support reality and resource for each child.

That central role for the mother of the child isn't always true and there are a number of exceptions, but when we look at the situation that exists for most children, the role of the mother tends to very consistently be at the center of each child's interaction with the world.

Mothers mother. That happens in every human setting. Mothers tend to be the heart of each child's support processes, and mothers tend to be the core of each child's support functionality.

In most homes, the mother is the primary caregiver and the mother is the primary source of both support and protection for the child. The overwhelming majority of the initial interactions for most children in most settings are with the mother.

We need to support those interactions. We need to make those interactions easy and safe. We need to make it possible for mothers to be with their children and we need to make it possible for mothers to provide that support to their children in those key times.

We need to support mothers in all of those early functions and roles for mothers, and we need to provide that support in ways that enable all mothers to very directly engage in the right levels of interactions with their children.

We need to have each and every mother understand the great opportunity that exists to show and demonstrate direct and responsive emotional support for their child in the first three months of life, and we need each and every mother to understand both the need and the opportunity that exists to exercise and strengthen their baby's brain by interacting directly and consistently with their child in the first three years of life.

Most mothers do not know that science and most mothers do not explicitly understand those biological realities today. Very few mothers and very few fathers in our country today know those realities in a clear, concise and science anchored way.

That lack of knowledge by both mothers and fathers about those early opportunities to help their children is actually a major and unacceptable failure of our public health agenda as a country.

That lack of knowledge by parents about those brain development biological realities is a public health deficiency of major magnitude. It is a significant and unacceptable deficiency that we need to correct soon because children are being damaged every day as a result of that information sharing failure.

Too many children being born in this country today are not getting needed levels of support in those key months and years because their families are unaware of the opportunities that exist to provide that support.

We owe it to every parent to make sure that every parent has that level of knowledge about how to help their children at those key points and times in their lives and in the lives of their children when that knowledge is most relevant. We need to change the current low knowledge levels about those issues because the consequences of parents not knowing those realities have negative impacts on far too many children.

The truth is that parents in every setting very much want to help their children — and parents in every setting very much want to know how to help their children succeed. That information exists, but we are not doing a good job of sharing that information with all parents today.

Parents can clearly do a more effective job as parents when that information is known and understood by each parent.

Parents who understand those realities can make informed decisions about the various ways of interacting with their child. Parents can make very different sets of decisions about multiple levels of parenting behaviors, and about various direct and indirect child support activities when that set of realities and opportunities to help each child is clearly understood.

Parents who know the absolute biological and functional value of those basic brain strengthening interactions can both do their own interactions with their child in ways that support that value, and — when resources are limited and when difficulties or logistical issues exist relative to their own direct activities — parents who have that knowledge can also work to seek out other resources in their families, or in their communities to help make those enabling and empowering interactions happen for their children.

Great creativity by parents and families on those issues and functions is possible, but that creativity for those issues will only happen in many situations if parents and families understand both the science and the opportunity that exists for their child.

We need every mother to know even before her baby is born what can be done to help her child achieve the high levels of success and the emotional security that mothers want for their children.

Obstetricians should communicate that science and teach that opportunity to each of their patients in the weeks and months before each birth. Obstetricians have great credibility with each mother and they have a perfectly timed opportunity to teach those points because those caregivers can share that information with each expectant mother in that highly important and highly motivated learning time that tends to happen just before each baby is born.

Pediatricians, family physicians, nurses, and other related caregivers for both mothers and babies also need to share that same set of information about the high value and the functional benefits that are created by those interactions with mothers as soon as each baby is born.

Many new and first time mothers are concerned about how to be a mother in ways that will provide the most benefit to their child. This knowledge about those very basic and direct ways of helping each child can help alleviate that concern by those mothers.

Both obstetricians and pediatricians can give comfort and a sense of security and direction to all new mothers by explaining the great value and the lifelong benefits that the mother will be able to give to her child by having those kinds of direct and loving interactions with her child in those first months and years of life.

Mothers who are concerned about their own role and their own activities as a mother can be helped with that concern when their caregivers explain clearly and explicitly that direct and on going talking, playing, and caring interactions with their child by the mother actually adds very real value for the child, and can create functional benefits that can last for the child's entire life.

We need to help all mothers understand that those kinds of basic, direct, nurturing and loving interactions with their child aren't just pleasant and emotionally rewarding things to do to get through the day. Those basic child focused interactions by each mother actually provide security, learning readiness strengthening, and enhanced learning capabilities for their child.

We also need to help each mother — often by generating support for the mother from family, community, friends, and appropriate caregivers — with appropriate resources and assistance in those times of early childhood opportunity and need. We need to help each mother with useful levels of functional support as those needs exist for each mother and each child.

All mothers deserve our support, because all children need that support.

Fathers Can Also Add Major Value in the Brain Strengthening Processes

We clearly should include fathers in that education and support process as well. Fathers often have a major role in the support systems for their children. Fathers are often key members of the parenting team for children.

Fathers can help and reinforce mothers in the mother's activities, and fathers can also be the direct and key parent for their children who creates highly useful support interactions with each child.

For a significant number of children, fathers are the primary support person. Mothers are usually in that primary direct support role but fathers are actually the key and primary caregivers for a number of children. Children can benefit significantly from fathers in that role, both doing those functions directly or sharing those functions in various ways with the mother and with the family of their child.

There are many fathers who do the basic and primary support functions for children — either alone or in partnership with the mother of their child — with great skill, competency, and high levels of benefit for the child.

The number of fathers in our country who read to their children and who interact directly with their very young children in those key years is large and growing.

Our culture is increasingly encouraging fathers to be in those roles, and the positive emotional rewards for the fathers that result from those focused and direct interactions with their children tend to reinforce those behaviors for the fathers. Fathers often fall in love with those interactions and find them to be a highlight and high point of their lives.

Even though that set of interactive and involved parenting behaviors is the approach used now by many fathers, a key point to understand relative to other fathers is that some fathers do not feel that their own functional and interactive parenting role is important to their child.

Many fathers do not know and do not understand that they are actually making a direct and positive difference in their child's life, and in their child's future abilities and future capabilities through their own direct parenting interactions with their child.

We need to do a much better job of communicating those realities and the value created by those interactions to those fathers who do not know or who do not understand their value to their child today.

It can be very empowering, motivating, and encouraging for fathers who don't know about those processes to realize that their own direct and positive parental interactions with their child in talking, reading and playing with their child actually creates and adds hundreds of millions of neuron connections in their baby's brain.

Caregivers and communities need to teach that reality to fathers as well as to mothers because fathers can be a key asset to their children with those interactions, and because many children would benefit very directly from those interactions with both parents.

The role of the father in those kinds of interactions is actually more than just pleasantly playing with their child. Those kinds of direct and loving interactions from fathers can add substantively to their child's sense of security, learning readiness and brain strength.

We Need Parents to Know That Brain Exercise Creates Strong Brains

As the most common experience, however, the usual pattern is that the primary caregiver who does most of those support behaviors for each child tends to be the mother. We need to honor, respect and support that relationship.

We need to very intentionally help mothers in those roles. We need to create ongoing levels of support for every mother. We need to help every mother help every child.

As part of the process of helping each mother provide the best support for her child, we need to be sure that we do what we need to do to help all mothers understand both the science and the basic opportunities that exist for their child. We need every mother to understand that her child can build strong muscles with physical exercise and that her child can build a strong brain with neuron connecting brain exercise.

We need to help every mother meet the neuron connection needs and brain strengthening opportunities for their child by teaching every mother that those needs and opportunities exist, and by teaching every mother in very practical and highly functional terms what she can do to help create those levels of neuron connection experiences, exercises, and brain strengthening activities for her child.

Parents Are the First Teaching Resource for Children

Both mothers and fathers need to realize that they are actually and clearly the first teachers for their children, and the first source of learning for their child. In some situations, someone other than a parent is in that role, but most of the time, for almost all children, the first teacher is the child's parent. The first place of learning for each child is almost always the home.

Education for each child obviously and clearly starts at home — and — education for each child also, very clearly, begins at birth. To some degree, new studies tell us, education even begins slightly before birth.[40,41]

Children may have many teachers in their lives, but parents are clearly the first and most important teachers for almost every child. The interactions of the parents with each child in those first months and years of life sets each child on the learning path that will guide their entire life.

We need all parents to know that they are the first teachers for their child. We need every parent to know how to do the sets of things that will functionally strengthen their child's brain and build his or her learning readiness levels in those first key years when they are the primary teacher for their child.

We need that understanding to exist with all parents so that parents can do their job as first teachers for each child in ways that can create the maximum possible benefit in those key areas and those key time frames for each child.

Most Parents Do Not Know That Science Today

This point has been made several times, but it is important enough to make it again. Most parents today do not know that basic package of science. That science about the development of their child's brain has not been explicitly taught to most parents in America in a clear and effective way.

Parents at all income levels and parents from all groups will be able to make better decisions and more fully informed decisions about their parenting activities in those key years when that knowledge about early brain development is known to each parent.

Even the parents who do almost everything functionally "right" today for their children in those first key years of life often do everything right now for their child for intuitive, emotional, or even cultural reasons and not because of a cognitive and intellectual understanding of the functional realities and the purely biological issues that are actually involved in the brain development of their children.

Doing things right for children based on emotional, intuitive or cultural reasons can be a very good thing to do. But doing things right for each child based on cognitive and intellect-linked reasons that are anchored in real functional realities, in solid science, in credible and effective research and in fully informed professional expertise about the science and practice of child development, and the processes of lifelong learning can be even better.

We need to make sure that every single parent and every relevant family member — mother and father, aunt and uncle, grandparents and cousins — understands the basic core science and the basic biology of early childhood development and understands the importance of exercising their child's brain in those first key months and years in order to increase the likelihood that their direct interaction with each child in their family will have the most effective impact, and create the greatest benefit for their child.

People Are Inventive, Smart, and Love Their Kids

People are both inventive and smart. Parents love their children. Parents and families want to do good things for their children. Parents all want their children to succeed in life.

We need to help all parents to be able to help their children succeed.

When people understand the goal and the role of creating direct interactions for infants and babies, and when people understand the value and the direct benefit to their child that comes from building brain connection stimulation experiences in those key years for both infants and babies, then the likelihood of individual people in each setting figuring out both creative and consistent ways of doing that support for their own child goes up significantly.

Knowledge is power. In this case, knowledge is both strength and power — because that piece of knowledge about brain development processes and time frames gives parents a set of very powerful tools to use to improve the life path and the brain strength of their child.

We Need Mothers and Fathers to Know That Talking, Playing, Reading and Singing All Build Brains

The actual processes and direct interactions that can be done by parents to help each child are not complicated. They are generally easy to do.

Parents need to know that they can exercise the brain of their child and make their child's brain stronger by talking, reading, singing and playing with the child.

Children who have those very direct "talk, read, play, and sing" interactions in safe and consistent ways with their parents, or with other caring adults, end up with stronger brains.

It is a very direct and simple process. Direct interactions between the parent and the child are the functional key to the neuron-connectivity building tool kit that exists in each child's brain. Talking, reading, playing, interacting and singing to each child strengthens the brain.

Parents who understand the value of those basic functional interactions can generally figure out how to make those particular sets of interactions happen for their children in the settings where they live, and where they interact with their child.

Talking, for example, can be done almost anywhere. Talking to a child directly is a very effective and powerful way to exercise the brain of a child.

Talking Directly to a Child Builds Brain Strength

Talking is often the easiest interaction tool to use and it actually leads the interaction list as a positive, useful and effective thing for a parent to do. Talking can have amazing benefits for a child. People too often do not know that those benefits exist and do not know that those benefits can be created for a child by that deceptively simple behavior.

Talking directly to a child is actually an absolutely essential tool that parents and families need to understand and use to create the needed levels of exercise for their child's brain. Talking directly in safe and positive ways is generally the single most useful brain-building tool for each child, in fact. Talking directly to a child also significantly reduces the risk of toxic stress syndrome in very young children, so that simple level of direct verbal interaction actually offers multiple levels of benefit to a child.

Baby and infant brains are stimulated in powerful ways when caring adults speak directly to the children.

Talking in direct and interactive ways to a child is a growth process and a brain exercise tool that strengthens children's brains and supports neuron connectivity processes very directly and effectively. It is overwhelmingly clear that children who are spoken to often by adults in those key months and years benefit directly and significantly from that process.

People used to think that talking to a baby was idle and useless chatter — simply a pleasant and enjoyable way of parents passing time. People also used to believe that talking to a baby when the baby was too young to talk back and too young to respond verbally was a waste of time for both mother and baby.

Those beliefs are both dangerously incorrect.

We now know that talking to a baby from the very first month of life actually very directly stimulates and exercises important neuron connectivity processes at very direct levels in each baby's brain long before any child can respond with words of their own.

Brain scans done of children by some important research programs show the positive impact of talking directly to a child. Multiple studies have been done that show better learning skills and much larger vocabularies for the children who have been talked to directly and frequently by adults in those key years.[40,44]

The basic packages of adult interactions with children that build strong brains all begin by having parents or other caring and trusted adults talking directly and talking often to each child. Parental interactions with babies and small children in those first years tend to generate major functional value for developing brains. Children's brains need those direct spoken interactions for maximum stimulation of the neuron connectivity process.

Children in those first years of life actually need adults to talk directly to them for both brain growth and for emotional security and stability.

The more that a child hears direct and positive adult conversation from a caring adult in those key months and years, the stronger the neuron connections are in each child's brain.

The new brain scan research programs show that baby brains get activated in important ways when adults talk directly to a child, and when adults interact verbally in various ways with each child. Dr. Patricia Kuhl and her team at the Center for Mind, Brain, and Learning at the University of Washington have done some powerful research into those issues, which everyone who is concerned about early brain development should know about.

Talking and Reading Should Lead Every List

If no other brain building exercise interactions beyond talking happen with a child, having regular and direct verbal interactions with trusted adults builds strong baby brains and those interactions also gives each child a sense of security that directly supports the learning processes.

Talking can be golden. Children respond well to direct verbal communications. Parents can help their children in multiple ways by talking and interacting with their child. Talking directly to children creates both brain strength and emotional strength when the communications with the child are done in a positive, accepting, and loving way.

Several key studies have shown that the children who hear the most words spoken in those key years tend to have much larger vocabularies in kindergarten. Those children who are spoken to directly and often in those key months and years tend to have better reading skills — both in the third grade and in later years of school — in comparison to the children who have had the fewest words spoken to them in those key first years.[4]

Some Talking Levels Have Been Linked to Income Levels

Even though the income levels of parents do not have a direct, operational and functional link to the numbers of words that are spoken to any child, studies have shown some very clear patterns for groups of people where higher-income people tend to speak more often in direct ways to their children.

We need to understand those patterns and those linkages and we need to know what they mean for the development of each child.

The patterns of speaking to children that are shown by those particular studies are clear. Higher-income children do tend to have more words spoken to them than low-income children in those key years. When you look at average numbers of words heard by each child each day, the average number of words heard tend to be much higher for higher-income children.

That does not need to be true.

There is not an absolute, direct, fixed, or actual functional link between income levels of parents and the number of words spoken to a child. People from any income level can speak with any frequency level to their child. Talking is free. It does not cost money to talk. Low-income people can speak to their children with no expense involved.

We know that to be true because it does happen for many children and no expense is involved. Some of the lowest income families can and often do have very high levels of words spoken to the child in their family.

The children in those low-income families who actually do hear many spoken words every day each benefit very directly from that experience.

But the very consistent pattern that multiple studies show us tends to be that the higher-income families generally speak many more words each day to their children than low-income families.

We Need All Children to Know Thousands of Words

The difference — on average — in words spoken to children at various income levels can be extreme. Low-income children often have less than one-fourth of the words spoken to them each day compared to high-income children.[4]

That pattern of hearing fewer spoken words results in too many low-income children who too often only know hundreds of words at age three, and who know barely 1,000 words at kindergarten — compared to higher-income children who generally know more than 2,000 words by age three, and who often understand 5-10 times that many words by kindergarten.

We need all children to hear thousands of words directly spoken to them in those key years when brain exercise levels affect the development of each brain, because we need all of our children to have that stronger learning capacity at age three — and we need all of our children to be learning ready and reading ready by the time they enter kindergarten.

That can be done. Parents, families, and child care settings for low-income children can very intentionally increase the number of words that are spoken to and heard by each child.

Communities and families at all income levels can support those processes. We need leaders from every community who understand those realities and who encourage all mothers and all families in each community to be talking extensively to their children. We need programs in all settings to encourage parents in each setting to talk to their children.

That support for the talking processes by community leaders, and by informed family members can very directly help each child who receives that support — regardless of family income levels. The final chapter of this book describes some of the successes that happen for children from every group when the number of words heard by low-income children in those key years increases.

The children in low-income homes who do hear higher levels of spoken words in those key years have life long positive impacts at multiple levels from that process and from that strategy.

We clearly need to have every mother and father understand that it is a very good thing to talk consistently and directly to their child — and we need every parent to know that talking can be a wonderful gift of love to give to a child.

Every Language Works

Too many people take talking for granted or assume that talking to their child is just a pleasant thing to do. We need all parents to know that talking can be a highly beneficial and literally life-changing thing to do, and we need all parents to know that their child will benefit directly from being talked to directly in loving ways with high numbers of spoken words regardless of the language used to do the talking.

90

Every language works. That is important to understand. There is no advantage for those learning processes to any given language. Every language works and all languages work.

Multiple languages can create even stronger learning abilities and multi-language strengths for children. We need all families and all parents, and the members of all communities to know that their children's lives can be enriched and improved when adults talk in loving, frequent, and direct ways to each child.

Reading Also Creates Major Benefits

Talking isn't the only brain and vocabulary building tool that parents and families can use with their child to create both a sense of security and strong brains. Reading is another very useful life enrichment and brain building tool.

Reading to children also has huge benefits at multiple levels that have been consistently confirmed by a number of studies and by the observation of parenting experts in a wide range of settings.[5,11,13,15,20,47]

Reading works. Like talking, reading also can happen almost anywhere — and it can help children everywhere. Parents in almost any setting can use reading as a brain-strengthening tool and as a vocabulary-building tool for their child.

Reading to a child is actually one of the very best interactions and one of the most effective interventions that parents can do for their children. The value of reading to children has been proven in multiple studies. Reading has clearly been demonstrated by experience in multiple settings to have value at several levels for the children who are read to regularly and often.

Parents who want to help their children build strong learning skills need to know that reading can be a very effective intervention and interaction approach for children. Reading is a brain building interaction that can be done and used in almost all settings by almost all parents and families, and it has a positive impact on almost all children.

Reading to a child creates several levels of benefits. Reading not only increases neuron connections — reading regularly also can help create a sense of safety, stability and security for each child.

Reading can help make children more kindergarten ready because reading to a child can teach each child that there is a cognitive link between symbols on a page and the meaning of words. Children who enter kindergarten without knowing that a direct link between symbols and meanings exist can have a more difficult time with some learning processes at that point in their education.

The children who enter preschool and kindergarten without having any significant number of reading experiences can find themselves at a significant disadvantage for some learning processes at that point in time.

We need to recognize and understand the fact that several studies have shown us that reading patterns for children also tend to differ — on averages — based on the income levels of families.

Several studies have shown us that higher-income families tend to own many more children's books than low-income families — and a number of studies have shown that high-income families tend to spend significantly more reading time with each child.[5,17,22,23,28,49]

Too Many Low-Income Homes Do Not Even Own One Book

Again — that overall pattern linking income levels and the average reading time for children in each group exists. When we look at those patterns, we need to understand that there is not a mandatory, fixed, or absolute linkage to reading levels and to reading frequency that is tied in some inviolate and functional way to the specific income levels of families.

Any parent — regardless of income — can read to their child. Any family — regardless of income level — can read to the children in their family.

Low-income families clearly can and do read to their children. Roughly 30 percent of low-income families read daily to their very young children now. Some low-income families currently read extensively to their children, and those low-income families who do read to their children often make reading a regular part of their child's life.

Unfortunately, however, several studies tell us that the majority of low-income families read rarely to their children, and a significant number of low-income families today do not read to their children at all.

More than half of the lowest income families do not have a single book in the home. More than half of the day care centers and the child care settings for low-income children also do not have a single book.[48]

The benefits that result for children who do have someone reading to them can be extensive. The opportunity that is lost for children who do not have reading done for them in those key years is significant, and it can be negative at several levels for the children for their entire lives.

One of the major reasons why low-income families do not read to their children is that most low-income homes do not know and explicitly understand the functional linkage that exists between early reading to children, and the ability of children later either being able to read or being unable to read.

Another major reason for low-income homes not reading to their children is the expense of books — a fact that can be highly relevant when every penny of income is needed to buy food and pay for housing.

Those of us who know that science and who understand those linkages should all be ashamed of ourselves for not teaching that set of linkages to all parents, and for not making adequate and affordable numbers of books available to children in all homes and in all day cares.

We need more low-income families to understand the benefits that result from the reading process — and we need more books in low-income homes and in the day cares that serve low-income children.

One study showed that making four books available to each very young child along with direct and explicit coaching to the parents about the value of reading had a learning growth improvement for the children with the books, which was roughly the equivalent of having those same children going to a direct coaching program by trained educators at that point in their lives.

That particular study only makes sense if we remember that giving those four books to each home actually resulted in the parents in those homes reading the books to the children, and creating new and additional levels of direct parent/child communications and parent/child interactions in the process.

The books that were placed in those particular low-income homes did not do anything magical just by being there to create those learning gains. The reading process that resulted from each family having the books in their homes created the gains. The sum total of those reading related interactions with the parents created the learning gains that happened for each child whose family received the four books.

Reading Works for Every Income Level

The actual biological benefit and learning capability improvements for a child that results from reading are not linked to income at any level. Parents and families of all income levels can clearly help their children build strong brains and build solid vocabularies by reading to their children.

Both strong brains and larger vocabularies are good for all children from all groups. Reading tends to increase vocabularies and reading tends to create brain patterns for children that make brains bigger and stronger for the children from every group, and from every income level who have someone reading to them.

The children who have larger vocabularies at age three and age five tend to do better in school. That particular linkage between early vocabulary levels and later scholastic successes has been shown to exist, and that linkage tells us that higher vocabulary levels need to be created for children from all groups in those early years.

The higher vocabulary levels that are created by reading are not simply due to the actual number of words that are included in each book. The higher vocabulary levels for children who are read to also result from the fact that when parents who are reading a book also talk to their children about the books they are reading, then the direct conversation that surrounds the books adds many words to the children's vocabularies, and does it in a way that is often anchored on the books and both inspired and triggered by the books.

The entire reading process also exercises and shapes baby and infant brains because it teaches each child the important intellectual concept that symbols can have meaning. That basic concept that written symbols have meaning can stimulate its own explosion in neuron connectivity in a baby brain — and that explosion can enhance each child's own capacity to actually read.

Reading Can Also Support Emotional Security

Reading can also help give children a very good sense of personal security, direct connections, and positive emotional linkages with the person who reads to them. Every parent who reads to their children can easily understand that connection and benefit — because the whole process tends to feel good at multiple levels for both the parents and the children.

Children tend to love having regular reading times. Millions of children also fall in love with particular books that are read to them regularly as part of a regular reading process.

Higher-income families tend to make daily reading rituals a regular, consistent, and comforting part of each child's day. That pattern can happen as well in many low-income homes — but it doesn't happen now in as many low-income homes as we need it to happen.

The linkage between being read to in those key months and years and later being actually able to read is an important one. Reading can clearly create a sense of intellectual growth for a child and can trigger a new skill set and a new mental capability for each child as the written words on the page become functional words in each child's mind.

Parents need to understand that the moment of linkage between words on the page and words in a child's mind can be almost magical in its own right —

and it can have a very positive impact on the bonds that exist at multiple levels between each parent and each child.

Reading Is Good but Talking Is Essential

Both reading and talking are key tools for early childhood brain development that all parents need to understand.

As a package, the truth is that reading to children is very good and talking to children is essential. Talking is actually the single most important tool. Even in settings where there are no books and no readers, children benefit hugely from having caring adults in those settings talking directly to them.

Children each need adults to talk to them. Mothers and fathers who talk to their children give the children a great gift of brain exercise, and that exercise can have great benefit for a child in those key months and years whether or not anyone reads to a child in that time frame. Major benefits can happen for children who are spoken to even when reading is not part of the interaction process.

Talking combined with reading is good, but talking all by itself adds great value, even if no reading is included in interactions with the child.

Playing with the child is also hugely valuable as a brain-building tool and as a source of emotional security and stability. Having toys for the child, playing with the toys, and talking about the toys creates its own sets of interactions that also help to build secure and learning ready children.

Too many parents do not know and understand how much benefit children receive just from having someone who the child loves and trusts playing with them and talking directly to them. Talking directly to a child on almost any topic is a very good thing for parents to do for their child.

Talking at mealtime is a very good thing to do. Talking while giving a bath or while helping a child get dressed can be a great thing to do.

Describing what you are doing in multiple settings — like shopping or cooking — can add real value for a child.

Experts tell us that it is most effective to talk directly to your child and to make regular eye contact with your child when talking.

Waiting for a child to respond to what you say can be particularly helpful as a brain development exercise.

The Center on the Developing Child at Harvard University has done some extremely insightful research into the value of what they call "serve and return" interactions with very young children.[12]

Several studies have shown that interactions that involve getting a response from the child — a smile, cooing, or actual words spoken by the child — all have particular positive impact for the learning process. The serve and return interactions approach can be taught to parents and those interactions can clearly be beneficial to the children.

The Harvard website has some very good materials that deal with those issues.

The research done on direct child/mother interactions in the first months of life by Dr. Beatrice Beebe and her team at Columbia University that is described in the Three Key Months addendum to this book also describes some of the basic impacts that happen very early in the parenting processes as a result of direct mother child interactions and mother child feedback responses in the first weeks and months of life.

Educators advocate a number of ways that can be used to talk effectively to a child. In talking to a child, rhyming is used often because rhyming has great power to teach word use patterns and because rhyming often is a good way to amuse the child. Rhymes have their own sets of learning process benefits, in addition to being fun and easy to hear and remember.

Rhyming books and reciting nursery rhymes all have powerful and positive impact on both verbal skills and thought processes.

The popular ABC song that has survived so long and is used so often as a parenting song continues to exist and to be extensively used because it is both fun and extremely effective as a lifelong learning and memory-jogging tool.

Significant numbers of adults reach into their memory and pull up that ABC song when it is time to alphabetize something.

That is a lifelong gift for everyone who uses that tool in that way.

Asking Questions Is a Great Learning Tool

Parents need to know that consistent and interactive conversation with their child can have significant value for the child. Pointing out things verbally to a child in any setting can be a very good thing to do for a child. Parents can do those pointing out processes at objects in almost any setting.

Asking questions regularly can also be a very effective thing to do for a child. Questions can be asked by parents in any setting — and the questions that are asked to a child about a wide variety of subjects can create very effective levels of interaction with the child.

We need all parents and families to understand that asking and answering questions can have a very powerful and positive impact on the conversation skills of children. Some studies show that having a dialogue and a give-and-take conversation on various points with a child can be a major building tool for brain skill levels and learning skills for the child.

Creating a dialogue that involves both the child and the parent is a particularly useful way to help children learn to think, and it is a great way to exercise their brain. That is true even in those early weeks and months when the children don't speak any words and simply make noises as their contribution to the communication process.

Making it a point to have a set of dialogues with each child each and every day can be a key learning tool for parents to use to help their children even before the child can clearly carry out his or her own side of the dialogue.

Any Questions Can Help Stimulate Brain Growth

The questions asked by parents to their child don't have to be based on any deeply designed agenda or specific curriculum. All questions are good. It's the

98

interaction with the child and the verbal dialogue and give-and-take interchange with the child that builds the most value for the child in that particular communication process.

"What color is that broom?" is a great question.

"What else here is yellow?" is a great follow-up question.

Other follow-up questions for the child tend to create themselves once the pattern of asking questions begins, and once that pattern and that behavior becomes part of parent-child interactions for any parent and child.

Twenty Questions Can Be a Great Intentional Interaction Tool

Deciding to ask the baby or child 20 questions each day can be a good starting goal for parents who haven't been asking questions of their children in the past. Too many homes ask no questions at all today. So having the parents of the child setting a goal of asking each child 20 or more questions each day can be very useful in those settings where questions are new to the communication processes with a child.

Twenty each day can be a good number of daily questions that can create and trigger the pattern, the behavior, and the practice of asking questions for an adult and a child.

One question asked to a child each day generally isn't enough to create a pattern and a give-and-take conversation. But 20 questions a day with questions asked each day to a child can clearly set up a patterned interaction with the child, and the 20 questions asked each day can often clearly and easily lead to 20 more.

Twenty Questions and Thirty Minutes of Reading and Direct and Safe Interaction Can Build Brain Strength and Security in a Child

Knowing what those tools are, it is possible for all parents to look at their own situation and setting and create both strategic plans and tactical approaches that can functionally build the brain strength for their child. Parents who want to build and enhance the brain strength in their child can build a plan for their child that sets specific parent interaction goals for their own daily interactions with their child.

Setting goals and setting up personal parenting plans can be very useful tools for parents to use in building strong brains for their children.

Setting specific functional goals as a parent about the number of interactions and setting specific working goals about the type of interactions as a parent can be a useful approach for parents who want to help their child, and who want to put a successful and achievable interaction strategy and brain strengthening approach in place for their child.

Twenty questions each day can be one good goal. Deciding to do 30 minutes of reading to the child each day can be another good goal.

If each parent sets a goal of asking their child 20 simple questions each day and if each parent also sets a goal of reading to their child for 30 minutes each day — maybe using two 15 minute increments for the daily reading time for the child — that combined set of interactions with each child can trigger neuron connectivity linkages and brain strength building exercises for each child at a significant functional levels.

Those simple and measurable daily interactions that are done as part of that parenting plan can create benefits for a child that can actually last for an entire life.

We could close the learning gaps that exist for many children in this country significantly if those kinds of direct parent behavior and child interaction goals — or similar sets of goals — were set and achieved for children who otherwise would not have those levels and volumes of interactions with their families or their caregivers.

That specific package of interactions each day with an adult can also give each child the safe 30 minutes of adult interactions that are necessary for each child to prevent and buffer toxic stress syndrome.

Twenty questions, 30 minutes of reading, and 30 minutes of safe interactions every day with a caring adult can have an almost magical positive impact on a child. Children need a sense of safety and a sense of security to thrive — so having a loving adult interacting in a safe and positive way with each child each day can create that opportunity to truly thrive.

More interaction minutes and more questions for each child can be even better — but 30 and 20 of each can be very useful — and being very useful is far better than not having any significant interaction support for a child.

Questions from each child also set up very useful interaction and communication experiences for the child. Children learn in large part by asking questions. Encouraging children to ask questions instead of just answering questions is also a very good thing to do.

"Why" Is Often a Key Part of the Dialogue

The question "why" is almost always a key part of that learning process for each child. It can be very good for each child to ask "why." It can create solid interchanges and useful learning for a child when the question "why" on any issue or topic from a child is answered in a positive and informative way by the adult in their life.

A major goal of the interaction processes between parents and children is to create intellectual capacity and to strengthen thinking ability levels for each child. Answering "why" questions can be a very useful part of that process and can build both vocabulary levels and thinking skills for a child.

We Need Useful, Fun, and Frequent Interactions

Perfect interactions are not necessary. We do not need perfect interactions with each child. We need useful interactions. We need safe and friendly interactions. Fun interactions are particularly good.

Frequent interactions are essential.

Loving interactions are wonderful.

We do clearly need consistent, frequent, caring, good, and often fun interactions in order to build brain strength levels in each child — and we need every mother and father to know how powerful those seemingly unimportant interactions with their child actually are in the development of their child's thought processes and their child's brain.

"Positive" Interactions Are Particularly Good

The whole interaction process for each child is particularly beneficial when the talking that is done to or with the child, or even when the talking that is just done at the child, has both positive and encouraging components.

Positive is good. Encouraging and supportive is even better. To do really well, children need positive and encouraging comments and interactions as part of the interaction process.

Unfortunately, the reality that we face is that too many interactions that happen with children today are negative. Too many comments that are being made in too many settings are negative and even critical — including scolding children, blaming children, or using angry words and angry tones of voice with the children.

Simply scolding a child doesn't create the most effective levels of value and benefit — and being critical of a child doesn't trigger the best brain growth opportunity for a child.

But saying positive things to a child does add value for the child at multiple levels. Saying positive things to a child helps to create a sense of security and comfort that makes learning easier for that child.

Positive Comments Are Better Than Negative Comments

That is another area where parents who learn about those realities in their own lives can chose to change behavior. As parents set specific goals for brain building exercise linked interactions with their child, including goals for the time spent reading every day, and goals for the number of questions asked of each child each day, it is also possible for a parent to very clearly and intentionally set the goal of having the clear majority of comments made to the child each day be positive.

A key point for all parents to look for in talking to, and talking with, their child is the relative numbers of positive comments made compared to the number of negative comments that are made each day to their child. Parents should set a goal of having more comments be positive than negative each day, and that outcome would move all children into the kind of positive feedback ratios that are now experienced primarily by children in high-income families.

Making sure that more positive than negative comments are made to the child each hour is a good way for parents to achieve their daily positive comment goals.

A baseline planning goal for parents who chose to deal with that issue can be to create a functional plan that calls for the parent to very intentionally make more positive comments than negative comments each day and each hour to their child.

Actually keeping a check list for even one day where all comments that are made to the child are rated as positive or negative can help identify both what kinds of comments are being made now, and whether the total mixture of words being said is sufficiently positive to achieve that communications positivity goal.

Many parents do not have a good sense of how many negative comments are made to their child in comparison to the number of positive comments that are made. Parents of young children are sometimes very surprised and even shocked when an observer tells them that they make more negative comments than positive comments to their children over the course of a day.

Positive comments do happen now in high proportions for some children. Many parent/child relationships and current parental communication approaches with children have positive, affirmative, and encouraging comments made by adults and parents to the child every day that far overshadow and significantly outnumber the negative, critical, and even angry comments that are made each day to the child.[4]

That situation of having the positive comments that are made to a child outweigh the negative comments that are made each day isn't true for all children, however. For some other children, the number of negative comments far outweighs the positive words said to the child.

Researchers have looked closely at those issues in several settings and some of their conclusions about those communication patterns were extremely useful to learn. This is important research and we will be well served if we use it to guide our thinking about parent/child interactions in ways that benefit children.

The researchers learned that a major proportion of parent/child relationships today, in a number of settings, have the number of negative or critical comments that are made each day to each child significantly overshadow the number of the positive comments that are made each day to each child.

Some children hear almost only negative comments now.

When that negative over balance of communications from adults happens for a child, the total weight of the negative comments made to a child can create negative perceptions and can even trigger some negative consequences and toxic stress issues for the child.

Some Settings Had More Than Twice as Many Negative Comments as Positive Comments

One important study showed that the parents who interacted the most with their children tended to be more positive, and those parents tended to have 3-6 positive comments made to their child for every negative comment that is said.

That same study showed that the families who interacted least with their children had twice as many comments made to their child in a negative perspective compared to their positive comments.[4]

Again, some of the studies that looked at that particular issue showed patterns that followed the income levels of the parents and connected the income levels of parents with the ratio of positive and negative comments that were made each day to the children.

One study that looked at the positive and negative comments by income level showed that high-income families in those key months and years for their child averaged six positive comments made to their child in comparison to each negative comment made to the child.

The middle-income families in that same study averaged two positive comments made to their child for every negative or critical comment that was made to their child.

The lowest income parents in that study averaged only one positive comment for every two negative comments that were made to their children.

The lowest income families, on average, made many fewer comments in total to their children, and most of those fewer comments that were observed in that study were negative.

Again — as with reading levels and as the research reflected relative to the total words that are spoken each day to individual children — there are many low-income homes that give very high levels of positive feedback to their children. There are many low-income homes where the ratio of positive and supportive comments to negative comments equaled or exceeded those same ratios in higher-income homes.

But — on average — the lower-income homes that were studied tended to have twice as many negative comments as positive comments made to each child as the daily experience for the children in those homes.

The overall impact on the personal development processes for each set of children by that balance of negative and positive comments that are made to the children is not hard to understand.

Negative/Positive Comment Levels Are Not Mandated or Inevitable

Those studies were — as so many of those studies are — based on averages. Those results and those patterns of negative and positive comments made to children are not based on anything inevitable or on anything that is fixed, required, inviolate, or even predestined as rigid and mandatory behavior levels for any specific family or for any particular set of people.

There is no law, regulation, or mandate that requires either set of behaviors for either group of people. Many low-income families now have much higher percentages of positive comments made to their children. Some high-income homes today have the majority of comments that are made to their children made in a negative way.

Those numbers that the researchers discovered about negative and positive comments made in various settings reflect patterns — not rules. Those patterns can each be changed for each family and they can be changed for each set of people. People who are aware of those patterns and who want different communications to happen for their own children can simply and explicitly decide to change those communications and change the ratio of positive to negative comments made in their own interactions with their own children.

We are more likely to have people decide to change the nature of those comments now in various settings and in our various family interactions, because we now know that those unfortunate negative comment patterns exist for too many children. That knowledge of the existence of those negative patterns gives us both the power to make informed choices, and the functional opportunity to make a change for individual children and individual families for future communications with their children.

That change in the ratio of positive comments to negative comments can happen for each child, one at a time. Low-income parents and low-income families who become aware of those patterns can now simply decide to make the number of positive comments exceed the number of negative comments each day for their child.

It Doesn't Take Money to Make Positive Comments

It doesn't take money, wealth, or resources to make positive comments to a child. It can take a conscious decision to make more positive comments — and that decision to make positive comments can be done one child at a time, one family at a time, one parent at a time, one home at a time, and even one community at a time.

When entire communities become aware of those patterns of communications with children, the culture of the community can sometimes be changed by the people who are in it. People in any setting can decide to create a culture of positive comments and continuous positive feedback to their children. Both families and communities who understand these issues can chose to encourage positive affirmations to the very young people in each family and setting.

The patterns we see too often now of having most comments made in a negative way can change for each child and it can change for each family if families decide to make having a high number of positive comments made to their child a chosen behavior for each parent and for each family.

All parents love their children. All parents want their children to do well. Negative comments are not, by themselves, a bad thing to make. The parents who are making critical comments to their children now are often warning the children about things that really do need warnings.

"Don't touch the hot stove" truly is a negative comment that can and should be made by parents at every income level to every child.

Warnings about those kinds of issues are a legitimate part of life and warnings and admonitions about various dangerous and undesirable behaviors are an important component of raising every child. Every home needs to make some of those negative comments to create a safe set of behaviors for each child.

What we need to change in a number of home settings now, however, is to very intentionally and deliberately add a number of positive comments to each child's daily experience of warnings and admonitions.

"Don't touch the hot stove" needs to be followed by — "What color is the stove?"

Or — even better — "Good girl. You are really smart not to touch that hot stove. You are really a very smart little girl and I love you so much. So let's not touch that hot stove. Why do you think we have the stove? What color is the stove?"

We Need to Add Positive Comments to the Admonitions

It can be very beneficial to our children if parents who make those kinds of admonitions also decide to very intentionally offer a range of positive comments to their children. That will be very well received by our children. Children love their parents and children tend to get particular joy from having positive and loving things said very directly to them by their parents.

Every child loves hearing those kinds of loving statements from their parents and from other trusted adults in their lives.

Children beam and glow when their parents say positive and loving things to them. It does not cost money to make positive comments to a child — and children in the lowest income homes may benefit even more when those positive comments are made.

We have not done a very good job of encouraging those positive communication approaches as a consistent part of our overall parenting culture as a nation.

We need to support behavior patterns for all groups of parents that enhance the likelihood of each child doing well in those areas by having both parents and families giving more encouraging and positive comments to each child.

We need to encourage parents and families from all income levels and all groups to deliberately and intentionally aim at having the clear majority of the comments that are made to each child each day in each setting have a positive rather than a negative tone.

Children who hear more positive comments than negative comments feel both loved and safe — and that creates a major opportunity for learning skill growth, personal security, and a sense of self-worth at the same time.

Some Negative Comments Are Inevitable

We need to remember that some negative comments will happen for any child. That is natural. Negative comments like "Don't do that" are inevitable in parent/child interactions. "Don't burn yourself" can be a very good thing to say to a child.

Even the most positive families who had a 6-1 ratio of positive to negative comments for each child did not have a 6-0 ratio. Children often need guidance from a parent or adult, and sometimes the needed guidance involves negative comments.

But if the only perceived feedback from an adult to a child every day is negative, then that experience can unintentionally slow the learning process for the children. An overwhelmingly negative balance on the comments made to a child can cause that child to be less eager to interact, less ready to learn, and less secure in his or her own sense of who they are.

Individual children can benefit significantly if the parents or the adults in their lives make a point of supplementing any basically negative words with positive words that, in total, outnumber the negative feedback given to a child.

As we build a continuously improving parenting culture for America, we would be well served by teaching parents to make a deliberate point of having the positive words that are said to each child each day outnumber the negative words that are said to each child each day.

That can be a good functional goal for parents to set for their own communications with their child as part of their overall strategy to build a strong brain and a secure future for their child.

Toxic Stress Can Be Reduced or Avoided

The brain development chapter of this book talked about the very real lifetime damage that can happen in the brains of very young children who face constant stress, and who have a set of basic stress neurochemicals constantly activated in their brains.[26,27,45,50-52,55]

Some extremely powerful research has been done into the life-long impact that can happen to children who have "Adverse Childhood Experiences" early in their lives. Researchers at Kaiser Permanente looked at decades of health care experience for children who faced stress and other adverse experiences, and discovered that there were a number of health conditions where the negative health consequences and the negative health outcomes for the children with early adverse experiences more than doubled in later years of their life.[55]

That research about the long-term damage that is done by early negative experiences for each child needs to be understood by every caregiver for young children, and by the families of young children as well.

Dr. Nadine Burke Harris has a current Ted Talk available on YouTube that explains some of those issues in a highly understandable, accessible, and family friendly way. The Center for Disease Control has looked at those issues as well and concurs absolutely with their impact.[51]

In some of the worst situations, the children end up fairly quickly with toxic stress syndrome. That outcome is not a good thing for children.

Toxic stress syndrome can do real biological brain damage that we should avoid if at all possible. We now know that the damage can actually be avoided. The risk levels for toxic stress can be buffered by having parents talking, reading, and singing in positive ways to their children in those key months and years.

All of the parenting strategies that work to build strong brains and that help develop secure children — talking, reading, playing, singing, and directly interacting with each child — work to prevent toxic stress as well.

110

A key risk relative to that issue that very much needs to be avoided is a sense of isolation for each child. Children who feel isolated can adopt a mind-set of "presumptive negativity" where they assume that future interactions with people will be negative, and young children who feel very isolated can develop actual toxic stress syndrome.

Texting Can Be Distracting and Can Functionally Isolate a Child

Interestingly, the risk of isolation for our children is entering a modern age, and there are now new factors that can increase isolation problems for the children who are being born and raised today.

Texting can, for example, increase childhood isolation levels.

Texting and other electronic connectivity interactions that focus the mother or the parent away from the child can also create their own levels of stress and isolation for each child.

We are a texting society. We text in high volumes and we tend to use our various screens and our electronic linkage tools a lot. That isn't going to change. We need to deal with that reality.

Texting is not a bad thing to do in itself. But texting can be bad and texting can be damaging if constant texting time is substituted for direct contact time with a child in a way that functionally and significantly reduces needed direct and personal, focused contact interactions for a child with a parent or caregiver.

People who text with significant frequency and who spend a lot of time texting need to be very sure that they also have sufficient, direct and focused time with their children. High levels of texting can create real levels of functional isolation for a child with no awareness by the parent that functional isolation exists for their child.

Texting can be interspersed and interwoven with a sufficient amount of direct face-to-face contact time for a parent with the child and not create damage for the child. That mixed level of interaction can be successful for the child if the actual parent one-to-one and personal contact time with the child continues to be very direct, very focused, and clearly involves real attention that is actually paid to the child when that direct contact time for the adult with the child happens.

The key to success for parents each day relative to their child in that area of their lives is to regularly stop texting for a bit and to focus only and very directly on the child for a period of direct time that very intentionally and clearly involves no texting during that time.

Putting down the texting device or setting aside the interactive screens for real periods of time — maybe creating at least two or three 20 minute direct contact, and direct focused interaction times each day with each child — can be golden times each day for each child. And that text free, pure child focus time can be golden time, for each parent as well.

Some experts are expressing concerns that the advantages that many children from high-income families have traditionally had from consistently higher levels of direct parent interaction time with their children might be significantly eroded if high-income mothers switch their attention from their children to their various connectivity tools — with texting serving to create and maintain new levels of completely unintentional child isolation and inadvertent levels of personal insecurity for very young higher-income children.

It would be unfortunate at multiple levels if we closed some of the most problematic intergroup learning gaps in our country by having lower scores in the future for high-income children who face and experience growing levels of unintended functional isolation by being ignored in those key brain development months and years while their parents are texting.

We Do Not Want to Create Inadvertent Isolation

The value of avoiding inadvertent adverse experiences relating to child isolation is clear. It is obvious that we need to do a good job of not ignoring our children if we want our children to thrive, and it should be clear that we don't want texting to undermine thriving.

Children do not need constant and perpetual attention from parents, but frequent, focused, direct and positive conversations, and regular interactions with the parent are needed by each child.

That means that setting up and creating regular and consistent daily text free interaction times with the parent and child can be a very good strategy that meets the clear need by the child for those times of direct focus, and times of direct and clear interaction with his or her parent.

Putting down the texting device can be painful — but the pain of a child being ignored and the functional negative consequences of having the needed direct time with each child each day replaced entirely by texting interactions for the parent can be damaging at several levels for each child.

A Reminder App Can Be Useful

This is actually a good time to use various creative and supportive texting processes to support parenting interactions. There are now some very valuable apps that can remind mothers who text a lot to periodically set down her texting device to focus directly on their infant or child in a more direct way for a period of time. Those are very good apps for mothers to have.

Some texting-linked pilots that have done versions of that work have had encouraging levels of success in improving parenting patterns for the children whose parents received those texts.[57]

One of the texting related pilot studies involved simply sending each mother periodic text messages that simply and explicitly reminded the mothers that direct interactions with their child will strengthen their child's brain development, and that it is good for their child when direct interactions happen.

The Children Whose Mothers Received Reminder Texts Were Two Months Ahead

That simple text sent to those mothers clearly changed some behaviors. Children benefited. Very real improvements in measurable learning skills actually resulted in the children whose mothers received that set of text messages.

Those children whose mothers received those simple texting reminders about their child's opportunities were two full months ahead in their learning skills by the time they were only 2 years old compared to the children from a matched set of mothers who did not receive those same texts in those same key months.

That pilot was a clear success. It was very simple. The mothers who received the reminder texts each figured out their own ways of helping their child. Mothers who were reminded of that brain building process figured out various ways to help their children. The array of ways that the mothers who received the reminders figured out to help their children actually worked at a significant level for that set of children.

The expense of that pilot was almost zero and the impact was significant. We need to work off that learning to figure out a variety of ways to use texting to parents in creative ways to improve outcomes for our children.

We need an array of innovative apps available to support parenting through text reminders that trigger specific behaviors and teach key information about child development.

Parents also need to understand that a constant level of attention to the child isn't needed for either infant stability or growth. Periodic attention works well, as long as the periodic attention is regular, dependable, and focused very clearly on the child for special and dedicated times during the day when direct focus on the child is the functional priority for the parent.

Texting apps that remind parents who text a lot to make those child-focused times part of each day can be a good thing to have.

We Don't Understand the Full Impact of Interactive Devices Yet

We actually do not know yet what the impact will be on our children's thought process and brain development from the experiences of young children, who are themselves, increasingly and sometimes almost obsessively, directly interacting with electronic devices. Large and growing numbers of very young children are interacting directly with those devices today and some of the interactions are extensive.

It appears from some of the first studies that when parents read electronic books to children using interactive electronic devices, that parent linked reading process can create some of the same value for children as regular book reading. But that positive initial benefit apparently only happened in those studies when the parent was also interacting with the child during the reading process and when the e book was held and shared like a paper book.

We know from other research that passive screens, like basic television watching, can actually slow the learning development in young children. Studies have shown that children in those key months and years who just watch television actually lose ground on their learning levels. The American Academy of Pediatrics has long offered warnings about negative consequences that can result from extensive watching by young children of standard television shows and content.

But children who interact with parents and with interactive screens seem to get at least some of the benefits that are created by other parental interactions.[58]

We need to understand all of those processes more completely. Those interactive devices are already a major part of the life experience for many children. We do know that pure electronic book reading has great value, and it appears that other interactive linkage levels by young children with various electronic information sources seem may add some value as well.

Many of the best children's books are now being made available for electronic reading. Used appropriately, they can function just like a paper book.

We should encourage those processes and those electronic access links to books because so many low-income homes have no books today, but many of those homes with no paper books do have electronic connectivity tools.

The final chapter of this book describes some of the programs that exist now to get both real books and video books into the hands of low-income children.

It is clear that the older children who interact with certain kinds of computerized games are creating faster mental response times for some functions. We don't know yet about the impact that whole area of brain development will have on major areas of our children's lives.

We need relevant foundations and various research funding organizations to fund studies of those functions so that we can have the best minds in academia able to spend time figuring out what those impacts are and how we can make them most beneficial for children.

That new world of connectivity for our children is not going to go away. We need to understand it so that we can create the most benefit for our children in the context of that clearly ongoing connectivity reality for our children and our society.

We Need to Encourage and Support the Parent Interaction Role

We do know now from basic life experience and from all of the new brain science, and all of the new developmental process research that parents play a huge role in the lives of each baby and each infant. Parents are extremely important to children. That has always been true and that will always continue to be true.

For best results for our children in the key areas of neuron connectivity and exercising young brains, we now need all parents of all children in those age categories to know how major that role is for the development of their child, and we need all parents to understand what can be done to give their child the best start in life.

Knowledge is power. We all need to have that basic knowledge in order to create the equivalent of a public health campaign to support brain strength development for every child. We need the information about those processes that is outlined in the first chapters of this book to be known by all parents and all families of young children in America.

We clearly need all parents to know that their children need direct interactions in those first months and years of life when the universal biological processes that happen in every brain create permanent neuron connections in each child's brain.

We also need all parents to know that if that opportunity to stimulate and exercise each brain is missed, the brain literally prunes out billions of neuron connections and those connections are gone forever.

We obviously can and should still help all children who need help after that point. Development of those capabilities after that point is more difficult, but it is not impossible.

There are actually many important levels of brain development that happen for every child after that point, and we should support all of those processes — but the very best times that give us the biggest benefit with each child for those levels of brain exercise and building basic brain strength are in those very first key months and years.

Rather than doing damage control and creating support processes for improving learning skills and resolving economic challenges later in the lives of large numbers of disadvantaged children, it is far better and more effective for parents and families to do things that reinforce and support those extremely useful neuron connections in that key time frame when those interaction activities with the baby and with the very young child have the most positive impact.

The purpose of this book is to make that point and to call for that support — for every child from every group in America.

Society Needs to Support Parents in That Role

Parents are and will be key to that process and to those goals. Every child has parents. That is a biological requirement of birth. We need to do what we can to help parents do the things that will give all children the best start in life.

That will be difficult and challenging in many settings and situations, but being difficult is no reason to abandon or give up on that incredibly important goal.

We need, for starters in that child support process, to have all parents — and all families — understand those issues. Parents who know about those opportunities become empowered to make decisions in the context of that knowledge.

In some cases, the decisions that are made can directly change and guide parent behavior. In other cases, the decisions can involve parents looking for other resources to help their children in the ways that their children need to be helped. Those are both good things to do.

We need to help and support parents in both of those approaches. We need to use multiple levels of reminders and supports for parents — and we need parents who decide to reach out to the various support programs — like early reading support settings or direct in-home nursing programs — where those resources exist and are a good fit for their child.

We need, as a society, to support and encourage that parenting role and we need to encourage and enable those parenting and learning processes for the parents of each child. All of that support follows patterns that parents want and feel good about relative to their children.

Parenting obviously can create its own very clear and positive emotional rewards for both parents and children at multiple levels. Parents love their children. Parents want their children to succeed in life and to thrive.

Knowing that those future consequences will happen for children is a good thing, but the immediate positive feedback that parents feel and receive from

118

those behaviors is even more important as a factor that guides behavior in the moment we live in

Many of the very best rewards for parents actually come from the direct interactions with their very young children, and we need to do what we can do to ensure that those direct interactions do happen in positive ways for as many children and parents as possible.

There is a very reinforcing and loving bond that happens with great benefit that triggers extremely positive feelings and levels of great affection for both parents and for children when those interactions happen.

Helping Children Can Be Extremely Difficult in Some Settings

The truth we need to all face, however, is that it can be very difficult in some settings to have the time, energy, or opportunity to make those connections happen for a child. Many parents are too tired at the end of a hard day of work to give themselves the time, or to find the time for those interactions to happen.

When a parent is in a low-income job — or sometimes in two or more low-income jobs — and when that parent faces transportation difficulties, and when the parent faces what can be functional child care logistical nightmares — and when the income level for the parent is so low that buying day-old bread, and buying basic food at deep discounts just to make eating affordable is a daily reality — then expecting that parent to spend money on a book, or to find time every night to read the book can be more than one bridge too far.

When a parent is exhausted and logistically challenged, finding the time to interact and to ask questions, carry on conversations, and read books to their child can be an insurmountable goal to achieve.

Parents who understand the brain development science and who understand the emotional development needs, and who decide and want to make the positive feedback levels and brain exercise levels higher for their children can just find it too difficult at times to do those activities at the levels that the parent would like to do them.

We Need to Figure Out Ways to Help Each Child

Exhausted parents can have a much harder time doing the key things that children need in those key months and years. Parents with no financial resources can face major barriers to doing those activities for their child in those high opportunity time frames.

When those kinds of realities and logistical challenges are true for a family, the rest of us need to figure out how we can help the parents of young children in those settings get the time and the resources that are needed to help each child.

We cannot abandon those children. Every child we help at that point in his or her life will have a better life if those needs are met at that point in time. We need to recognize the need to help each child and we need to accept the ethical and moral obligation to help each child now that we understand what those processes and those risks are, and how they change actual lives of very real people every day.

All children will do well and we will close and prevent the learning gaps that are crippling too many of our schools today when we figure out how to do what needs to be done to help make those needed interactions with each child in those key years a reality for each child in every setting.

Parents are very clearly the essential place to start. All parents need to have a clear sense that their own direct interactions with their children — particularly in those first years of life — are essential and invaluable to their children. The rest of society needs to help mothers and fathers and families with those kinds of pressures find the time and the resources to focus on their child, and to have their child's needs met in those key months and years when lives can be moved to better trajectories.

Every child we save is a child we save.

We Need Both Books and Support Resources in Homes and Day Cares

We need various kinds of support programs — like the visiting home nurses programs — that teach mothers useful sets of parenting skills in the home and that can even model those skills by helping the actual child. We need to support those programs and make them available where they are needed to change the life trajectory of a child.

We also need other programs that help by reading to children and by getting books and educational support sources into homes. Children need toys to learn — and helping all children have basic building blocks and other logistical toys that teach function and structure to each child can be a very good thing to do.

We need day cares for low-income mothers that very intentionally and deliberately help to meet those brain-strengthening processes for each child.

We need to help low-income mothers to seek out day care settings that provide those services, and we need to all expect all day cares to do those activities for the children they serve.

The logistics of daily living for low-income people truly can be draining and exhausting, and the available resources for helping children in many homes can be slim or non-existent.

We Need to Make Books Available to Low-Income Children

In many low-income settings, every single available amount of money is spent on rent, food, and basic living expenses. Having discretionary money for parents to spend on books for their children can be extremely difficult.

We know from several studies that between 50 and 61 percent of low-income homes have no children's books today.

We also know that low-income mothers are eight times more likely to read to their children if the mothers are given books, and if the mothers are also told about the benefits to their child that are created by reading.

We also know that even though more than half of our low-income mothers do not read to their children now, more than 30 percent of our low-income mothers do read daily. We know from that information that it is entirely possible to have reading done in low-income homes.

The number of low-income homes that read to their children will go up significantly when more low-income homes have books in the homes. The number of low-income day cares and custodial settings who read to the children under their care will also go up significantly when more of those settings have books in them.

Those facts all create obvious opportunities. There clearly are a set of actions that we should collectively encourage and support — providing resources of various kinds to low-income families as effectively and often as we can to encourage the right levels of interactions with an adult will happen at some level for each child in those key years.

We Clearly Need Day Cares to Support Parents in Those Activities

We very much need our day cares — both the institutional group day cares and the various kinds and levels of in-home day cares — to have books that they read to their children, and we need our day cares to very intentionally and very explicitly be part of the support system that creates needed brain exercise opportunities and processes for each child.

Our day cares need to be part of the brain development resources team for each child. Too many day cares today function totally as custodial, baby sitting sites with minimal interactions with the children. We need that to change and we need day cares to also understand their role in the overall development processes for the children in their care.

Many day care workers will love having that knowledge and that opportunity. People don't go into day care jobs because they hate children. People tend to very intentionally self select into day care settings and day care jobs in order to be with children.

Teaching those day care workers who are in those jobs because they want to be with children and to care for children about the great value they can add by reading and talking in positive and reinforcing ways to children can make those day care jobs better and even more meaningful for a number of day care workers.

Day cares are clearly a functional, but often underappreciated component of the relevant education infrastructure for each child.

We need the people who run our education programs for states and communities to understand that day cares are actually already a part of the educational continuum today for the children who they will be teaching in their kindergartens and in their elementary and high schools.

We need the people who lead those education systems and who run our various education institutions to do what they can do in creative ways to help those day cares with those activities, and to educate parents about those issues in various ways in order to have more students learning ready when the students actually get to the schools.

We also need to help mothers and fathers from all groups find child care support settings and approaches that provide those interaction processes and that meet those development needs for their children.

We know that low-income families can benefit from multiple levels of support — including having good day care programs that read, talk, and sing to their children and having support people who are able to visit homes and coach parents and help parents with that whole range of activities that build strong brain connectivity levels.

We all need to recognize that it can be an extremely rewarding and highly beneficial investment for us all to invest in those resources at the point in time, and in the settings and situations where that investment can change the life trajectory for a child.

Each child we save is a child we save.

We Need to Give Parents the Gift of Being Able to Help Their Children

Parents are the key to the future for almost all children.

Parents love their children. Mothers and fathers very much want their children to succeed. We need to give parents the gift of understanding about how parents can very directly help their children, and we need to give parents the gift of being able to do the very beneficial sets of things for their children that can make entire lives better for their children.

Both families and communities can help with that process. For the maximum benefit to our children, we need community leaders, community cultures, and family level understanding and support for that whole early child development process.

At the most core level, we need to focus on the family — on the mother and the father for each child. We need to help parents do the things as parents that will create real benefit for each child.

We will be making a huge mistake as a country if we do not create the equivalent of a public health campaign to teach that information about those key months and years to every single mother and to every single father as soon as we can relative to the birth of each child.

We need our full caregiver team — obstetricians, pediatricians, hospitals, and relevant nursing staff to share that science and to support that process. Another chapter of this book explains how that support from our care teams can be used to help each family and each child.

We very much need our communities and our families to support those parents in those processes. We need the whole village to support both the parents and the children so that we can, in fact, help every child in those key months and years when that help creates the most value for the child.

124

We know what to do. We need to do it.

This is a time and an opportunity for leadership to make a difference. We very much need leaders for all of our communities and settings who understand these key issues and who do what needs to be done as leaders to make the future significantly better for the children in the settings they lead.

CHAPTER FIVE

Families and Communities Can Help as Well

FAMILIES AND COMMUNITIES can both help our children build strong brains.

We need the family for every child to support strengthening the brain of each child — and we absolutely need every community group — every racial, ethnic, cultural, religious, ideological, and community-centered group — to make building strong brains for the children in their group a major priority for the group.

We need all groups to win. We need children who are born into every group to have the support needed for academic, economic, and functional success in their lives.

We have some significant differences now between groups relative to average group performance in a number of economic and academic performance areas. We are facing learning gaps today in many communities that are alarming at multiple levels. We need to make the learning gaps between groups that are so troubling in so many settings today disappear — and we need to do that by bringing up the performance levels of all groups.

We need to prevent the gaps — because it is so very hard to close those gaps once they exist.

We are seeing significant learning level performance disparities in too many settings for our Native American, African American, and Hispanic American communities. We can make those gaps disappear for the next set of children by focusing our efforts on the children, infants, and babies who are being born today.[2-4,22,34]

The children who are facing learning deficits in our schools today are the same children who had very small vocabularies at age three and very small vocabularies when they entered kindergarten. We need to provide every level of support to those children who have those challenges in their lives and we also need to make sure that the current generations of very young children does not face those same challenges.

To make that effort a success, we need to support all groups. We need children from every single group to get the brain exercise needed in those key years to build strong brains.

We now need to create a sense and a belief in each relevant community that we can make those gaps disappear in the future and then we need leaders from each of those groups to be leading the way toward helping the children in their group improve their learning capabilities in those key years for each child.

Leaders will be extremely important. Leaders from all groups in each relevant setting need to make sure that infants and children in those key years are getting the support that will allow each child to have the best chance of success.

Families Can Be a Major Resource

Helping each child can be done as groups and communities and it can also be done particularly well in families.

Families who want their families to do well and families who want to have their family members succeed in today's world can make that success happen by helping all of the newborn children and all of the infants in their family receive very real and functional brain enhancing support in those first key years.

That process can start today for each family — and the benefits for each family that does that support for their children will be immediate — because brains are developing now in the children who are born in each family.

Families who want to help their families succeed can use this basic understanding to figure out a variety of ways of helping the children in their families grow strong brains and to also help children born into their families avoid the damage created for the brains of children by toxic levels of stress.

Families often function as a direct resource to make life better for each child who is helped by their family.

Similar support can be provided within communities and by groups of people for various people in their group.

People in any ethnic, racial, religious, or cultural group in any community can decide to put the people in their own group collectively on a better path by making sure that the infants and the very young children in their group get their needed levels of brain strengthening interactions that each child needs in those key years of life.

That Work Can Be Done Individually and Supported Collectively

That process of helping children can be accomplished in specific settings for families, and for ethnic, cultural, or racial groups by people in each group who understand those issues and who want to help each child in their group do well.

That work can be done one child at a time. It can be done collectively for multiple children in a family if the collective approach that is used also provides direct and individual support to each child.

Each group who chooses that pathway of helping their group's children in those key years will have almost immediate benefit for group members.

We Don't Need to Wait Decades to See Results

The benefit to the family or group from helping children in those key months and years is almost immediate because it only takes a few years for a newborn child to get to kindergarten. Having all children in a family or all the children in a group "learning ready" at that kindergarten entry educational crossroads moment for each child can create entirely different educational pathways for each child who is helped.

Kindergarten participation for the group members can be different for the entire group in just a few years if groups make that goal a priority and if group members do what needs to be done to make it happen for each child.

The impact can be felt very quickly. The future dropout rate for school students can be cut by half or more in just three years — by functionally having many more children "reading ready" in each group when they get to kindergarten.

Each Family and Community Needs to Teach Each New Parent About Early Brain Exercise

As a starting point for getting more students in each setting reading and learning ready, both families and communities can simply, directly, and very intentionally help every single new mother and every new father understand and appreciate the great and important opportunities that exist for strengthening the brain connections for each child.

Group wisdom on that issue can add great value.

Families and communities can also help all new mothers and all new fathers understand the major negative consequences and the very real risks of not providing that support to each child in those first key years.

That information needs to be understood by all family members. It needs to be understood so that entire families can create enhanced interactions and appropriate and effective supports for the children and the new parents in their family.

Families can add functional value in many ways. Family members can read, talk, sing, and play with those very young children. Family members can support the mother of each new child to both have the time to interact with the child and to bring books and other basic learning tools to each other or primary caregiver for the child.

Families can also encourage mothers to have those kinds of interactions and can praise, congratulate, and celebrate the mothers and fathers who are having those kinds of interactions with their children. Peer approval can be a powerful reinforcing mechanism for having those behaviors happen.

We Need Ethnic, Racial, and Cultural Leaders to Understand This Opportunity and Process

We need all groups in America to do well. We will not be successful as a nation if we end up with widening learning gaps between groups and if we have significant and growing numbers of children who are left behind in those key areas of development.

We need each ethnic, racial, cultural, and community group to be part of the agenda for success, as well as having each family support those efforts.

That information about early childhood brain development clearly needs to be understood by all of our various ethnic, racial, cultural, and geography-linked communities and by their leaders. We very much need our community leaders in each of those settings from each of those groups to support those activities.

We Need Community Cultures to Support Learning

We need our community cultures in all settings to include basic values that call for supporting all children in each community in those early months and years when that support for each child sets key paths for each child's life.

We need communities to create resources to do that work where those resources are needed by parents who are overworked, under pressure, and who have significant resource issues and financial difficulties.

We need communities to support parents and families in that process when support by the group in various ways can make a difference in parenting approaches for each child in need of support at the time when that support is most needed.

We also need each of our communities to have a culture of continuous learning.

We need all group members to appreciate the value of a learning process that starts at birth and then continues through the life of each person.

We need both community leaders and family leaders who teach and preach the values of continuous learning and who both understand and support the processes that are needed to give each child the best set of opportunities to learn. We need those same leaders to support and celebrate the parents who are giving those levels of support to their children.

Aunts, Uncles, and Grandparents Can Provide Direct Support

Multiple layers of family members can be involved to help each child. We often see very useful functional child raising roles for grandparents, aunts, uncles, and other family members in the support processes that exist now for our children in those first years of life.

For many children, the main support resource for child raising that extends beyond parents for a child is, in fact, other family members.

Grandparents play a major role in that entire process for many children. Grandparents often interact directly with the children and grandparents often very directly help the children's parents in the parent's support of their grandchildren.

Grandparents also often serve as a source of wisdom, experience, direction, and guidance for parents and families on child-related issues. Raising children is an area where shared family experience and years of related knowledge can be particularly useful and important.

We now need all grandparents also to understand the science and the function of brain development in those first key years for each child.

Some cultural traditions have actually — entirely unintentionally — caused some grandparents in some settings to give advice about child raising to parents that have worked against the most effective brain exercise practices and that hinder and reduce some direct child interactions in the time-limited

132

opportunities that are available in those first months and years to strengthen children's brains.

Some cultural practices in some settings have included having grandparents advising new parents in their group and family to not interact directly with their children in several ways in those first key years.

That advice from the perspective of an older culture to avoid some levels of interacting with children and to avoid responding to inquisitive or emotionally needy children has unintentionally and inadvertently weakened the brain development process for some children in some settings. The children who have been at least partially ignored as a result of that advice and who were "not spoiled" in those settings where that particular advice has guided parental behaviors are less likely to get the brain exercise needed to strengthen their brains in those key years.

We need the family elders and the grandparents who gave that old advice of having minimal direct child interaction in those early months and years to parents in their families to understand the new science and to know and support the need for mothers and fathers of infants to actually increase — not decrease — those interactions with each child in those settings.

We Need Grandparents to Teach and Use the New Science

In the best situation, we can have grandparents both interacting directly with children in positive ways and teaching this new science to new parents in the family. That teaching by the grandparents is needed and can be very useful if the parents of a child do not know the biology or the science, and do not know what the most effective approaches are for raising their child to be reading ready by school and to be richly endowed in neuron connectivity for life.

For many children, a grandparent is actually a primary caregiver. Sometimes the grandparent is the only functioning caregiver for a child.

For many reasons, grandparents can be both direct caregivers and a major direct resource in helping directly in the care of each child. That can be a wonderful thing for a child.

We need the grandparents who care directly for children to understand this new science of early brain growth in order to give the best support to each child.

We Need Grandparents Who Talk, Read, Play, and Sing with Children

We need the grandparents who care directly for our children to have the same kinds of talk/read/sing interactions with the children under their care that parents need to use to strengthen the brains of their children in those key years.

Grandparents and other family members who do their own direct read/talk/ sing and personal interaction support functions for each child under their care can transform the lives of those children.

The number of successful people in the world who point back to a grandparent as the key person who helped them personally in those all-important early years of their life is a very long list.

A grandparent who provides personal care to their grandchild in those early years can have a transformational impact on the child. Many grandparents have played that role for many children for as far back in our past as grandparents and children have existed.

Again, each child saved is a child saved. When a grandparent is there to help the child directly or to help a child's parents with various levels of support — and when the grandparent is able to read/talk/sing and to interact directly with their grandchild in those high impact years — then children's lives can be enhanced and transformed.

Families Tend to Care About Family Members

Other family member — aunts, uncles, cousins, and older siblings — can also do those same basic interaction functions that help create success for each child. Families tend to help and care deeply about their family members.

134

One of the most loving and one of the longest lasting things that any family member can do for another member of their family is to be there for their newborn babies and for their infants and small children in ways that help strengthen those needed neuron linkages for those children in those key months and years.

That support from family members for a child doesn't need to be constant to have a positive impact on the child. Each time that a child in that age range has an interaction with a trusted and caring adult that builds those neuron connections, the impact of those connections for that child can last a lifetime.

Security Can Be Enhanced by the Sense of Having Multiple Caring Adults

Each interaction with a child can have value. Family members with intermittent child interactions can add permanent value for a child.

Children's emotional security can clearly be enhanced by a sense that the child has a number of loving adults in his or her life who care for and enjoy being with the child.

There is a level of security created by children being in a loving family setting that adds value that reaches beyond the neuron connections. Families can and do make very real impacts on the life of each child and we need to make sure that we get the very best benefit from the family interactions with each child.

Communities Need to Provide Support, Guidance, and Leadership

Communities of various kinds can also help in extremely important ways with the development of our children.

Each and every community can add value for the child related developmental issues. Racial groups, ethnic groups, religious groups, and cultural groupings can all have a positive impact on children in those first key years. Fellow residents of a city or a geographic setting can add value as a form of community alignment when those opportunities to align in the context of neighborhoods or cities exist.

Mayors Can Play Major Roles

Mayors of cities can have a particularly strong impact on child development issues because mayors are often seen as the leaders of the entire local population. Mayors also tend to benefit as stewards of their cities when all members of the population they serve do well in both education and employment levels.

Mayors all tend to be leaders — or they would not be in the role of mayor. Mayors need to use their leadership skills and leadership leverage to create community support for the continuous learning of all children and for the reduction or elimination of any learning gaps that might exist for groups of people in their jurisdictions.

Mayors can help teach those issues about early learning opportunities to each community as well. For the most positive impact on children, all communities and groups should be aware of those early childhood development issues and all communities and groups should be doing what needs to be done in each setting to ensure that each child in that setting gets the support needed by that child in those key years.

Support for Children Can Be Volunteer or Funded

That support for brain development in children from various communities of interest can be organized and somehow community funded or that support for children can be volunteer-based, cooperative, and basically unfunded or self-funded. Various kinds of child support and parenting support approaches can work. The key is to have someone in each setting who is helping each child.

Volunteers in many settings can step in where parents need additional levels of support for the care of their child. Volunteers don't need to make lifetime commitments to each child to have a major positive impact for the child. Short-term and well-timed commitments to children by volunteers can actually sometimes make a lifetime difference for each individual child who benefits

136

directly for life from that kind of immediate, timely, and situational support from someone in those key time frames.

Every day of safe and secure interactions of the kind that strengthen neuron linkages for a child is a day of benefit for that child. Incremental and intermittent support from a caring adult on a volunteer or assigned basis for a child is functionally far better for the child than no support for that child.

Volunteers can help with that effort in a number of settings. Paid staff who are assigned in a focused and intentional way to provide that support directly to parents and to our very young children can also add needed levels of assistance to both families and the children who receive their support.

Students, Adults, and Retirees Can All Add Value

We need all of our day care settings to understand those key sets of issues and we need all day care settings — particularly the ones for very small children — to be having the direct contact interactions with each child that exercise the brain of each child.

We also need all day care and babysitting settings to have books to read to each child.

We need to think of day cares as an extension of our education system — the institutional support that educates the children long before kindergarten and prekindergarten.

We also need support in each home. Professional caregivers can do that work and volunteers of various kinds can also add major value to those processes and those children.

Volunteers to do that work of helping a child in those key years can come from many sources. Student volunteers have helped children in some communities. Adult volunteers can have a huge impact in the right settings.

Retired people who have already raised their own children can sometimes have the time needed in their own lives to help change the lives of a child.

Retiree volunteers can add value at multiple levels.

Retiree Volunteers Can Read to Children

Volunteer grandparents — retirees in each community who have time to give to change the lives of real children — can be a wonderful resource for our children in that time of high need.

Retirees are a significantly underutilized resource in many settings. Retirees often have both skill sets and dispositions that can benefit children — and some retirees may also have time to spend directly benefiting children.

We need better ways of facilitating that kind of helping opportunity for retired people who want to function as people who can add real value to children. Volunteers can literally transform lives by being there in a consistent way for the children who need that consistent and direct support in those first years of life.

Retirees don't need to make a 10-year commitment to a child to add lifelong value. A 10-month commitment at a peak time could add life-changing value for a child or for small children who are helped by that volunteer. Five months could change a life. Billions of neuron connections can happen in five months.

Community Reading Programs Can Also Help

We need more children to benefit from reading. Large percentages of our children have no one reading to them.

Community reading programs can be a great way of helping with the reading aspects of the overall early childhood development effort. Various organizations can and do set up places and times where children can be read to by adults. That reading can be done to groups of children or it can even be done for individual children who are brought by their family to those reading-focused settings.

Serving as volunteer readers in libraries, religious settings, and even in day cares or community gathering places can also give people a very pleasant thing to do that can also help make a real change in the trajectory of children's lives.

That process can be particularly helpful when the settings who provide the reading opportunity and who set up the reading resource also have free or low-cost books that are available for the children to take home and to use in their homes.

We also need all day care settings to include reading as a basic component for their care and interaction with each child.

You Can't Read to Your Child If You Have Nothing to Read to Your Child

A couple of studies of low-income mothers found that more than half of the low-income homes did not have a single children's book. Communities of various kinds can correct that deficit by making good and fun books available free or at very low cost to the homes and to the day care settings that have no books or very few books in them.

You can't read to your child if you have nothing to read. The logistics of that reality are self-evident. You can't read a non-existent book.

So we need books to exist and be available in all of those settings where we want children to be read to. Various programs can make that a reality. The best chapter of this book salutes several of those programs. They are very much needed. Making books somehow available to families who want to read does need to be done somehow in all settings if we want reading to happen everywhere.

There may be very few investments that a community can make that create higher levels of benefit than making books available to low-income homes. Between half and 60 percent of the low-income homes have no books today. Making books directly available to those homes along with information about the benefits of reading actually can increase the likelihood of reading for low-income mothers by a factor of eight.[5,22,28,47]

Homes with More Books and More Reading Have Higher Learning Skill Scores

The homes with more books and more reading times, tend to do better on all measurable outcomes for children.

Children with more reading time tend to have higher reading skills.

Preschools and day care settings for low-income children also need books. One study showed that 80 percent of the day cares for low-income children had no books at all. We need to do a much better job of getting books into those settings as well because low-income children spend a major number of hours at those locations.[48]

Daycares can have a major impact on the life of each child and we need to be sure that our day cares are encouraging reading and have books to read.

That set of consequences that links reading with other success levels is not just true for the U.S. A study of 3,000 homes in Germany showed that the number of books in the home strongly predicted reading achievement levels for children and that was true across all income levels.[48]

Another study of 29 countries showed that the number of books in a home was a better predictor of reading success for a child than the family standard of living — and that the positive impact of having books in the home was the highest for the least educated and poorest families.[48]

Book distribution can change lives — particularly when the parents of a child learn the new science of early year brain strengthening and are ready and eager to have access to actual books in order to use reading time to strengthen their children's brains.

Leadership Is Key

We do need our leaders for all groups to be promoting all of the direct interaction efforts — reading, instructing, and talking to our children. Our leaders should now be leading us all to helping every child succeed. It is hard to imagine a more important priority for any leader than having the children in the group they lead succeed.

Having the right levels of leadership in each community on those specific issues is key to getting us all down those new paths.

We very much need community leaders in each setting to help with this early childhood development support for all children in their groups.

Every group of people has people who are the respected, admired, trusted, supported, and emulated leaders of their groups. We need those respected and trusted leaders in each group to be leaders on this specific issue in order to save all of our children.

Each ethnic, racial, cultural, religious, and community group needs leaders who want to improve the future and the destiny of their entire group by leading on these issues. We need leaders who help the children from their group each be on a path that leads to success for each child and that will also lead to success for their entire group because all of the children succeed.

We have patterns of behavior today that are not creating those positive outcomes for too many children. The negative outcomes we face will not change until someone does what is needed to create change. The status quo will prevail unless leaders take us to a better future. We need respected and trusted leaders for each of our key groups and communities need to teach, preach, lead, and model behaviors that will help the parents in their groups improve the lives of their babies and support the brain development in those key early years.

Each Group Needs Respected Leaders Who Lead on This Issue

There are major learning gaps today relative to average performance levels for our American Indian, Hispanic, and African American students. Multiple studies show the existence of those learning gaps and the reality is that some of those gaps are growing larger.[2,18]

That should not be happening. We need people in each group to help the children in each group in those key years to keep those gaps from happening in the future for each group.

We need trusted and visible Hispanic leaders who explain those issues to the Hispanic community in each setting. We need African American leaders who have an equally powerful and equally influential leadership impact on the African American community to explain those issues to African American parents of young children in each and every setting.

We need leaders from each refugee group and from each local minority group of any kind who also has measureable learning gaps today to also help their groups with those issues in each setting.

We need leaders in every Native American group who are taking a leadership role on this specific set of issues for the children in their groups. Multiple studies have shown that there are major problems in the education levels of far too many American Indian children today.[61]

Some of the Native American early reading readiness levels have deteriorated over the past couple of decades. The number of school dropouts in a number of Native American settings has increased significantly. There are almost no children going on to college and less than half of the students in some communities are even graduating from high school.

That situation could be reversed in each of those settings if each child in each setting received the right support and the right set of direct interactions from an adult in those first key years of life. Children who are on a path to failure and major difficulty today can be helped to be on a path that will lead to success.

The only way to reverse that negative pathway is for people who lead in each Native American setting to figure out ways of achieving those goals for the children in those settings.

Each setting's leaders should figure out what resources are needed to break those cycles by intervening now with each child born in those settings.

There may be internal resources available or there may be a need to use external resources. In either case, the cycle will not be broken until and unless someone does what needs to be done to break it.

All Groups with Gaps Need the Same Sets of Strategies

That same strategy is needed for the leaders of every group where learning disparities exist today. The specific processes and approaches that can make success for children happen in each group will need to be specific to each setting.

Leaders in each site need to set the goal of having each child in their group helped. Then leaders need to have parents, families, and other group members figure out what the approaches and resources are that are needed to help and save each child.

That opportunity to save each child exists. It can be done one family at a time and it can be done one setting at a time. Each child who is saved in each setting can take advantage of a very different set of site-specific resources to use to address their own lives and their own learning pathways.

Today, the outcomes for far too many children in far too many of those settings are dire and grim. Learning gaps abound… some of those gaps in some settings are getting worse.

Those learning gaps can all be made to disappear.

Learning Gaps Disappear When They Are Prevented – Not Healed

For all of the groups in this country that have reading gaps today, we need to recognize that there is knowledge that needs to be shared about early childhood development with each parent, family, and group. We also need to recognize that there are some cycles of learning deficiencies that need to be broken in those first years for each child, each family, and each group.[23]

Leaders from every group need to break those cycles. Leaders from every group need to set up functional pathways to success.

We need leaders from each of our community groups who serve as credible teachers and as support resources for the parents of young children in their groups, as well as leaders from each group who help the parents get the resources each child needs to break the cycle of failure.

Group Success Is Improved by Having Group Members Succeed

Group success, for any group, over time, can obviously be affected very directly and significantly by having more people in each group who have benefited from the best early learning exercises and opportunities.

Breaking the cycles of disadvantaged children can be helped in each group, one child at a time, by getting the right support from parents, family, and friends to help each child in the group.

We also need our city leaders, our legislative leaders, our education system leaders, and even our congressional and governmental leaders to be part of the solution strategy for those issues. We need all of those levels of our society to be supporting the processes that are needed to break the learning cycles for each child in each group.

We need to build targeted community resources to help each child. We need parents who reach out to use the community resources and who use those resources for their children because the parents understand the value of helping their children in those first key years.

To create those beliefs and to support those behaviors in the parents of all of the children, we need community leaders from each group who are teaching and encouraging all parents in their groups to help their children in those specific ways.

We Need Early Learning to Be a Cultural Value and Behavior

We need to very intentionally and deliberately embed those beliefs about those capabilities and those achievement goals in each culture.

If we are going to break some of the negative cycles that exist in some settings and communities, we will need credible and trusted leaders in each group who work to enhance and modify the culture of their group in that setting to make early childhood support both a cultural value and a shared cultural behavior for their group.

If we are going to eliminate the learning gaps that exist by racial, ethnic, and cultural group in this country today, we will need to do the only thing that can make those gaps disappear. The only strategy that can make those gaps disappear is to help all children in each group in those first key years with their personal and individual neuron connectivity building process and do it well enough for each child so that those gaps never appear for those children.

We need to prevent the gaps — not close them. We need the culture of each group to support that process and to encourage the behaviors that can make it a success.

We need group cultures in every setting that support, protect, and celebrate the early learning successes of children in their culture.

Some Group Cultures Support Early Learning Now

We know from looking at multiple cultures that not all cultures hold the same beliefs about early childhood support today. There is clearly a very mixed set of beliefs between cultures on those issues.

Some cultures in our country do place a very heavy emphasis today on those times of early learning for their children. Books have been written about the "Tiger Moms" from some cultures who now focus high levels of energy on their children's minute-by-minute development opportunities from birth on — and who focus intensely on the immediate needs and opportunities for their child in the early years of each child's life.

We now know from the perspective of biological science why those cultures have had the success they have had in the high academic achievement levels for their children. Biology and timing have made those cultural approaches major successes for the children who have had that support from their family and group.

Some aspects of those cultural beliefs about focusing direct support on each child in those early years need to become realities for other cultures as well if collective progress for all group members is going to be a goal and an achievement for all groups.

The Focus on Early Learning Clearly Does Work

That early learning focus as a behavior and a cultural belief clearly does work for the groups of people who use that approach now.

The lifetime pathway results that we see for the children whose parents share those cultural beliefs about early childhood support can be seen in their children's on-going academic success — stretching on far past kindergarten into their college years and even into their post-graduate education levels.

The patterns and the consequences of those workable approaches to early childhood support are both fairly visible. Which cultures and groups of people are sending their children to graduate schools today? Those numbers have been studied and they have been reported. We know what those academic admission and success patterns are for those children who have that level of early support.

The Success Levels Are Not Genetic

What we need to understand and remember is that those success levels for those groups of successful children are not genetic. A high percentage of those very same children who are each doing so well today in all of those academic settings would be non-readers and many would also be school dropouts if each of those children from those same groups had been isolated and if each of those children had not been given those early years of direct and focused support that they receive.

Those levels of success that we see today for that set of children are based on clear patterns of parental and family behavior — literally beginning in those first days of life and continuing through those very first months and first years of life for each child. That level of support in that key time frame had a huge positive impact on the life of each child.

We can send all children from all groups down that same path to success, by using that same approach for each child from every group for those same key months and years.

The trajectory that is being created now for those children who get that direct and early support from adults in their world can exist in the future for children from every single group — that success can happen for all children from all groups if the first years of life for each child give a strong start to each child from every group.

We Can Help All Children Reach Their Potential — by Exercising Every Brain

Again — those basic and core consequences for those children who do well and those basic consequences for those children who do poorly in those areas are purely biological. The basic biology of early brain development is the same for every brain.

The time frames for that brain development process are the same for all brains.

Those differences we see in groups of children and in our collective learning gap data by group are not ethnic or racial at their core. All children from all groups have the same potential to develop and strengthen neuron connections in their brains in those first key years of life. We need to help all children achieve that potential by exercising every brain.

We need the cultures and the leadership of all groups to support the needed processes for each child so that all children get that needed support in those first key years of life. We also need to change cultural beliefs that create impediments to the learning processes for our children.

It is time that we understand clearly the fact that there are some cultural beliefs today that drive parental behaviors in ways that have either a negative and positive impact on that particular consequence of our brain biology.

We Can Change Our Cultures to Include Those Values

We need all cultures to expand their behavioral expectations to include shared beliefs about the value of helping children at an early age.

We need to change some beliefs in some cultures. That can be done. Cultures can be changed. All cultures are simply invented. No culture is genetic. No culture is innate or functionally inherent to any of us. DNA doesn't create any specific cultures. Each and every culture is invented and then each culture is learned.

We can choose to change cultures when culture change is in the best interest of the group that is using the culture.

That process of culture change for a group generally requires leadership of the group to be involved. Cultures can be changed if key people in leadership positions in a group take direct steps in intentional and deliberate ways to change the culture of the group on any specific point or belief.

We Need to Embed Continuous Learning in Every Culture

Leaders need to lead that process of changing cultures relative to those learning issues. We need all cultures to include those cultural values and to include the key cultural expectations about helping each child in those first years when that help is most needed by each child.

The book "Ending Racial, Ethnic, and Cultural Disparities in American Health Care" deals explicitly with some of those issues. That book says that there are major differences and disparities in American health care by group. That book explains that the very real health care disparities that exist between groups in this country are caused by three main basic factors — bias, biology, and behavior.

Bias, Biology, and Behavior Create Disparities

That particular health care disparities book describes how to fight bias and it explains how to influence behavior. We need to use exactly those kinds of strategies for children in the first three years of life. We need to fight bias and we need to influence behavior so that every child gets the full benefit of their own personal biology.

We need each of our community groups to explicitly understand and to directly support those strategies and we need to make those strategies real and functional for each family.

Celebrating Success in Learning Is a Good Family Culture Practice

Family members and group and family cultures can also help create success for their children by celebrating the successes of the children who do receive the right early year support.

Families and community groups should each celebrate the children in their group who have vocabularies that contain thousands of words rather than having vocabularies that are limited to hundreds of words at the point when children enter kindergarten.

The disadvantaged children in each group at that point in their lives will continue to need the support of family and the community far into the future. That need to help the children who fall behind will not change.

What we do need to change is to also now very intentionally celebrate the children who have been successful and who have been advantaged in their personal vocabulary building and learning skill set.

Children who have been successful in their personal neuron connectivity growth should be recognized and applauded for their successes by their families and by the culture that each child is part of.

We Need a Culture of Success

We need a culture of success and we need cultures that celebrate success. Success builds on success. Winners win. Cultures reinforce behaviors.

Success can be a foundation for success. Doing well and being recognized for doing well can be both beneficial and emotionally rewarding for the people who are recognized in any setting by their own group for doing well.

It can be very reinforcing for the children who are doing well in the learning process to have their personal learning successes receive the quiet but clear approval from other members of their family and from other members of the community who are most relevant to each child.

We Are Becoming Bi-Polar in Our Developmental Realities

Families do matter. Cultures matter as well.

Some mothers, fathers, and families in our country today are very highly focused on their infants and children. Children in those families and groups who benefit from that focus have a huge advantage over children who do not have that support.

Some children are surrounded from birth with a culture of support that includes a wealth of direct adult contacts, frequent and direct interactions, significant reading times and embedded and consistent reading rituals, as well as a set of constant learning experiences that happen daily for each child.

Some families have both the time and the resources to provide that broad support for their children as a top priority. Some mothers do those kinds of functions for their children at an almost total emersion and full commitment level for the mother.

Some of those highly supported children have almost constant conversations and constant interaction with their mother and with other focused adults. Those parents have extensive direct interactions with their children.

When they use day care for their children, that set of parents often insists that the day care settings they use for their child be solid, intentional, well supported learning experiences for their child as well.

The consequences of those extensive and positive interactions with parents and other adults are obvious for those fully supported children. Those children benefit directly and individually from that support.

There are many children in our country who are doing extremely well in school and in their various life activities — and the scores for the top children on the standardized tests taken in school settings are at very high levels now and are growing higher.

Some Children Have No Readers, No Talkers, and No Books

Some other children in our country are at the other extreme. The children at the other extreme have no one reading to them. There are no books in their homes. Reading isn't part of their lives.

The interaction for those children with adults tends to be inconsistent and low volume. The lower levels of interactions that do happen for some children with their adults can too often be angry, impatient, rude, critical, cold, and even sometimes, cruel. Children who face primarily negative interactions with adults do less well on their learning levels and capacity and they do less well on their emotional security and their interaction skills and approaches.

The chapter on our parenting tool kits pointed out that the most advantaged children in our country today tend to hear positive words for nearly 90 percent of the time in their interactions with adults. Those same studies show that the more disadvantaged and lower income children often hear negative or critical words for two thirds or more of their adult interactions.[4]

Those children who receive minimal support, minimal reading time, minimal adult interactions, and who often also hear a high level of negative communications, too often go down paths that will make their lives difficult and often painful and dysfunctional.

Where that channeling into negative pathways is happening for a child, we need to break that particular negative feedback pattern for that disadvantaged child. We need to turn the damage into a strength and an asset.

We need to set up positive interactions for those children. Many of the most effective positive interactions and comments made to children don't cost money. Making supportive comments to a child can be affordable in every setting. Children benefit significantly at multiple levels when positive feedback shapes their adult interactions.

We need all families to understand the value of positive interactions. We need parents, families, communities, and relevant groups of people to understand those interaction direction issues and to have their own interactions with the children in their family be positive reinforcement for the child.

We Need to Bring the Lowest Performers to Higher Levels

We need to help the children now who have the lowest levels of interaction, the lowest level of reading, and the lowest level of support in those key years.

If we do not help those children, we need to recognize that we are currently are on a path as a country of creating significant and growing bi-polarity relative to the capabilities of our children. We can't succeed as a bi-polar country. We need to lower that degree of division between our children by bringing up the lower performers and by giving more children with the lowest levels of support more support at the time when that the support is most needed for each child.

We Need to Offset and Balance Financial Resources with Human Resources

For those families where financial resources are slender, those financial advantages that create early childhood support resources for the most affluent children need to be offset for low-income children by very real human resources and by various functional resources that can spring from our families and our communities.

152

We also need organized and functional support systems in various settings that mothers can reach out to and use. We need approaches that can bring support staff into homes when that support is needed in homes to help both mothers and children. Communities need to have those resources available when they are needed for the children and parents who need them most.

We Need the Interaction Needs Met for Each Child

Children need that support and need their neuron connecting interactions from some source. It can work just as well for an individual child to have that support resource spring from the family and from the community as it does to have that same resource spring for higher income children from the children's parents' bank account.

We Need Families and Communities to Support Every Child

We need each child to have a parent, family member, or other caregiver to provide those needed interactions in those key biological windows of opportunity when those interactions add the most value for each child.

For the parents who have resource limitations and barriers to providing that support, we need to figure out support tools that can and will help the parent and the child achieve those goals.

The key to success is to have the biologically relevant direct interaction need filled for each child in that key time of opportunity.

We need community leaders from all groups who see that need to help every child in that key time frame and we need leaders in each community and each family to lead us to ways that the need can be met in that time of opportunity for each child.

There are programs like the visiting nurses services that can bring very important and highly useful support and services to mothers and fathers in their homes. There are a variety of support programs that can strengthen in-home parenting.

We need to support those programs and make sure they are available when they are needed.

The communities that have major reading and learning gaps today will not see those gaps disappear until each group does what is needed to prevent those gaps from occurring in the children from that group.

Those major learning gaps between groups of people used to be a mystery. No one knew how those gaps came into being or what caused them. We can now work backwards to see how those gaps came into being for each child on either side of each gap.

We now know how to prevent those gaps. Because we know how to prevent them, we all need to do what needs to be done to prevent them — and we need both our education system and our various government programs to help us with that effort.

The next chapter of this book explains both how our education system will benefit when those gaps are closed and what our education system of leaders can do to make those gaps disappear.

CHAPTER SIX

The Education System Will Benefit Heavily from Better Early Development Efforts

No segment of society has more to gain from having more children with strong neuron connectivity levels than our school system.

When children enter kindergarten with small vocabularies and when children can't learn to read by the third grade, those children present major problems for our schools. Those children with those challenges are much more likely to drop out of school. They are significantly more likely to drop out of school than the children who can read in the third grade.[7,13,61,62]

That makes perfect sense. It is extremely difficult for any student to stay in a reading dependent and reading focused school setting when the student personally cannot read. Dropping out of school can reduce stress, pain, and even embarrassment levels for non-readers.

The drop out problem for our schools is amplified by the fact that our children with significant reading issues are also much more likely to become pregnant while in school and the children who can't read are significantly more likely to be a behavior problem while they are still in school.

It can be really hard for a child who can't read to sit through classes that are based on reading day after day without responding in some negative ways. Negative responses clearly happen. We now know that 85 percent of the children who are in our juvenile justice system today are either functionally illiterate or can't read at all.[11,62]

Children who can't read are much more likely to go to jail.[9,10,65-67]

Before they end up in jail, those children tend to have behavior patterns that disrupt schools, absorb the functional energy of their teachers in highly unproductive ways relative to the teacher's basic teaching functions, and take away teaching resources that are badly needed by the other students in each school who are ready and even eager to learn.

That makes the job of teaching in those classrooms extremely difficult and it makes learning for other students in those settings significantly more difficult as well.

Schools Start in a Deficit Position When Students Are Not "Reading Ready"

Schools in too many settings start with a huge deficit relative to academic success when their classrooms have high numbers of children who have those problems and challenges when they enter school. Those children who have those challenges absorb many of the key situational and functional resources of the schools.

The schools with many students who are not reading ready can too often become caretaking settings for the other students in each classroom because significant teacher energy in each classroom is spent helping, supporting, or even constraining the children who have those personal learning challenges.

Behavioral issues can happen in schools both for the students who can't read and for the students who actually can read but who don't have teachers who have the time available to teach them and help them learn.

Some schools currently have very high levels of students being suspended, and that kind of situation involving many suspended students creates its own set of dysfunctional problems and issues for both the students and the schools.

That is particularly true for the students who suffer from Toxic Stress Syndrome. The children who had negative neurochemicals buildups in their brain because of early stress levels are significantly more likely to have behavior problems in school and in society.

156

Researchers tell us that the children who face emotional deprivation in those key time periods have their brains organized around fear conditioning and vigilance rather than around self-regulatory thought processes and complex thinking.

Schools Would Be Better Off If All Students Were "Reading Ready"

So schools would be much better off and schools would clearly be better able to accomplish their educational missions if the students in the classrooms were all reading ready and not suffering from toxic stress when they got to the actual school.

The answer to making more children reading ready is not to improve kindergarten. Improving kindergarten is one of the most commonly mentioned and most frequently proposed strategies for improving reading readiness for children. The goal of improving kindergarten as the strategy to end the learning gap is proposed by good and well-meaning people in full good faith.

That strategy, however, cannot succeed alone as our primary approach for getting more children reading ready. Improving kindergarten is doomed to fail as a stand-alone approach for reducing those gaps because most of the problems occurred for the slow learning children who are in kindergarten several years before they arrived at the kindergarten doors.[1-3]

Biology and the timing of the key brain infrastructure development in the first years of life for each child is the reason why that strategy of just improving kindergarten will not achieve the goals of having more children able to read and stay in school.

We need to be very honest with ourselves about the fact that kindergarten is too late to have the needed neuron connectivity impact that is needed for those challenged children. The pre-kindergarten year is too late to achieve full benefit for those children as well.

Pre-kindergarten is generally not the answer for the children who have fallen behind in those first years because pre-kindergarten usually starts at age four and the most important and relevant neuron connectivity opportunities actually happen for children before that very young age. We need to solve those learning problems for each child before that time.

The time when the children who can't read most need our support to strengthen their learning capacity and their ability to learn to read is actually in those first three key months and years of their life before they even make any attempt to actually read.[3]

Kindergarten and Pre-Kindergarten Add Major Value for Learning Ready Children

That does not mean that kindergarten and pre-kindergarten do not add real value for children.

Both pre-kindergarten and kindergarten can be wonderful, life-enhancing, and highly beneficial growth and educational opportunities for children — but that is basically true for the children who are learning ready when they get to kindergarten. The right kindergarten and the right pre-kindergarten settings can do almost magical things to help learning-ready children into wonderful lifetime paths of learning... if the children are actually ready for those paths when they enter the pre-kindergarten settings.

The sad and painful reality, however, is that those kindergarten and pre-kindergarten years cannot change the trajectory and eliminate the learning issues for the vast majority of the children who are not learning ready by age four. For the children who are not ready or not able to learn by age four and five, the pre-kindergarten years for each child function more as a level and type of day care and as a child maintenance setting rather than being a time and place of major educational growth and learning.

Brain plasticity does not disappear at 3 years old — and those children who fall behind in those first months and years can be helped with both learning and behavioral skills, but that is much harder work to do when it starts after that golden neuron connection time has passed.[21,29,66]

Birth Through College (B to C) Is a More Useful Educational Continuum Than K to 12

People who talk about education issues often refer to the "K to 12" years — kindergarten through twelfth grade — as the relevant times for learning and as the right years for public policy focus relative to our education systems. For a number of years, we have focused our schools and our thinking about education issues in that "K to 12" context.

We need to stop thinking of our overarching education continuum for children as being built around a "K to 12" time span and functionality level. That particular continuum is flawed and deficient at both ends. "K" is too late. Twelve is too soon.

If we really want the best lives for our children and if we really want our education processes to support best lives for each child, then we need to start thinking about our overarching education and learning continuum for children as actually being a birth through college continuum. We need to replace "K to 12" with "B to C."

Birth through college makes sense as a way for our education planners and policy thinkers to think of the relevant functional learning continuum for each child. College should be included in that thinking because society does tend to provide college as a funded resource and because college is an important and highly relevant piece of the learning reality for large numbers of children.

College, for that thought process, includes any and all of the training programs that exist for students beyond their high school years. Professional schools, trade schools, and various technical training levels all should be part of our overall education policy thinking and planning. The students who are reading ready at kindergarten are also much more likely to do well in technical schools at age 19 than the students whose vocabularies in kindergarten only contain hundreds of words.

We need to think of parents as being the first teachers for each child and we need to think of day cares and various babysitting support systems as being the next set of teachers and as the first levels of institutionalized learning. Instead of thinking of our child care centers and day cares as separate babysitting processes that are irrelevant to the actual education process for our country, we need to recognize the reality that our day cares and child care settings interact in an educational context with each child in those key learning years and we need to take advantage of that reality.

We actually need to very intentionally build on that reality and we need to make each of those settings better learning tools for our very young children.

We need to include those settings as key pieces of our overall education strategic continuum — and we need to do a much more intentional and effective use of those settings as part of our child brain development strategy and approach.

We need to have parents very intentionally filling that first teacher role for their children and we need the various child care centers, day cares, and family support processes for child care to be very intentional next-step components of the education continuum for each child.

Focus on Education at Birth Leads to Grad School Success

We need both family cultures and group cultures to support that entire continuum and we need both families and groups to assign priorities to helping each child in those first key years.

Embedding those early child support behaviors and beliefs in group cultures has been shown to have positive outcomes for the groups who use them.

We know from a number of studies and from obvious observation that the cultures, families, and parents who provide the most focused support for their children in those first three years of life are also the groups who have the highest percentages of children graduating from college and also the highest percentages of children going into various kinds of graduate and post-graduate training.

The complete B to C continuum is clearly both relevant and real to those children from those settings and family cultures. Some cultures and settings emphasize high levels of interaction with their children in those first months and years. Those children from those families and settings benefit individually and those children each tend to do well as students at the very back end of that education continuum because those children were each so well supported at the very front end.

We need the people who do our education planning for our educational systems, funding, and educational infrastructure to think in the context of the overall B to C continuum and we need our planners to figure out how to create equivalent success levels for all children from all groups at each stage of that total process.

Our school systems need to support that process and need to explicitly support a culture of continuous learning as well.

Whether we end the continuum and planning for our education experience for each child at college or at graduate school, birth is the obvious and uncontestable place that we need our planning about education and development for each child to start.

Education Leaders Need to Address the Full Continuum

Our schools in each community need to encourage, teach, preach, and, where possible, provide support for parents and for children in those first years of life. Our leaders in the education profession and education infrastructure need to become leaders for that entire learning and education process and continuum.

We need our school systems in each setting to be community teachers in lifetime learning. We need to have everyone understand the values and the virtues of early childhood development activities. We need our formal education processes to create and deliver a full continuum of education support and education approaches that can allow us to achieve the full potential for each child.

We need to have our school leaders reaching out to each community and to each community group to help make the B through C continuum a community understanding and a belief system for all groups and a shared goal for all families in each community and setting.

We need the educational leaders in every setting to be thinking about the key role that day care, babysitting, and organized child care setting play in that educational process. We also need those who regulate day cares in each setting to understand the key role those day cares play in the brain growth of each child and to put basic standards in place in each setting that support that process.

We don't need to mandate that day cares have only licensed staff for dealing with children in those key times, but we should mandate that day cares have books in them and we should mandate that day care settings both read regularly and interact regularly with the children in ways that create learning readiness results for the children.

Our education leaders in each community should extend their thinking from just the K to 12 context to figure out what best practices could be for those day care settings and for those children.

We Need to Help Students Who Give Birth Understand Those Issues

At a more mundane level, we also need to recognize the fact that a number of students in our schools become pregnant and become parents while they are still students. We need the teaching programs in the schools for those students who have babies — and for the fathers of those children — to have a clear message and a situational teaching focus that explains the neuron connectivity opportunities that exist for each child to each new mother.

We need to break some multi-generational cycles of not having children able to read by having those newborn children of the students given the support each child needs to be able to read.

That can be a high value goal. Very focused teaching and support opportunities for the children of children who are at major risk of not being able to read can help influence a particular highly relevant set of people's lives in very beneficial ways.

We Also Need Our Day Cares to Support Those First Key Years

We very much need to think of our various day care settings — and even our more structured and ongoing babysitting settings — to be part of the teaching and learning continuum for each child.

A very high percentage of parents use either formal group day care settings or various kinds of home-based day care settings to provide care for children while the parents are at work. Some parents hire individual babysitters — often family members — who care for children in their own home or in the child's home. Some well-to-do parents even hire nannies to provide care in those early years.

Regardless of the type of day care that is used by parents, we need to make the day care process to be part of the brain growth and earliest education experience for each child. We need day care to be part of the education team.

To the extent possible, we need both day cares and babysitters to provide basic levels of read/talk/sing interactions with the children in their care. Regular reading time, for example, can be and should be built into those day care and babysitting settings whenever possible for each child.

Very large numbers of children in America receive day care at one level or another. We need the people who provide day care to understand the key development needs of the children in those first key years.

We also need day cares to have children's books and to have talking and reading time with children whenever possible.

States tend to license day cares of various kinds in many settings now. The licensing requirements often — a very appropriately — have safety components to them.

We need to take advantage of that licensing process to also require that the people who care for children in the settings have at least a basic understanding of the brain development biology and time frames that are relevant to all children. We also should expect day cares to have books and some levels of safe and educational toy elements in them.

It might be very useful to at least develop a kind of grading system and some kinds of measurement processes that can identify some key activities and then tell us which day cares provide those key activities and how often those activities happen in each setting.

When we get to the point where all parents more clearly understand those child development opportunities and issues, the expectations for day cares as a key part of the learning tool kit for each child should increase.

It would be good for people who study and understand those issues to develop tools to help parents understand whether or not their day care provider or their baby sitter is meeting those key needs.

In Home Support Resources Can Also Add Value

As part of our overall education agenda and infrastructure, we also need various kinds of support resources that can help parents in their homes with various levels of assistance for those key issues.

A number of communities are now building additional levels of direct parental support resources. In some settings, home aides exist who can visit the homes to help the mothers in various ways relative to their children.

Those home aide and in-home support resources that are available to help mothers in their homes vary significantly from place-to-place and site-to-site.

Where those in-home support resources do exist, we need to have those resources clearly focused as well on helping the mothers with the specific support processes that can help meet the neuron development needs of their children.

That support can involve having those in-home aides coaching mothers and it can involve those aides helping mothers to perform those functions.

It can even extend in some settings to having the aides, themselves, actually doing some reading and directly interacting in various ways with the children. That can be particularly useful in settings where the custodial parent for a child personally cannot read or has logistical issues that impede reading.

Each of those levels of support and approaches for that process can add value. Some very promising results for children in some settings have been achieved by having either volunteers or paid aides working directly on a regular basis to have the children in a setting get their regular daily stimulus and some level of regular direct interactions with an adult in ways that their baby brains need at that point for best growth.[29]

We Need Group Learning Sessions for Parents as Well

Those programs have been supplemented and enhanced in very effective ways in some settings by having mothers getting together in small groups to do group learning and to offer group reinforcement to each other for each other's efforts.

We need our various communities to expand those kinds of efforts as well — to have mothers supporting, reinforcing, and encouraging other mothers in their child support and learning efforts and processes.

Those group interaction approaches have been very popular and well received by mothers when they have been piloted in various settings.

We learn well by example. Seeing other people interacting in fun and effective ways with their infants can be a very powerful learning experience for a parent.

The learning by example process may be most effective in person, but various YouTube support examples and testimonials can also be good tools that add real value for parent education.

We need a rich array of YouTube types of examples that parents from all cultures, ethnicities, and economic levels can look at easily to see how other parents who are very much like themselves are achieving their own parenting goals and interacting with their children.

The YouTube-linked teaching process may be the single best way of teaching some mothers and fathers good and effective ways of providing both brain exercise and emotional support for their children.

All Students Should Be School Ready When They Get to School

Many of the support programs that are being created in various settings have highly beneficial and extremely encouraging impacts for the children who benefit from them.

Both communities and families should look at the available learning tools and support tools in their settings and should use those programs that work best both as direct support and as models for helping each child in various situations and settings.

Our goal as an overall education system should be for all of our children, to be learning ready when they enter kindergarten and to be reading ready students when they get to that point in their education process. We need teachers to have classrooms full of reading ready students if teachers are going to add the most value to the students they teach.

People become teachers to change lives for the better. Teachers who can focus on changing lives and on helping learning ready and reading ready children can have a major impact on those lives. That collective positive impact can make us stronger, safer, and more successful as a country.

We Will Be Stronger and Safer by Succeeding in Those Developmental Efforts

Being safer as a country is actually a relevant issue for our education system. We will be safer and we will be more secure as a country when we can create a reality of having very real educational and school successes for more of our children and when we have our schools create alignment rather than division in our communities and our country.

Too many schools have significant levels of internal division today. We need to look at the division that exists in our divided schools and we need to create alignment in each of those schools around the shared community goals of helping every child.

Division between groups of children is exacerbated in any educational setting when higher percentages of children in any group in that setting can't read or stay in school.

Those issues need to be addressed at the earliest point in the developmental process for children from every group — and we need to show clear evidence to all groups that there is goodwill and real efforts being aimed at those sets of problems and issues.

We Need Better Schools in Our Jails as Well

Looking at the full continuum of education opportunities that we can work with for our people, we also need to look at our prisons as teaching venues and as education support opportunities as well. Some of our illiterate prisoners don't have the capability of being ready to read, but some of our prisoners do have that capability to learn to read. We need to take advantage of that fact and that learning potential for those processes. We need to help those prisoners who can learn to read actually learn to read.

One study of prisoners showed that the overall recidivism rate for readmission to prison for illiterate prisoners exceeded 70 percent — but when illiterate prisoners were taught to read, the recidivism rate for the new readers dropped to under 30 percent.[62]

The personal benefits to those specific prisoners of not being sent back to prison are immense. Those are life-changing and very real benefits. The benefits to society of not having to re-imprison those reading capable people are also extremely high.

We should not ignore or overlook that particular high leverage opportunity for our targeted education efforts as we look at the total continuum of education opportunities that can help all of the people we can help.

We Need a Culture of Perpetual Learning

Schools will benefit significantly if we get early childhood development right for more children. If we created a massive campaign to have a culture of perpetual learning that helps each child from their moment of birth and if that campaign helped every child who can't read now to be able to read, that change in the student composition of our schools would transform our schools. It would also transform our society.

Schools Need Students Who Can Learn to Read

No segment of society will benefit more from getting the early childhood development issues right than our schools. The results will be almost immediate.

The benefit that schools will realize from helping those children in those years doesn't need to be realized in decades. Benefits can happen for our schools in a very few years. The benefit to schools of helping very young children can start almost immediately — with the children born today who are directly helped by someone today each coming to their pre-kindergarten settings much more learning ready only four years from now.

Four years is possible as a time of significant change for individual children. That time frame can be highly relevant to both schools and students. We can change a lot of lives and we can modify a significant number of almost immediate school realities if communities decide now to make a difference for their children.

We can also have a major impact on individual lives in those same few years when parents, family, friends, communities, and our educational support resources all help create the needed brain exercise for individual children.

The cost of failure is huge. We are failing far too many children today. We need to recognize that cost and we need to do what needs to be done to put us as a country on a better path than the one we are on today.

CHAPTER SEVEN

We Need to Reduce the Number of People We Send to Prison

WE IMPRISON FAR too many people in our country today. We disproportionately imprison people from our minority populations, and we disproportionately imprison people who have reading problems and who have dropped out of school.

Those are bad, dysfunctional, and damaging things for us to do. It will be very difficult for us to succeed as a prosperous and thriving country who is at Peace with ourselves if we continue down the path of putting far too many people in jail, and if we are clearly discriminatory in who we imprison.

We need to be a country where all children from all groups have an equally high opportunity for success. We need to help every child from every group avoid the pathways that lead to both financial difficulties and jail.

We need to make helping every child a clear and conscious goal and priority for us as a country and in our various communities, and we need to provide that support in a way that eliminates the discrimination and the disparities that are too often linked to ethnicity, culture and race. The book *Ending Racial, Ethnic and Cultural Disparities in American Health Care* deals very directly with a range of those issues relative to key areas of health care delivery. We need to apply some of the same principals that can be used to eliminate disparities in care, to the problems of disparities in our education and learning processes.

We need to be a country where each and every child is given the support that each and every child needs in the first key years of life to do well in school and to do well in other key aspects of their lives — and we need to do that work to the point where we do not have disproportionate numbers of people from any group being imprisoned.

We know now that 60 percent of our prisoners either read poorly or do not read at all — and we also know that over 80 percent of the children in our juvenile justice system today have those same problems.

We know that high school dropouts from all groups have a much higher likelihood of going to prison.

We need to be a country where every child from every group gets the kinds of direct and supportive interactions with adults that build brain capacity, language capacity, functional neuron connectivity growth, and basic underlying mental capability reinforcement in those first key months and years of life when biology dictates the building processes and the neuron connectivity levels that happen in each child's brain.

We need to provide that support for all children to the point were we significantly reduce the number of children who can't read, and significantly reduce the number of children who drop out of school and end up with the kinds of major economic shortcomings and logistical problems that tend to follow the children who can't read for their entire lives.

We need to be a country where we accept accountability together to help every child during that time of high opportunity for neuron connectivity — because every child who we do not help in those key years can end up with disadvantages that can last each child for their entire lives, and we need to recognize the painful fact that those disadvantages actually push far too many of our people today into our jails.

We need to change that pattern of putting so many people in jail because putting large numbers of people in prison is ruining far too many lives and it is creating massive burdens on families, on communities, and on our society across multiple levels.

This is not a hypothetical or theoretical problem. We put far too many people in jail. We have more people in jail per capita today than any country on the planet by a wide margin. We have more than six times more people in jail per capita than Canada. No other country on the planet puts so many people in jail and the gaps between us and other countries on that point is widening.

That painful reality is relevant to this *Three Key Years* book because the processes that end up putting too many people in jail tend to begin at an early age and because there is a clear link between reading and learning skills and large percentages of the people we imprison from every group in America.

We all need to understand the situation we face today. We should not pretend that this problem does not exist. We should be collectively — and painfully — aware of the reality that more than 84 percent of the children in the juvenile justice system today actually either read poorly or do not read at all.[11,62]

The basic pattern we see for far too many lives today is fairly obvious and highly visible. The children who cannot read tend to drop out of school. Those children who have dropped out of school from all groups have a much higher likelihood of being arrested, jailed, and ultimately imprisoned.

We should do what we need to do to have all children from all groups ready to learn to read when they enter kindergarten so that we create those disadvantages for far fewer people, and so that far fewer people have lives that are scarred and damaged by being incarcerated.

We Are All Better Off When We All Win

We need to think of this as an opportunity to create clear and intentional win/win outcomes for every group of people. We need to stop putting disproportionate numbers of people from each and every group in jail, and we need to take very clear steps to help every group prosper and thrive.

To succeed as a nation, we need children from every group and setting to do well and to succeed. We need all of us to win — so that we have the collective strength as a country and as a society that comes from everyone doing well and from everyone functioning at levels that create the best chances for success in life for each and all of us.

We are weaker as a country when we have significant learning gaps and when too many children are headed down a path that will lead to dropping out of school, being unemployed, and too often being imprisoned.

We are far stronger as a country when we have all groups succeed. We are stronger when all groups succeed in achieving basic economic goals. Collective success leads us to shared success. Shared and mutual success is very clearly and very logically a rising tide that can actually lift all ships in this country.

We all do better when we all do better. We all win when we all win. That is a simple logic that we all need to understand and embrace and then apply in functional ways to the basic neuron development realities for our children.

We Need to Support Neuron Connectivity for Every Brain

For us all to do better, we need to do the things that need to be done to help every child in those months and years when neuron connectivity levels can be exercised to build and structure a strong brain. We should all very clearly understand those processes and that science and we should collectively make a commitment as a society to provide that support for every child in those time frames when those interactions provide the most value to each child.

We need to do that work one child at a time.

We need to do that work one child at a time because our best new science teaches us that those processes happen separately for each brain. The basic underlying biology is the same for every child, and the time frames are the same for all children from all groups. The basic developmental process happens, however, one brain at a time.

Each brain develops based on its own pathway in that key period of time that means, from a pure logistical perspective, that we need to figure out ways of providing that support to each child at the time the support is needed for that child.

We All Do Better When We All Do Better

That process and that commitment to provide that support is important at a very individual level for each child — and that process and its aggregate consequences are also very important for us collectively as a nation at multiple levels.

We should do that work to help our children for purely ethical reasons. We should do it because it changes individual lives for the better and that knowledge creates an ethical obligation for people who now know it. Ethics and a sense of basic accountability that is created by having that knowledge about those processes require us to do that work for every child.

The Economic Benefits Are Painfully Clear

We should also do that work for very clear and important economic reasons. The economics of these issues is remarkably clear. From a pure economic perspective, economists who have studied these issues tell us that there are huge financial dangers and costs that result from doing those processes badly, and there are huge financial rewards and financial benefits — both for society overall and for individual people in our society — when we do it well.

Highly credible and well-regarded economists from a wide spectrum of economic thought have looked closely at those issues. The economists who have studied those issues have reached important and highly consistent conclusions about what they have seen and about the impacts of those realities for us as a country.

We now know that very credible economists in important academic settings believe that those early childhood brain growth processes and their consequences have major functional, financial, and economic implications for us as a nation that should be a priority for our policy thinking at the national level.

Several important economic studies have shown that the pure financial return on our collective investment that comes from helping our children in those first years get to a path for each child that includes being employed rather than being unemployed (and far too often actually being incarcerated) is conservatively a multiple of the program expenses that would be spent to achieve those goals.

James J. Heckman, Nobel Laureate and Economics Professor at the University of Chicago, has done some remarkable work focused very directly on those issues. His work should be studied by every government agency and legislature process that is focused on early childhood economic realities.

Dr. Heckman points out — from the perspective of a Nobel Laureate — that the right investment in high risk children at that age is the best and most effective way to break the failure cycle for that group of children, and he demonstrates that the economic benefits of breaking the failure cycle are huge.

Dr. Heckman shows us that it makes very clear economic sense to make the right investment on behalf of those children at that point in their lives because the pure economic return on that investment for society is so high.[21]

Other economic analysts in other settings have reached similar conclusions.[29] Economist Aaron Sojourner has done some important research at the University of Minnesota that has reinforced those findings. His papers on those issues are worth reading.

A Minneapolis Federal Reserve Bank study estimated in 2003 that the pure economic return for that investment in early childhood brain development would exceed an $8 gain for each dollar spent on the program.

Work done by economists Arthur J. Rolnick and Robert Grunewald for the Federal Reserve on that issue make very similar points with painful and persuasive clarity, and they also deserve everyone who cares about the economics of those issues reading their thoughts and their conclusions.[30]

Federal Reserve Chair Janet Yellen gave a talk in October of last year reinforcing those positive economic impacts of helping pre-kindergarten children.

A Harvard Economics study released last year showed a return of $4 to $9 for every dollar invested in early childhood support for children. That study was done and released by the Center on The Developing Child at Harvard.

The evidence assembled by those economists about the economic benefit of helping children at that early point in children's lives is fairly compelling. In addition to making lives better in important ways for all of the children who are helped, we now know that there might not be any other functional economic investment in our people that creates a better pure financial return and a higher economic benefit for us as a society.

We do well financially as a country and we will do well financially as both states and communities by doing well and by "doing right" for each child in those key years. We will do better societally and personally at multiple levels when we have more children able to succeed and when we have fewer children on a path to failure, unemployment, negative economic realities, and long term and far too frequent incarceration.

We Will Not Succeed as a Society If We Continue to Fail and Jail So Many of Our Young People

We need all of our people to do well. That can happen — but it will only happen if we take very deliberate steps now to help all of our children get the needed levels of support in those key years when that support is so badly needed and when the opportunities for changing the life trajectory of each individual child away from prison into lives of success are so great.

We will not be able to succeed as a safe and prosperous nation or succeed as safe and prosperous communities if we fail increasing numbers of our children relative to their personal life paths and trajectories. We will not prosper as a nation if we end up with growing numbers of people who are permanently unemployed and unable to make significant and regular contributions to our society as either employees or taxpayers.

Our cities and our states will not do well with large numbers of people who are permanently functionally unemployed or significantly perpetually underemployed. Gangs thrive in those conditions, and gangs are not good for the residents of our neighborhoods and cities.

We could face a future of having major population segments in this country unable to succeed and increasingly angry and divisive because of the obvious differences in life outcomes and the major differences in levels of success that will continue to exist for our various groups of people if we don't deal with these issues successfully and soon.

We Will Be a Nation Divided Against Itself If We Don't Change Incarceration Realities

We run the risk of being a nation divided against itself in a number of angry, cruel, dysfunctional, and damaging ways if we don't address a number of key disparity issues now and create the opportunity for children from each and every group to do well because all children from every group are learning ready when it is time for each child to learn.

We need to be honest with ourselves about the fact that we are failing too many of our children today — and we need to be honest with ourselves about the fact that the consequences of that failure reach into multiple areas of our societies and our lives.

We Imprison More People Than Any Country on the Planet

We need to be brutally honest with ourselves about a very important reality. We have three times as many people in prison as any other western country. We have more than six times more people in jail per capita than Canada. We imprison more people than any country in the world today by every measure, and the number of prisoners in our country has been growing for decades.[69]

We do many things very well as a country. In some areas of our performance, we lead the world in ways where we can be justifiably proud of our successes.

Putting world-leading numbers of people in jail is not an area where we can take any pride. We are failing badly in our imprisonment realities.

We need to change that reality — and in order to change that reality, we first need to clearly understand that reality.

Two key points need to be understood about that overall incarceration reality. One key point that we all need to understand and acknowledge is that hugely and painfully disproportionate percentages of our prisoners today come from our minority populations. We clearly have discriminatory arrest and imprisonment rates. We have very high percentages of minority Americans in jail.[67]

The second key point that we all need to recognize that most people do not look at in dealing with our imprisonment issues is the basic functional reality that a high percentage of our prisoners can't read. Reading is a relevant issue that we need to think about and address. We imprison non-readers. Roughly 60 percent of the people in our jails either read poorly or do not read at all.[70,71]

We Discriminate by Race, Ethnicity and Reading Levels Relative to Who Goes to Jail

Undeniable and painful data shows us very clearly that we discriminate in our imprisonment practices as a nation and in communities by race and ethnicity, and equally important data shows us that the people from every race and every ethnicity who can't read are the most likely people from each group to go to jail.

The disproportionate imprisonment rates that exist by race and by ethnicity in this country are so extreme that they are hard to believe. Hispanic Americans are more than three times more likely to go to jail than White Americans, and African Americans are more than six times more likely to go to jail than White Americans.

More than 10 percent of all African American males in their 30s are either in jail or on probation today. Current projections from credible experts predict that more than one in three African American males who are in their 30s today will end up in jail over the course of a lifetime if we continue with our current pattern and our current pace of incarceration.[67]

We have far too many people in jail — and we imprison people from our minority populations at a painfully disproportionate rate and level. The numbers are beyond dispute and the consequences of those grossly disproportionate incarceration rates are divisive, damaging, and destructive to us at multiple levels.

We Are Putting People in Jail from Each Group Who Can't Read

As we look at those levels of discrimination, we also should recognize that within each of those groups, an extremely high percentage of the imprisoned people from the group either read poorly or do not read at all.[65,68-71]

For each group of people in prison, highly disproportionate percentages are non-readers. That is an important point to recognize. Non-readers from every group are much more likely to go to jail. When you look at the imprisonment rates for people who are readers, those rates are significantly lower for the readers compared to the non-readers in every group.

When you look at the rate of imprisonment for African American males who have attended even one day of college, that imprisonment rate drops to levels that are only slightly over the level for all White males in the country, instead of being six times higher.

When you look at numbers that link dropping out of school with going to jail, a study at Northeastern University showed that one in four young black male dropouts is in jail today. Other reports have indicated that nearly 60 percent of male African American dropouts in their 30s are likely to spend time in jail over the course of their lives.

It is clearly not a good thing relative to incarceration to be a dropout.

It can be very difficult at multiple levels to be a high school dropout from any group. Dropouts are much more likely to be unemployed. Unemployed people who cannot find a job and who need to get access to money for all the basic reasons that people want and need access to money are more likely to do things that result in incarceration to get that money.

The unemployment rate for black male dropouts in this country last year was 69 percent. The unemployment rate for Hispanic dropouts was 47 percent. For White dropouts, the unemployment rule was 54 percent.

We need to understand the reality that we are putting people in jail from all groups who can't read. We also need to understand that the people from all groups who drop out of school and who can't read create higher rates of being unemployed and going to jail.

The positive way of looking at those realities and numbers is to know that people who can get through school because they can read are much more likely to have jobs, and the people who can read from every group are significantly less likely to go to jail.

People with Low Levels of Interactions in Those First Three Key Years of Life Tend to Have Low Reading Levels

That very clear fact base about who is unemployed and who can't read and who is in jail ties back in obvious logistical and highly linear ways to the main points about early childhood brain structure and neuron connectivity opportunities and development that are at the core of this book.

People who had low levels of neuron linkage support from the adults in their world and who received low levels of brain exercise in those first key months and years of life are less likely to be able to read.

That inability to read can lead those people who did not get that neuron connectivity support in those key months and years down those negative pathways that too often include a much higher risk of going to prison.

We Can Measure Differences at 18 Months – Based on First Year Interaction Levels

We should not think of this as being just a long-term problem. Those brain strengthening processes that happen in those first months and years of life affect children immediately. We can identify with a high level of accuracy the children who are on that path to not being able to read by age three.

Some newer studies point to very powerful indicators of differences in learning status for children that can be measured at only 18 months old.[2]

Eighteen months is a very early age. The reality that we all need to understand is that good research is telling us that some children have already fallen behind by the time they were 18 months old.[3]

The children who fall behind by 18 months and who fall significantly behind by 3 years old are each more likely to be behind when they get to kindergarten. The children who have low vocabulary levels in kindergarten tend to be much more likely to have lower reading levels by the point at grade three when we tend to measure and compare reading levels in our schools.

We know that the people who can't read by third grade are much more likely to be unable to read in high school. We know that the students who can't read in high school are more likely to drop out of school, and we know that those students are also much more likely to end up in jail.

Those are not academic, ideological, hypothetical, speculative, theoretical issues or purely suppositional concerns. Those are very functional issues and realities, and they affect real children at each of those age levels every single day.

Brain development is a functional and biological issue for each and every child from every group of people in those key years. Functionally, that set of realities means we are pointing too many people to a life of crime and to major economic shortcomings in their lives by not giving each child the support needed in those first three years of life — and even in the first 12 and 18 months of life — that each child needs to be a reader and to have academic success.

Many Factors Lead to Imprisonment

Context is extremely important and relevant as we are looking at and thinking about all of the incarceration issues. Those points about those sets of life influencing factors and processes for each child need to be understood in the complete context of our overall imprisonment factors and our full set of incarceration realities.

We clearly put people in jail at much higher levels if the people can't read. That is true of all races and ethnic groups.

It is also a pattern that we can see in other countries. Studies in Great Britain show that roughly 60 percent of the people in jail there also read poorly or do not read at all. There are similar patterns in the Scandinavian countries.[66]

Those countries all imprison far fewer people than we do — but they each also have a higher percentage of non-readers in the populations they do imprison.

So as we look at those issues, we need to recognize the clear linkage between high school dropout levels and both unemployment and incarceration. We need to recognize that reality and those linkages.

That is, however, only part of our problem with incarceration in this country. The biggest problem that we generally focus on when we look at those issues is that we clearly discriminate heavily in our incarceration rates based on both race and ethnicity.

As we aim at reducing the number of people we send to prison, we all need to recognize that the racial and ethnic discrimination that we see today exists in ways that are independent of any factors created by reading levels.

Reading proficiency is clearly one relevant factor for who is arrested. It is also clear that arrest rates vary significantly and even massively in some areas and settings by race and ethnicity with no regard to the reading levels of the people being arrested.

Race and Ethnicity Are Both Major Incarceration Factors in Too Many Settings

A number of studies have shown us that minority Americans get arrested more often than White Americans for the same kinds of crime in all of our major urban areas. We also know from statistical analysis that minority people who are arrested and who go to court in many settings tend to have measurably higher average penalties than White criminals who are convicted of the same crime.[72]

One New Jersey study of traffic arrests showed that black drivers made up 15 percent of the drivers, 42 percent of the stops made by policemen, and 73 percent of the arrests. That study reported that the actual speeds for drivers were equivalent for all groups.[72]

The reading levels of the drivers were clearly irrelevant to those arrests.

Another Florida study done using video footage showed that racial minorities in that setting were 5 percent of the total drivers, but more than 80 percent of the people stopped and searched by police.[73]

There is no functional way that reading levels of those drivers could have created those disparities in police behavior.

A number of related studies and reports tell us that discrimination, disparities, bias, and prejudice clearly have an impact on many parts of our judicial and law enforcement systems and that impact of those factors can be shown at statistically validated and functionally significant levels.[74]

The book, *Cusp of Chaos,* addresses some of those issues.

Equal Protection Under the Law Is the Official Goal for Our Country

Equal protection under the law is our goal as a country. It is the right goal and it is a goal we all need to support. We do achieve that goal a significant proportion of the time.

Many law enforcement people work very hard to keep racism and ethnic prejudice — both conscious and unconscious — out of their practices and decisions. That is true and that is good. We need to encourage, recognize, honor, support and expect that behavior.

It is also true that basic patterns of discrimination clearly do exist today relative to some areas of arrest rates and penalties.

We need to understand that entire context of law enforcement realities and behaviors as we look to using our early childhood development strategies and approaches as strategies to ultimately significantly reduce the number of people we are sending to jail. We need to understand the issues relating to illiteracy and we also need to understand the full set of negative and discriminatory issues and practices that relate to ethnicity and race.

As we look at the link between not being able to read and being sent to jail, we need to recognize that those bias-related linkages to incarceration do also exist — and that they exist in an overall context that we need to understand and acknowledge as we work to solve that set of problems.

We Need to Understand the Full Set of Factors

We can't take a simplistic approach to any of those issues. We do need to look honestly and directly in each of our settings at the full set of key factors that clearly influence that entire law enforcement and incarceration process.

The book *Ending Racial, Ethnic, and Cultural Disparities in American Health Care* deals with those issues of bias and behavior in health care delivery very directly and addresses ways that we can address those issues in health care settings. The book, *The Art of InterGroup Peace* also deals with those intergroup issues and their consequences in other settings.

Biased behavior that is relevant to which people are being arrested and who is being imprisoned clearly exists in too many settings today. There are significant trust issues relative to law enforcement in a number of settings, and those trust issues in those settings tend to have a history that is based on actual negative inter group experiences of people in those settings.

We need to address those incarceration-related issues directly in each setting where they are relevant. We need each of our communities to address the issues that can result in biased behavior by law enforcement and in biased judgments by our courts.

We need police departments in all settings who understand those issues and who act in ways that cause the police to be people who are trusted by the full populations they support and who are aligned with the full communities that they serve.

A Number of Police Departments Are Reaching Out to Create Better Linkages

Many policemen do an excellent job of enforcing the law without prejudice or bias. We need to recognize, honor, and support that reality and those behaviors.

A growing number of police departments are recognizing that there have been some historic intergroup issues and that there continue to be some current intergroup issues as well. Many of those police departments are reaching out in increasingly effective ways to the communities they serve in order to have better linkages with the people they protect.

Those issues are all real and valid in a number of settings. That particular set of issues has been addressed and discussed in *The Art of InterGroup Peace,* *The Cusp of Chaos,* and *Primal Pathways,* three books that deal specifically and explicitly with intergroup issues.

We need to recognize that there are levels of discriminatory behaviors by both police and courts in some settings that have had a significant negative and prejudicial impact on who is in jail today.

This book about the future of our children accepts that reality and recognizes how much damage those behaviors do and have done.

This book also, however, says that those levels of discrimination and that context of too often intentionally functional bias are not the only relevant realities and factors that determines who spends time in our prisons.

We also very clearly do imprison people who can't read.

We need to deal with both sets of issues if we want to significantly reduce the number of people in our jails.

A major message of this book is that we do need to address and change the functional realities of our childhood development challenges and we need to deal very intentionally with the real world child development opportunities that we can affect and change if we want to change the number of people we put in jail and if we want to change many lives for the better.

For this book about the impact of not being able to read and having a higher likelihood of dropping out of school, being unemployed, and being incarcerated, the focus for our thought process needs to be to get us all to look hard at the key and indisputable link that very consistently exists for all groups between not being able to read, dropping out of school, and going to jail.

We need to address those issues with focus, clear intent, and even some courage — and we need to figure out how to offer alternative pathways for those children who need better pathways for their lives.

We tend to imprison non-readers from every group. We need to take steps to increase the number of children who can read from every group so that we can, in fact, reduce the number of children from each and every group — every racial, ethnic, and cultural group — who end up in jail.1876

We Can't Allow Prejudice, Bias, and Discrimination to Divert Us from Nurturing Infant Brains

We will be doing our children a huge disservice, and we will damage many lives if we allow those other sets of biased, discriminatory and prejudicial behaviors relative to race, ethnicity and even culture that do exist in multiple settings to distract us and detour us from the key job we have today of helping all children from all groups take full advantage of the biological brain development opportunities that happen for each child in those first months and years of life.

We need to save each child by strengthening every brain. We need to do that work one child at a time — and we need to do it in spite of any other levels of bias or prejudice or discrimination that might exist in any situation or setting. We can't ignore those negative factors, but we can't let them keep us from our focus on helping children.

We Can't Change People's Hearts – But We Can Strengthen Neuron Connections in Children's Heads

We all need to understand that we will actually reduce the number of people who go to jail if we help children from every group with that key set of learning processes in those key months and years of brain development opportunity.

We can't change the prejudice or the bias that might exist in people's hearts, but we can strengthen the neuron connections that do happen and do exist in children's heads. Those connections in children's brains need to be strong to give every child from every group the best pathways to success in life.

Let's do what we can do now to make those connections strong for each child — and let's have many children's lives be better because we have done what we have done for each child.

So we need to recognize, understand and even address those clearly discriminatory practices. We also need to understand the clearly economics linked disparity issues. We need to deal with prejudice and help people reduce their levels of bias when we can make improvements in those areas.

But we should not let dealing with those issues distract us from helping every child. We need to reduce the risk of each child going to jail even though all of those other discriminatory factors will continue to be relevant to the lives of too many people from too many groups and settings.

We all need to collectively understand and address very directly the high correlation that we can see for all groups between not reading and going to jail and we need to reduce the risk of imprisonment by helping every child at the time when the help offers the most benefit to each child.

For this set of issues, there is great power and opportunity that results from knowing what we now know, because that knowledge allows us to take action at a time in the life of each child when that action will provide the highest levels of benefit for the child.

We know what to do.

We know when to do it.

We Need to Help Children Before the Kindergarten Years

We know the things that we need to do to make a difference in the lives of many children and we know why that difference will happen for each child. The mystery of the learning gaps in our communities and schools that has puzzled and frustrated good and well-intentioned people for so long in so many settings is no longer a mystery.

We know that we can make some direct early support changes for the lives of our children that will significantly reduce the number of children who can't read, and that will also significantly reduce the number of children who end up in the juvenile justice system and in jail.

We need to talk, read, sing, play and interact in loving and supportive ways with each child.

Talking, reading, playing, and interacting in safe and caring ways with children in those key months and years can change lives and the functional consequences of those interactions with each child can put each child on a path that significantly reduces the likelihood that the child will end up in jail.

There is a golden opportunity today for us as a nation and as communities and families to make a major difference in many lives. We now have the ability to save children from the fate of learning deficiencies by helping more children be ready to read when the time comes in their lives for them to learn to read.

We need adults who interact with each child in those key first years of life when the right sets of interactions exercise each child's brain and build stronger brains for each child.

We very intentionally need to talk, read, interact, play and sing in very direct and individual ways to each child in those early months and years to change the trajectory of their lives.

Each child we save is a child we save. Each child we lose in the most damaging ways because of very low levels of direct and positive adult interactions in the time frames when the neurons in the brain of that child are making their vital and beneficial connections, is a child who will probably face major difficulties and who could easily be an ongoing challenge to the rest of society in a significant way for their entire lives.

Negative paths loom for those children.

Each child who doesn't get that early support and who goes down those most negative paths of non-support is a child who is highly likely to be angry, damaged, and significantly disadvantaged for far too much of their lives. The likelihood of dropping out of school is much higher for children who do not get that early support.

We need people to not drop out of school — and we need to do the things we need to do to keep people from going down the economically and functionally disadvantaged life paths that are the reality for far too many dropouts.

Ex-Prisoners Who Can't Read Can't Even Fill in Job Applications

We need to create a collaborative goal for us all to do the things that will keep people out of prison in the first place.

Once the prison cycle starts for any person, it's a very hard cycle for anyone to break. Recidivism is the rule. Readmissions to prison happen in very high percentages for far too many people.

Far too many people who are released from jail end up back in jail. It's an ugly and painful cycle and it is even harder to break that prison cycle when people who are in the cycle can't read.

That makes logistical sense. We know that when a person in prison who can't read or who reads poorly gets out of prison, those released prisoners can't apply for many jobs. They cannot apply for a high percentage of available jobs because those freed former prisoners who can't read can't even fill in any of the job applications or complete any application forms that require the applicant to read.

The Only Economic Infrastructure That Consistently Accepts Non-Readers Is Crime

People who can't get jobs in the normal economy too often find that the only economic infrastructure in their communities that accepts them and creates a cash flow for them is gangs and crime.

Gangs are growing in America today. Gangs functionally rule many of our prisons now and gangs also now have a powerful and even defining role in many of our neighborhoods and communities.

Gangs do a lot of damage. Gangs can make life miserable and unsafe for people who live in their turf and who are subject to their very primal behavior and impact.

Non-readers in both our communities and our prisons too often find joining gangs to be one of their few available life choices and one of their few available economic options because gangs often do accept the people who can't read as gang members. Gangs directly accept non-readers as workers for their various criminal enterprises and gangs give those people who can't read work assignments of various kinds that do not require the person to read.

That access to an economic infrastructure is a major and important economic and logistical difference in the lives of the people who are in our communities and who can't read and it is an even more attractive source of alignment, connection and group identity for large percentages of the people who are prison and who can't read.

Gangs recruit those workers who can't read. The rest of society rejects them. Loyalty to gangs by those particular members can be intense. That loyalty and sense of personal and group identity that is tied to gang membership can be powerfully aligned with people's basic packages of instinctive behaviors and thought processes for all of the instinct linked reasons that are discussed extensively in the book, *Primal Pathways*.

We Need to Break the Economic Cycles as Well

Those are cycles that we need to break and those are both economic and societal alignment realities that we need to address.

Finding jobs for people who can't read and who want to work to break one piece of the crime cycle in their own lives might be part of that answer. People who want to leave gangs and who need a source of income need other options to break the hold of gangs on their lives.

We need to build strategies in our communities that reflect the economic and functional reality of gangs in those settings.

We also need to take the larger view and the longer view and we need to help each of our very young children get that needed set of interactions that build neuron connectivity levels in each child's key time of high potential and dire need so that gang membership is not an attractive and functionally incented life choice.

We need to provide that help to each child so that those children do not drop out of school and so they do not end up in trouble with the law.

We need to take stands as a nation and as communities on those sets of issues. We would be well served by setting goals in each community to cut the number of people who go to jail by half or more.

We could meet or exceed that goal by helping all of our young children have that full opportunity for personal brain connectivity growth in those three key years, and we could also help achieve that goal by having all police departments focused on being aligned and linked in direct, supportive and clearly collaborative ways with the communities they serve.

We need to focus now on the reading readiness levels of every child as an anchor to that process. Eighty-five percent of the young people in our juvenile justice system today can't read. That is a chilling number. We can change it, but we need to start now if we want that number to change.

We Need to Begin with the First Month of Life

We need to begin for each child with the first month of life. The new science of brain development and educational processes supports that time of beginning for each child.

We now know that we can see differences in the learning levels of children at only 18 months old. Those new studies showing those time frames for early learning point us in very good and useful directions. They create a sense of immediacy that is extremely good to have.

We actually don't need to wait decades to see changes in children's lives. We can see real changes for real children inside of two years. Those new academic studies about those first year learning impact levels are golden in their power to help us set priorities for what we do now to help children who are being born today.

The impact of those basic interactions is immediate for each child. We now know that there are measurable differences in learning readiness levels that happen almost immediately, and we know that we can make a real difference for each child by beginning the interactions immediately.

The long-term impact of those basic interactions can be massive and will change our communities for their future paths, and the short-term impact of those basic interactions can be immediate and can change our children today. Immediate is a good time frame.

If we help our children today, each child we help today will be more learning ready one year from now. The percentage of children who are non-readers will change for children entering kindergarten in less than four years, and that set of basic interactions will change learning readiness levels for children entering grade school in less than six years.

When those children who have had that brain exercise support in the first months and years of life hit high school, they will transform the schools. Those learning ready children will break the school failure cycle that we see in too many schools today and they will break that failure cycle in those schools by not failing.

The Future Trends for the Percentages of Non-Readers Are Not Good

We need to take a hard and honest look at where we are today on some key trends. A chilling, sobering, alarming, and critically important potentially damaging point for us all to understand and consider is this: Some key trends that we see today relative to the future numbers of non-readers in our society and in our country are not good.

We are currently seeing significantly more children born into settings where reading levels currently are low and where the direct interaction levels with each child are too often even lower. The children who are born into those settings are at high risk of seeing those low levels of interactions happening for those key years of their lives.

We have multiple studies showing that high percentages of our lowest income families are not reading to their children or interacting with children today in ways that enhance brain connectivity levels for each child. High percentages of our low-income homes today have no one reading to the children at all.

The children in those homes with low levels of adult interactions today face challenging and logistically difficult futures through no action of their own.

The positive news — and this is extremely positive — is that roughly one-third of the low-income mothers do read daily to their children. Studies show that about 30 percent of our low-income mothers read to their children every day.

Studies also tell us that when low-income parents learn about reading opportunities, the number of readers can and does increase significantly.

But important studies also tell us that more than half of our low-income mothers currently do not read to their children at all.

One study showed that the lowest income mothers are reading — on average — less than 30 hours in total to their children over the five full years leading to kindergarten.[17,22] That compares to more than 1,000 reading hours for the children in the higher income homes during that same time frame.

Those children who average less than 30 hours of reading time between birth and kindergarten, and who also have very low levels of direct adult talking time in those key years, are ending up with very low vocabularies when they get to their prekindergarten years.

Too many children have only hundreds of words in their vocabularies rather than thousands of words at those early key points of their development and learning. It can be difficult for those children to catch up with the other children in their schools after that time.

More Than Half of the Births in the Entire Country Last Year Were to Low-Income Mothers

That set of facts and those patterns of behaviors and specific interactions with children for a high percentage of low-income mothers are both increasingly important to us as a country today because last year — for the first time ever in the history of our country — more than half of our births were to our lowest income mothers.

That trend needs to be both understood and addressed. It gives us an opportunity that we need to focus on with a high level of immediacy.

Those are very real and sobering numbers and realities. We know from a number of studies that our low-income mothers are less likely to be talking and reading to their children. More than half of our births last year for the entire country were to low-income mothers.

We can be on very negative paths and we can far too easily face a very divided and difficult future if we don't figure out how to help each and all of those children avoid the patterns that we have seen in the past for the majority of children in our lowest income families in all of those key areas and activities.

If we don't do what needs to be done to help more of our children in those high need years in the growing number of families where the reading levels today are low and where the interaction support levels in those key areas for children are not happening at sufficient value for each child today, then we could actually be on a path to significantly increase the number of people in our jails.

That truly would be a crime.

Only Interactions Can Turn That Tide

Now that we understand those issues, we have an obligation to deal with those issues. We need to do real things to help with very real problems and challenges and we need the courage to do the right things, because lack of courage on those issues at this point in time will create damages for many lives.

Wishful thinking or politically correct — but unstructured and situationally and functionally unsupported — optimism will not turn that tide. Blaming anyone will also not turn that tide.

Hoping that things will get better also very clearly will not turn that tide.

The only thing that will turn that imminent tide to save more children from difficult and under advantaged futures is interactions — one at a time — with each child on those key months and years when those interactions change and shape each child's brain. We need the courage and the insight to do what needs to be done now to make those interactions happen.

We Need Trusted Messengers to Teach Those Realities and Opportunities

We need to support parents and families in their efforts to help and support each of their children. We need to teach those issues very clearly to every family and we need to help every family help every child. More than half of the births in America this year will be affected very directly by how well we handle those issues.

This book deals with those issues and those opportunities in every chapter. Parents are critically important. We need to support parents.

We need parents to provide needed levels of support to each child. Parents need to be a key part of the solution set and the strategy for success for our children.

We also need families who are committed to the children in their families and who are working to provide those effective and direct levels of support for each child.

We clearly need our caregivers — our doctors and nurses who work directly with each child — to be part of the care system and be on the team that helps each child with that key set of issues.

We need trusted messengers of many kinds who understand these issues and who are giving those messages to all parents.

We need to create "surround sound" on those issues.

We also need people in support roles who can go to each family where support is needed to help with the interactions and interactions that are needed by each child.

We need volunteers to do that work and we need trained professionals to help with that work for families and children who need the help of professionals in that key window of time for each child.

We need all of our day care settings to function as an asset for brain exercises and neuron connectivity levels for each child. We spend billions of dollars on day cares, and we need those settings to be reading, talking, and interacting with their youngest children in ways that support this entire process for each child — with approaches happening in those settings that build billions of neuron connections in each child.

We Need Child-Centered Education Strategies

We also need the people who run our education systems to be thinking of the full education process for each child to involve and include the full continuum from birth to college, not just K-12. We need to replace K-12 with B-C.

If we want to increase the number of students who do not drop out of school — and who avoid ultimately going to jail — we need our educators to be supporting the earliest childhood education efforts across the full spectrum of child development as an anchor for that continuum.

In the same way that health care gets much better and more effective when it transforms from provider-centered care to patient-centered care, we need our education systems and our education agendas to transfer from provider-centered education to child-centered education.

Parents, families, communities, and childcare settings can all change the life of a child. Each community needs to build its own strategy that fits the needs of that community and that setting for its children.

Communities that do not do that work for their children are communities who will face bleak futures of collective dysfunction and collective failure. Far too many people will be in jail in those settings.

Communities who do actually do that brain development support work for each child will create a future where all children can succeed and where the communities will prosper because the learning levels are strong.

We all need to support the teams for each child that help each child thrive.

The tides we face today with all of todays births are fairly clear. The time frames we face are painfully clear as well.

We need to create a future for all children that will increase learning readiness and learning skills, and reduce the rate of future dropouts, future unemployment, and future incarceration.

196

Everyone in society — and particularly the children — will benefit when the pattern for each child is positive and when each brain gets the exercise it needs to create life pathways that lead to success.

As part of that agenda, we should decide as a nation and as individual communities to do what we need to do to cut the number of people who go to jail by at least half.

The path we are on now of putting millions of Americans in prison should be unacceptable to all of us. We need the people who lead each of our communities to understand those issues and we need each of those leaders to very intentionally make a difference now so that we have a very different future.

Our leaders can leave legacies of great value if they go down those paths. We need to encourage that to happen and we need to encourage it to happen now.

CHAPTER EIGHT

We Need Our Government and Community Leaders at All Levels to Support the Success of All Children in Those Key First Years

WE ARE AT a point in the history of our country where we need the people who run our local, state, and national governments — and where we need the people who lead each of our communities — to understand clearly the key issues that are involved in early childhood development.

Far too many of the people who lead us today in those areas have almost completely failed to either understand those issues or to address them in any relevant, meaningful, or useful way.

There are a few cities where local leaders have become aware of the potential to help children in those months and key years and a small number of people in legislative positions in various settings have begun to be aware of those issues — but the vast majority of relevant leaders for both our government and our various community groups have been entirely unaware of those issues and opportunities.

We need our leaders in all settings to do a significantly better job of dealing with those issues of early childhood brain strengthening and development.

We can't afford to have our leaders in governmental positions ignore those issues and we can't afford to have leaders who do not know the biological fact and functional reality that those first three years of life are the time when our children build major elements of brain capacity for their entire lives.

We need leaders to understand those issues and we need leaders to do what needs to be done at local, community, state, and national levels to make sure that we help our children get the support that each developing brain needs in those key years.

Community Leaders and Governmental Leaders Have Failed Us on Those Issues

Almost our entire current leadership has fairly consistently failed us on that particular issue at every level of government up to now.

Government leaders have not been alone in that failure. Far too many of our community leaders for our various ethnic, racial, cultural, and religious groups have also not done a good job of leading for their own groups on those key, life changing issues as well.

Groups of people who are experiencing learning gap issues for their groups have had leaders who are deeply concerned about those learning gaps — but those leaders have been almost unanimously silent and universally unaware of the underlying first years of life brain exercise realities that are actually creating those gaps.

The government policy that has been created to deal with that set of issues for those specific years is almost a void.

Leaders in a number of settings have encouraged support for our kindergarten programs and there is growing prekindergarten program and preschool program support as well in many settings. But our leaders have almost completely ignored, overlooked, or misunderstood the fact that those kindergarten and prekindergarten support efforts that engage with each child only after children are four or five years old will fail to close the gap for all of the children who did not get their needed brain building interactions in those first three key months and years of their life.

Major First Year Gaps Can't Be Erased in Kindergarten

The reading deficits and the learning problems for children who have fallen far behind in those first months and years of life cannot be erased in the kindergarten years or even in the immediate prekindergarten years for those children.

The children who enter kindergarten with vocabularies of only hundreds of words rather than thousands of words are far behind at that point in their lives and — for no fault of their own — the vast majority of those children will never catch up.

Scientists can measure brain differences in children as early as 18 months — based directly on whether or not the brains of children were individually exercised in the first year of life for each child.

The people who lead us in both our community groups and our government need to understand those issues.

That understanding about those key early year brain development issues has not been happening. That particular set of issues, risks, problems, opportunities and functional failures that exist relative to early childhood brain development for our children has been entirely invisible and off the agenda for the people who make the laws and who create both the processes and the cultures that govern us and guide us in almost all settings.

That Is Not Intentional Ignorance

That is not intentional failure. That lack of leadership support for children's development in those first key years is not because our leaders in any settings want any child to fail in any of those key areas of development.

People who are serving in government and in-group leadership roles at multiple levels do care deeply about the fact that many children are falling behind other children and those sets of leaders are also concerned about the functional problems and the learning gaps that exist for groups of children in too many school systems.

The fact that we have reading capability deficits so extreme that we have settings where the average score for the white children is actually double the reading score of Black, Hispanic, or American Indian children has become a huge cause of concern for many of our leaders.[2]

In the school districts of Minnesota, 51 percent of the eighth grade white students were proficient readers, compared to only 21 percent of the Hispanic students and 17 percent of the Black students. Those numbers and those kinds of differences in reading level skills between groups of people are echoed today in multiple other communities across the country, where the capability levels of students are being measured by group.[72]

People in government do care about those issues and those disparities — and people in leadership roles in each group in each community do care as well about teen delinquency, about school dropouts, and about the widening functional gaps in other areas that also exist in too many settings for far too many of our children.[2]

But very few people in our government settings has been linking those problems and those significant gaps between groups of children back to the early year child interaction levels for each child and to the fact that we did not do a good job of supporting neuron linkages for the children who have fallen behind in the three key and invaluable development years that happen at the beginning of each child's life.

Those gaps in learning levels were all created by not helping each of the children who have fallen behind in those key first years. The gaps are painful and damaging to many people — and those gaps did not have to happen… because the children from each group who do get that help in those key years do not need to fall behind.

Our Government Bodies Have Not Been Holding Hearings on Those First Year Issues

Almost no one in positions of power in major areas of this country has been aware of those specific functional and operational issues or time frames. Almost no one in governmental circles at any level has been spending time thinking about those issues and then holding hearings and coordinating public discussions about how we can deal with that reality and how we can take advantage of the obvious and high value opportunities for our children and our society that those facts about early brain development create.

There have been some encouraging exceptions to that pattern — and several communities have begun to do work of helping their children in those first years. Cities like Seattle, Boston, San Antonio, and Oakland are all beginning to work with children in those age categories to stimulate the early year learning capacities of their children.

New York City has a voluntary early literacy-learning program and a mayor who is focusing some attention on those issues. Chicago has some independent programs — like the very impressive Thirty Million Words program started by Dr. Dana Suskind — that are now set up to help a number of their children. The city of St. Paul and the city of Minneapolis looking at some early childhood years child development efforts.

Those programs are all encouraging, and all need significantly more momentum to close the relevant learning gaps in those settings.

People Are Concerned About the Learning Gap

The learning gaps themselves are very visible in many communities and school systems.

There has been a major and very real level of concern expressed by many people in many settings about the large and growing learning gaps that exist in their communities. The reading gaps showing very different average performance levels for our Native American, African American, and Hispanic children have been well documented by a number of sources and people in every setting are alarmed about those gaps and want them to be alone.

Those gaps in reading levels and a similar set of gaps that exist between groups for basic mathematic skills for children are major and those gaps are beyond dispute.

People in multiple settings are increasingly concerned, alarmed, and even angry about those gaps. All of those reactions are entirely appropriate because those gaps represent much more difficult lives for the children at the low end of the learning level continuum.

Policy leaders, governmental leaders, and community leaders have all looked at those numbers and many leaders across the full political spectrum have expressed major interest in doing things to help reduce those gaps.

The learning gap issue is not being ignored everywhere. People in several settings now see the gaps and some people are proposing solutions and strategies to close the gaps in various settings.

The problem is that most of the programs that are being set up in various settings to close the gaps are focused on the wrong set of interaction.

Most Proposed Solutions Have Minimal Chance of Success

A major problem relative to those proposed solutions in many settings has been that most of the plans and efforts to deal with those learning gaps have been targeted at solutions and strategies that have very low likelihood of actually succeeding in shrinking those gaps because those proposed solutions have been directed at older children.

Most of the current set of programs, proposals, and approaches in governmental settings that are intended to reduce or end those learning gaps have either not understand or simply missed the point of the early year brain development reality for each child — and many of the gap closing strategies have been directed at children after they are already in school.

People are trying to fix those gaps by fixing our schools. Schools in some settings are being blamed for the gaps and various programs to make our schools better to close the gaps are getting support in many settings. Significant energy is being focused on figuring out how to improve our schools and how to enhance our teaching processes for the students who are already in school in an attempt to close the gaps that currently exist for the children who are currently in school.

We Can't Eliminate the Learning Gap by Improving Schools

As this book has pointed out multiple times, closing those learning gaps after the children are already in our schools is too late. To solve that set of issues and to have a gap free educational reality for our children, we clearly need to prevent the gaps before children get to school.

We need to prevent gaps rather than close gaps if we really want our gaps to disappear.

Making schools better is a very good thing. Every child who is learning ready will benefit from having better schools. There is no downside to improving our schools. There are many benefits that result from improving our schools.

We should not, however, expect to close the learning gap that we see in so many settings by improving our schools. That will have a relatively small impact on that particular problem because the learning gap for each child who is challenged was created for each child in the first three years of each child's life.

A growing number of policy people, government leaders, and education leaders are now focusing their efforts on the immediate preschool years. Preschool is also too late for the children who have fallen behind by three.

Preschool improvement is a good thing to focus on — but that focus on improving the preschool years will have its focus on our four and 5-year-old children. Four and five aren't the major times of biological brain strength opportunity for each child. That time of great biological brain-building opportunity for each child happens in the years before the age of four.

Therefore, the approach and strategy of improving our preschool programs is good to do, but it falls short of the real time of major need and the great opportunity to close the personal learning gap for individual children.

It is a good thing for the country and it is a good thing for children that we are seeing significant and growing support at the local, state, and national levels for various categories of preschool support for children. It is good for children that our kindergarten and pre-kindergarten programs are getting increasing levels of support from various governmental leaders and agencies in various settings that will make those programs better in a number of ways.

Making all of those programs better will be a very good thing for all of the learning ready children who are in those particular educational settings.

Preschool Programs Have Growing Support Levels

Unfortunately — those particular preschool programs will not close the learning gaps that we see today because they happen too late in life for the vast majority of the children who are already in a deficit position for learning readiness by age three based on the support that was received by each child in the first three years of their lives.

That time frame and those highly functional issues have been invisible in most policy settings. Helping children in those first key years has not been a part of the most commonly proposed legislative packages or strategies for most governmental settings.

Well meaning governmental leaders have tried to close the learning gaps by improving high schools, improving grade schools, and improving kindergarten and prekindergarten programs. All of those improvements are very good and highly beneficial for learning ready children and all of those improvements will fail for the child who has fallen behind by 18 months and who has a tiny vocabulary at age three.

Helping those children at age four is too late for most of those children. We should not give up on those children and we need to do what we can to improve learning for each child who has fallen behind. But to fully succeed, we need interactions and interventions that begin before age one and that actually peak before age four if we hope to make those learning gaps vanish for all of our children.

We need children who are spoken to constantly and who have thousands of words in their vocabularies by the time they go through the prekindergarten classroom door.

Charter Schools Can Be an Asset

One of the fascinating sets of programs that have helped many children are the charter schools that have been set up in many settings. Some of the charter schools have clearly helped create a different learning trajectory for a number of children from low-income settings.

One of the key points to keep in mind about charter schools is that those schools tend to be voluntary enrollment schools. Parents make choices to have children attend those schools.

We know from our research that over half of low-income mothers read almost no books to their children. We also know from the research that roughly 30 percent of low-income mothers now read to their child every day.

The low-income mothers and fathers who read now to their children every day may well also to be more likely to voluntarily enroll their children in a charter school — and to make the effort needed to get their child to the charter school every day. The low-income mothers and fathers who do not read at all to their children today could well be more likely also to not enroll their child in a charter school.

That set of relationships has not been studied, but it could be relevant to those issues based on what we know of that biological science and based on what we know are the very different pathways to reading levels that exist today for our lower income families.

Many of those schools have the potential to do great things for the children who are most ready to benefit from them. There is some likelihood in a voluntary enrollment situation that the parents who choose to use those schools do so because those parents are highly supportive of their children at multiple levels.

We Can't Blame Our Leaders for Not Knowing That New Science

We now know that the entire set of processes for learning are anchored in the science of those first three years of brain development for each child.

We can't blame our leaders in either the government or in our community groups for not understanding those issues about those first three years of life for children in the past. We can't blame our leaders for not dealing with those issues in the past because some of the best and most useful science about brain development in children is relatively new.

Almost no one who knows what all of that research into early brain development tells us has actually been taking that science as a package and as a combined set of relevant and useful factors to our leaders — either to explain to our leaders in clear terms why so many children are failing in their personal reading and learning readiness or to propose actual solutions that our leaders can use to provide support for the children who are failing and to close the gaps for future years.

We can't blame leaders for not acting on any information about early childhood brain development that our leaders did not know. That lack of knowledge on those key issues has been the situation for almost all of our leaders up to now. It is entirely logical that our leaders have not used information that they did not know.

Up to now, our leaders have not had the knowledge base needed to lead us to better outcomes for each of our children using strategies and approaches that are focused on helping each of our very young children at those key points in the development process for each child.

The Days of Ignorance on Those Issues Should Now End

The impact of those first three years has been invisible for government decision-making, so we have not seen bright leaders creating processes, approaches, and cultural learnings that can help all of those children avoid being unable to read.

Those days should now end.

Those days of ignorance for our leaders on that point should now be gone. The science is now clear. The consequences of the biology-based early year brain exercise time frames for each child are now clear. The functional impact of helping all children in those key years is also now clear.

Now that our leaders can each know that science and now that our leaders can finally understand those basic time frames and those universal brain-building processes, we need basic decisions made by our leaders about public policy, public education, and public health to be more fully informed and directly influenced by that set of facts and by those clear and indisputable functional realities.

Brain Strengthening Should Be a Public Health Agenda

We now need our leaders to lead on those issues — beginning with a public health campaign aimed at building better connections in baby brains.

We need a full boat public health campaign focused on helping our children build strong brains. We need the entire community to understand and support that campaign so that we can help every child.

We need all groups of people to help the people in their own group and we need all groups of people to share in the collective benefit as groups that we all receive from helping the children in every group.

We are all stronger when we are all stronger.

We need a public health campaign aimed at the biological development of stronger brains in every child, so that all groups do well as the result of that campaign.

That set of public health issues relative to our early years of childhood is as basic at a biological reality level as not having poison in our food supplies or not having damaging bacteria in our drinking water.

Brain growth is a basic biological issue that lends itself to a public health approach and a public health commitment. Keeping dangerous bacteria out of our drinking water has been addressed as a public health issue and that water safety issues has been addressed well for most of our country because we made safe water a universal public health issue.

We all understand the relevant science of safe water. We all know that the consequences of dealing with our water safety issues badly would create collective damage to everyone in those areas and those settings where dangerous water would create a danger and do real harm.

We Have Failed Too Many Children at a Pure Biological Level

We need a similar public health campaign to protect us against the damage done to children by not helping our youngest children build strong brains. We need a commitment to support that process for each child in those early years when each brain is built.

We have failed too many children in our country at a purely biological level. Not supporting children in the times of early biological brain development has an extremely negative set of public health consequences for the children who are not supported in that period of time.

The positive consequences that will result for our population from supporting all children in those key years can benefit all of us collectively when the issue is handled well. The negative consequences of not providing children with early brain development support can damage us all collectively when we deal with that issue badly — because we end up having people who are in real need at multiple levels for their entire lives if those brain strengthening needs are not met in those early years.

We Need the Learning Gap to Disappear

We need to make the learning gap disappear. The Health and Human Services Department of the U.S. Government has released studies showing the major gap in learning for high-income families compared to low-income families and also showing significant differences in learning levels by race/ethnicity.[2]

Current research shows us that the gaps in learning for each child can be evident as early as nine months of age.

We know what interactions with children in those first three years create higher levels of learning capability — and we know what the impact is for low levels of interaction with each child in those years.

We also know that the levels of interaction with children tend to be different based on the income level of the parents for each child. Higher income children tend to have high levels of interaction with adults. Lower income level children tend to have lower levels of adult interactions in those key years. We need to understand and deal with those differences to help all children.

Income Levels Do Not Directly Affect Brain Growth

Income levels do not directly impact brain development or brain growth. Activity levels and brain exercise levels — not income levels — change brains. Income, alone, doesn't change the lives of children. Income, alone, has no impact on the biology or on the timing of brain development for any child.

But direct interaction with each child that is aligned with the biology of the brain development processes for each child does change lives.

Higher income parents tend to give their children higher levels of interactions in those key days, months, and years. Studies clearly show that those patterns exist for children based on the income levels of the family of each child.

Lower income children who get the same level of direct adult interactions as higher income children receive the same high levels of benefits as higher income children from those interactions.

We need children from all income levels to get those levels of adult interactions from trusted and caring adults in those key development years.

The patterns for groups of people that exist today relative to those interactions are pretty clear. There are many exceptions to the patterns, but the overall trends by group are highly relevant.

Both Word Gaps and Reading Gaps Exist

Studies tell us that lower income parents in our country, on average, spend less time reading, talking, and interacting to their very young children. We need to change those interaction patterns for those children.

Some low-income parents do have high levels of beneficial interactions with their children and the low-income children who get those higher levels of interactions clearly benefit, but there are studies that show that, on average, our lower income families tended to speak fewer than 1,000 words per day to their infants.[4]

That number of spoken words in low-income families compares to 5,000 or more words that tend to be spoken to babies each day in higher income families.

Similarly, the average reading time per child for low-income families averaged less than 25 hours per child for low-income families for the prekindergarten years — compared to more than 1,000 reading hours per child for higher income families.

Higher income families had over a dozen children's books in their homes — and there was only one book in 300 very low-income families in one study.[22,28]

We need to recognize the reality that one study showed that nearly a third of low-income mothers actually did read to their infant or baby every day. Those infants and babies in those low-income families who read every day were helped significantly by that reality in their own key times of development.

But that research has shown us that over nearly percent of the low-income mothers who were studied had no books in the home and over half of the low-income mothers and fathers did not read to their children at all.[28]

We Need All Parents to Know the Science of Brain Exercise in Those First Years

We need to recognize the significance and the reality that it is possible to read daily now to children in some low-income homes — and we need to recognize the reality that most children in most low-income homes are not being read to today.

We also know from their research that almost none of the low-income mothers who are not reading now to their children currently know the science or know the processes that are needed for strengthening their baby brains. We need to teach that information to every mother as part of our public health campaign to strengthen all brains.

All of that data points us clearly to the fact that we need to help lower income families read to their children and to interact directly with their children verbally in those key years of high opportunity — and that we need books in all homes regardless of income levels in those key first years.

That entire set of studies tells us that we can change the learning status and ability levels for low-income children by increasing the interaction levels for each low-income child with caring and trusted adults in those key years of great biological opportunity.

That strategy is not magic. We can close the learning gaps by group by improving those interaction levels for each child from every group.

We need the people who run our government and who set our laws to understand those issues at a very basic level and we need our leaders in each community group to take steps to create the right levels of support for all of our children in each of our settings.

Over Half the Births in This Country Last Year Were to Medicaid Mothers

That information about the difference in words spoken and the differences in the number of books read based on the income levels for the families of our youngest children is particularly important for us as a country because we are now, for the first time in our history, seeing the majority of births in this country coming from our low-income families.

Medicaid is, by definition, a program for low-income families. You have to have a very low-income level to be eligible for Medicaid. Medicaid pays for health care for low-income people and Medicaid, therefore, pays for births for low-income mothers.

Last year, for the first time ever, the majority of births in this entire country were to Medicaid mothers. For the first time in our history, most of the births in our country are being paid for by our government. Most births in this country now are coming from families who are at our lowest income levels.

Our government actually paid for 51 percent of the total births that occurred in this country last year and that number and percentage will increase this year.

That fact, all by itself, tells us that the government has a direct level of opportunity and direct potential leverage and influence relative to over half of the births in this country. That leverage and that opportunity for our public programs begins at the moment of birth for all of those babies.

Medicaid Needs to Make Early Brain Support a Top Priority

Medicaid now needs to do what it can do to change the basic patterns that we have seen in the past for the early child neuron connectivity process support for the children in our low-income families.

Our state governments run the Medicaid program in each state — so we need all state governments to recognize that reality and take steps to ensure that the caregivers for Medicaid inform all mothers of Medicaid babies about the

214

births and the science of exercising brains in those key years to build stronger brains.

Medicaid needs to incorporate early childhood learning into its expectations for care delivery and Medicaid programs in every state need to incorporate those sets of goals into a wide range of Medicaid-related communication processes and support systems that will help each of the children who are linked to the Medicaid system.

Cash Flow Should Support Early Childhood Learning

Cash flow has influence. We need to take advantage of the major opportunity that now exists with our care delivery processes and teams because Medicaid is paying for all of those births and is paying as well for the follow-up care for each child.

Medicaid now needs to make brain development support for infants and babies a top priority. Our Medicaid program should now require the caregivers for mothers and for children to educate new mothers about the brain nutrition, brain exercise, and neuron connection and growth issues for every baby.

Studies and pilot programs have shown that parenting patterns tend to improve when mothers learn about those opportunities for their babies. Medicaid should insist that caregivers teach parents about those issues and that Medicaid caregivers should also periodically evaluate whether the children are having problems in those early months and years when interactions and interventions can have huge impact and change lives.

Our Medicaid program already has benefits that provide immunizations and preventative screenings for each child. Our Medicaid program should now create a learning and teaching template for all of the caregivers who see newborn babies to have the caregivers educate each of the Medicaid mothers and families about the neuron connectivity biological realities and about the brain exercise opportunities that exist in that brief and important time frame for their new babies.

Medicaid is a combined state and federal program, but the states themselves functionally run our Medicaid programs. That means that we need each of the states to recognize the opportunities that are presented by those newborn babies and their care and we need each state to take action to teach all Medicaid mothers the basic facts about how to strengthen their baby's brain.

States should mandate a basic and explicit level of public health education on those issues on the part of the caregivers who care for Medicaid babies and who treat Medicaid patients.

States should each figure out ways that work in the context of each state to provide the right support to that growing set of low-income mothers.

When states have a majority of their total births from mothers who are in the income levels where there historically have been no children's books in the homes, then states and communities need to figure out ways of getting those books into the homes and having those books used for the children.

The Likelihood of Going to Jail Goes Up 60% for Dropouts

Every birth that doesn't get that needed level of brain linkage support in those first key years is a birth that is much more likely to end up as a child who drops out of school, becomes pregnant, and/or ends up in jail.

Those are very real consequences for both children and for states, cities, and school systems of not getting that early support do happen for each child.

This book has outlined those risks in some detail. The likelihood of ending up in jail increases by 60 percent for the children who dropped out of school because they were not reading ready when it is time for the child to learn to read.[10,61,69]

Having students who drop out and who go to jail affects state and local budgets in several negative ways. Many states are facing major cost pressures now from having growing numbers of people in prison. Prisons now take up continuingly increasing amounts of state budget dollars.

States need to look at the cold hard reality that the number of people in jail and prisons will increase if the incarceration rates for non-readers holds constant and if the total number of non-readers in each state grows substantially because most children who are being born today in each setting are being born into low-income families that continue to have those patterns of early childhood interactions that were described earlier in this chapter and earlier in this book.

Many states are trying hard to improve reading levels for their students and to reduce dropout rates. There have been some excellent and well-meaning efforts in the country that have had minimal levels of success in most settings.

Having state control over the Medicaid programs and having state control over related services provided to the low-income mothers gives each state a tool kit to use to help address both the reading deficits and the prison population growth by dealing proactively and intentionally with the early childhood issues that start people down those negative paths.

WIC Could Become a Brain Strength Support Tool as Well

At the combined state and Federal level, there is a very useful program called Women Infant and Children or WIC. WIC now skillfully counsels and coaches Medicaid mothers across the country individually and directly about the nutritional needs of their children. WIC even provides some food purchasing subsidies to buy healthy food for low-income mothers.

The current WIC program counseling for Medicaid mothers about food-linked nutrition should be extended immediately to cover direct counseling about direct brain nourishment for each child as well.

Both physical nourishment and brain nourishment qualify as public health strategies that we need to support.

The First Five Commission in Los Angeles County is doing a pilot program now to show how the WIC program can help with brain development issues for those children who are supported by WIC.

The Federal Government Supports Schools

On another relevant level, the Federal government also provides subsidies and financial support to education systems in all states and settings. Those subsidies that flow from the federal government to schools should be modified to add a requirement that schools in each setting work in some ways with the local community agendas and community resources to help educate mothers and fathers on those early childhood development issues and to also provide support of some kind where needed for parents of newborn children and infants who need that support to help their children.

State legislatures who are looking at their school systems and their state academic programs should all be fully aware of the early childhood biology and brain support needs as each state builds its education programs and agenda.

Legislatures who want schools to succeed at the highest levels should be thinking about the continuous learning continuum for children from birth through graduate school. State Legislatures should support and mandate programs in each setting that can provide the needed support to the children and their families who most deeply need help for their children in those first key years.

Legislatures should look in particular at the day care settings that are used by working mothers for millions of children to make sure that the day care settings support the brain exercise processes needed by our very youngest children.

Instead of thinking of day care settings as purely babysitting environments, we need to figure out a variety of ways to have those settings read and talk in interactive ways with our children.

Day care can be an education tool at a very basic level and our legislative bodies should understand that opportunity and that reality.

Legislatures who only focus on the issues of prison costs and on the issues of school dropouts and who think of reading deficits and learning gaps as isolated and unrelated issues and who ignore or don't understand the upstream reasons for all of those behavior issues and upstream reasons for the learning failures for children are likely to spend far too much money on each of those expensive downstream areas with minimal success.

Those legislatures who ignore those first years are at high risk of spending too much money simply to remediate the damages done by those downstream issues without really improving anyone's life or getting better overall outcomes and results in either area.

The University of Chicago did some excellent research showing the sheer economic logic and impact of investing in early childhood to reduce the economic burden for the people who end up in prison because they did not receive early childhood support.[21]

Legislative bodies who are wrestling with those issues should look at that research.

Legislatures Need to Hold Hearings on Early Childhood Support and Development

Legislatures should require whoever leads their state school systems — the state superintendents of schools or state commissioners of education — to present plans to the legislature that explain how they will help all children be school ready when each child enters school.

Local areas can come up with local programs to do that work in very creative ways. Various levels of community support programs can be created to help children in each setting. Communities can help children because the issues are specific to each child.

Brains develop one child at a time. Support, therefore, can and does also happen one child at a time.

Mayors Can Be Community Leaders on Key Development Issues

Cities and mayors can take lead roles on those issues and build stronger cities and more unified cities by creating approaches and programs that succeed in each city.

Mayors can have a very high leverage impact on those early brain development issues for children in the communities they lead.

Legislatures need to be supportive of a wide array of approaches in various settings that end up helping each child.

Solid and useful programs that are focused on those earliest years are more likely to happen in multiple places if the legislatures clearly support those efforts and even require them to happen and exist in some settings.

Legislative committees should hold very explicit hearings on those issues to figure out best practices and to create alignment around making those issues a key part of the complete learning strategy for each state.

The people who run the education system in each state and community need to have a clear sense of the obvious value and advantage that can exist when all students are school ready when they get to school.

Legislatures can use various funding leverage points to ensure that the people who run the educational systems keep that full continuum of learning in mind for each child.

Creativity is needed at this point in time. We don't know all of the answers yet and we are still figuring out best practices. We need to be creative on building that support for our children.

We need to figure out best practices and we need to share what we learn about what works with one another in systematic ways.

We Need Leaders from Each Group to Lead on Those Issues

We also need the people who are our religious leaders and our community leaders for various groups in various settings to help create support for those children in each group for those key years of each child's life.

Chapter Six talked about the need for our ethnic, racial, and community leadership to understand those issues and to support both approaches and cultural beliefs in each setting that help our children in those key, life changing years.

We need to address the learning gaps that exist today explicitly and effectively. There are major learning gaps now, on average performance levels, in our Native American, African American, and Hispanic communities.[2,18] Those gaps are not genetic. Those gaps exist today because too many children in each of those groups in each of those settings did not get the early neuron strengthening support that each child needed in those first key years.

There are Native American communities where the vast majority of students today have low literacy levels and do not complete their school years. We have both Hispanic and Black communities in multiple settings with low reading levels and high drop out rates.

Those numbers could be reversed in each group in each site if all of the children in those communities received the support levels that are needed in those first years to make each child reading ready.

We Can't Shy Away from Those Issues

Political correctness has caused some people to shy away from discussing those issues. Not discussing those issues and either pretending they didn't exist or simply not being aware that those issues exist has meant that many children's lives have been damaged and impaired in multiple situations and settings.

Being too politically timid to point out the problems and the opportunities has been a timidity that has damaged too many of our children.

We now need to make children a higher priority than political timidity.

It is time to stop the damage and end the impairment in every setting where it exists and we need to do that by creating help for each child who needs that help.

Our leaders now need to take the steps needed to save every child.

Each Community Needs to Help with Solutions

To do that, we need to help each of those communities with challenging outcomes to now help figure out ways to help each of those children in their communities.

All groups care about their children. Deeply. There are some horrific and personally damaging cycles for far too many children in some settings that can each be broken — one child at a time — if we get the groups who are most relevant to each setting to be part of the solution. We need those cycles to break. We need to save each child.

Each setting, each group, and each family needs to be part of the solution process.

Each child saved is a child saved.

We need organizations and we need leaders who are credible in each of our minority communities where learning gaps exist today to lead public health awareness and parenting education at levels that can create a culture of early learning within each group.

We clearly do need our leaders to lead in that effort. Leaders steer cultures. We need all cultures to be steered by themselves and by each group's leaders toward early learning support — with credible leaders making that new belief system and that new set of behaviors happen in each setting.

We Need a Culture of Health and We Need a Culture of Continuous Learning

Leaders can change lives by leading on this set of issues. There are very few things that leaders can do that will have a bigger impact on people's lives.

Overall, our leaders from all groups and all layers and levels of government need to set the tone by leading us in the right directions and by setting up a culture of continuous learning for us all that starts with birth.

As the book "Ending Racial, Ethnic, and Cultural Disparities in American Health Care" points out, we will all be well served and we will all be healthier when America creates a culture of health and then proceeds to build that culture around basic issues like active living and healthy eating.

We also need to put in place a culture of continuous learning — supported by all of us for all of us in ways that will create aligned behaviors and supportive collective approaches that meet the needs of our children from all groups and settings.

We need the people who run our communities, our schools, and our legislatures to understand that set of issues. We need the people in our Congress and the people who run our education departments at national levels to also recognize that set of issues and the problems and opportunities they create.

Ignoring Those Issues Will Not Allow Children with Small Vocabularies to Do Well

Ignoring the problem will not help the children whose vocabularies before kindergarten contain only hundreds of words to do well, learn to read, and somehow succeed in a world where far too many children start so far behind the other children after those first key years. We need to help each child take advantage of the golden time for all children to build the strengths and the tools that will create success for entire lives.

We need leaders to understand those issues and we need leaders at multiple levels to help us all build a better future for all of our children. We have never needed our leaders more to help the children of this country than we need them now.

Leaders tend to be intelligent people. Leaders tend to have solid problem solving skill sets. We need those skill sets and those problem-solving behaviors applied to this set of issues and we need those skill sets and creativity applied by the people who lead us on this issue now.

CHAPTER NINE

Caregivers Need to Be Part of the Solution

WE NEED THE caregivers who care for children in the first years of each child's life to make brain development support for each child a top priority for the care of each child.

There is almost nothing that a pediatrician or a child care team can do for a child in those first three years of life that will have a more significant lifetime effect and impact on each child than strengthening the child's brain.

Pediatricians, pediatric nurses, and other physicians who treat children in those first key years of life are almost always major influences on the parents of each child. We need to use that leverage and that credibility to help each child build a strong brain.

Pediatricians see children on average, roughly a dozen times in those first years of life. Those encounters create a major opportunity that can be focused very directly on helping each child build strong brains.

Those direct encounters can be a number of high leverage and high credibility times when mothers, fathers, and other in-home caregivers for children are advised directly about the neuron connectivity opportunities that exist in those key years for each child.

Parents come to those pediatric interactions to learn from the caregiver about best care for their child. In addition to the basic and standard teaching by the caregivers in those encounters about topics like nutrition and infections, those interactions should now be used very intentionally and deliberately to help each parent understand the biological time frames for brain development and the various levels and kinds of parental and family interactions with their children that can support brain strengthening processes for each child.

We Need All Pediatric Care Teams to Help with That Teaching Process

Pediatricians should also incorporate some basic assessments of infant progress in those key areas in their examinations and in their direct developmental analysis process for each child.

Some pediatricians and child care teams are doing that work extremely well now — but the truth is that we are not currently getting that level of support from our pediatric care teams on those sets of developmental issues for far too many of our children today.

Too many caregivers for both mothers and young children do not make that set of developmental issues a priority or a focus in their care delivery interactions with parents in those key years.

Not all caregivers make those issues a priority or even a topic of discussion. Too many caregivers today do not educate and coach each new parent effectively and consistently about those early brain strengthening opportunities and about those brain development issues and opportunities that exist for each child.

Some care teams do not mention those issues to parents at all.

That is unfortunate. Not doing that teaching directly to parents in those care related settings in those key time frames is a huge lost opportunity that is lost forever for each child. No one is more trusted by mothers and fathers than their child's pediatric caregivers, and that trust can translate into better parenting practices for many children if the teaching opportunity about brain strengthening approaches is used consistently and used well by our caregivers.

We can't afford to lose any of those opportunities. A dozen opportunities can be lost for each child by the caregivers who do not make brain development for children a priority in their care delivery approach.

We need all caregivers to be on the side of the very young children on that very important issue and we need each caregiver to do what each caregiver can do to encourage the parents of each child to help their child directly in those key areas of development.

The American Academy of Pediatrics Is Taking a Lead Role

The American Academy of Pediatrics reflected that basic position last year when the Academy officially advocated having all pediatricians recommend reading and early development support to very young children and even began supporting programs that help get needed books to mothers of young children who don't have books in their homes.

The Academy of Pediatrics also collaborated very directly with the Zero To Three National Center for Infants, Toddlers, and Families in September of 2013 to produce a document about brain development in those first years that all caregivers and policy makers should read. It is an extremely well written set of articles and papers.[5]

The joint publication was labeled "Early Brain and Child Development" and is available from the Zero To Three website.[1]

That report should be mandatory reading for people who are working on policy issues relative to very young children.

The Pediatric Academy is exactly on the right track with its current agenda and coaching. We are fortunate as a country that our key national association for pediatricians is doing the right thing for children on that key issue.

We Also Need Our Obstetricians to Directly Teach That Science

We need obstetricians to also be a key part of that education process.

To have a maximum educational impact on all new mothers from caregivers in the most effective time frames for the brain development of each child, it would also be very useful to have the doctors who care for prospective mothers during pregnancy to also be a source of wisdom and teaching on those key issues.

To help all mothers-to-be to understand the opportunities that will exist for their children, we would benefit significantly if we could get direct and equivalent support for educating parents on those issues from the doctors who care for pregnant women.

For maximum positive impact on mothers and infants, we will be very well served if the obstetricians and midwives who care for mothers during pregnancy join in that public health agenda and make the point of teaching each perspective mother about the wonderful and immediate opportunities for brain development in their child that will begin for their child with birth.

If we are going to have to highest impact from extremely credible and trusted experts with the parents of new babies, then our obstetricians and our midwives and our pediatricians and our pediatric nurses all need to be key parts of the learning process about early brain development for the mothers of very young babies.

Caregivers Have Great Credibility and High Degrees of Opportunity

Missing that opportunity during the pregnancy and during the first episodes of care after the child is born to teach each and every mother this information is very unfortunate because of the consequences to each child whose parents do not know or understand what they can do to help their child build strong brains in those key periods of time.

Each and every child we help and save is a child we help and save. Each child we don't help and each child who does not get that support and basic brain exercise in those key years faces a challenging life — through absolutely no fault of their own.

Ideally, that teaching can begin before the baby is even born.

Almost no one has higher credibility levels with new mothers than the obstetricians and the midwives who help the mothers through their pregnancies into birth. Those caregivers are respected, trusted, and have great influence with mothers. When those caregivers tell mothers that they will be able to strengthen their babies' brains by interacting with their babies in those first years of life, many mothers will take that message from those highly credible messengers to heart and will begin to plan their life as a parent accordingly.

That extremely high credibility level that the obstetrician team has with mothers then tends to be shared after their baby is born by the pediatricians and by the pediatric nurse practitioners and other child care team members who advise each mother about her infant child for those first years of life.

Those tend to be very special, high impact, high credibility, and effective patient/caregiver relationships. The caregivers for pregnant women and the caregivers for their children after they are born all tend to be given very high levels of trust, credence, and even behavioral compliance from the new mothers and their families.

That might be particularly true for first time mothers who are deeply hungry for information about their pregnancy and their new child, but it is true for all parents for each child. Pediatricians and other primary care team members for infant and children tend to be trusted and that creates an impact that can benefit each child when it is used intentionally to teach those issues about the value of exercising each child's brain to the parents of each child.

Mothers Should Know That Information Before Leaving the Hospital

Hospitals can and should also be support resources on that key set of brain support issues. Hospitals should add information about the brain strengthening opportunities for new mothers to the take home materials that hospitals give to each new mother.

It is important to start that teaching as soon as possible from each set of caregivers because the time to make an impact begins immediately and because far too many parents have no idea that those opportunities to strengthen their baby's brain exists.

A recent set of surveys done in California found almost no mothers of young babies who knew that science or who explicitly understand those developmental opportunities.

Almost none of the surveyed parents had been told about those issues by their care teams in ways that the parents remembered the messages and were able to build that set of factors into their parenting approaches and strategies.

Mothers and Fathers Become Enthusiastic When the Opportunities Were Explained

The mothers and fathers who are in the surveyed groups became excited and enthusiastic about the opportunities to help their child strengthen their brain and become better learners when those opportunities were explained — but those parents had not been taught that information before that time.

We need to do much better than that. We need all parents — every single new mother in particular — to know that information.

We need care teams who teach each set of parents the functional link between brain exercise and brain strength for their child. Just telling parents to talk, read, and interact with their children because interaction of various kinds is generically a "nice" thing to do for a baby is much less useful and much less respectful of the decision making role of the parent than telling the parent that brain exercises in those key years will help their baby have a stronger brain and will have an enhanced ability to learn.

Parents love their children and parents are accountable for their children in key ways that make sharing that specific linkage between behavior and their child's future clearly the right thing for the caregiving team to do.

Parents deserve the chance to understand that science and those behavioral realities in direct and clear ways. Caregivers should make teaching that set of opportunities to each parent a high priority.

Our obstetricians can begin that teaching before birth and the hospital where each child is born can also be an intentional part of the teaching process relative to those brain-strengthening issues for each new mother.

Our caregivers, as a team, should set a goal of never having a new mother go home from the hospital without having received a focused and solid teaching session on those specific brain development issues and opportunities for their child.

We Need Parent Teaching Tools to Reinforce the Teaching

That teaching process for each new mother in that hospital setting after the birth doesn't need to be long — but it does need to be clear.

It can be very useful to tie a set of the teaching tools that exist to do that work to that coaching encounter. Having that specific learning supported by video pieces, Internet links, and written materials can all reinforce the message in ways that make the learning process more effective and can continue to create teaching links after the baby is taken home from the hospital.

In the best set of circumstances, we need all caregivers — beginning with the obstetricians and the hospital care team and then extending to the pediatric care teams who see the baby for follow-up well baby and sick baby visits — to be teaching the basic facts about brain development opportunities to the parents of each child at the time when that teaching can provide the greatest benefit to each child.

At the core, hearing those messages about brain development opportunities in our babies from each of those trusted caregivers at each of those highly leveraged moments in the care relationship is an opportunity we need to utilize in the most consistent and effective way for each child.

We Need All Key Caregivers to Support Those Key Issues

We need to get the maximum benefit for each child from those highly credible caregiver relationships with each new mother. To begin the process, we need that set of caregivers to understand the key issues. Not all caregivers are current on the relevant science and biology. That needs to be an early teaching focus for any caregivers who do not know that science now.

We need those caregivers who are helping each mother with both pregnancy and childcare to understand the brain development functionality and to throw the most current information about brain growth science, processes, and interaction opportunities that exist for their child.

We need all of those caregivers who take care of our children to understand the science so all caregivers can to teach that science and that opportunity to parents and to each other as teams. We need caregivers to share that opportunity with each other in ways that create team care for the babies and their parents and families.

We need care teams who understand the extremely high benefit levels that result for a child from the parent talking directly to the child and interacting in loving and safe ways with the child.

Spoken interactions with each child build brain strength at levels that can exceed all other interactions. Too many parents don't know or even suspect the value to their child relative to brain growth that speaking to their child can create.

Reading to each child also has layers of benefits. The reading process, itself, creates a set of safe and direct interactions that babies tend to love. The vocabularies of babies who are read to tend to be significantly higher than the vocabularies of children who do not have books read to them. Multiple studies have shown that to be true.

A key point to understand about that relationship is that the books, themselves, often contain only a simple set of words. The major growth in vocabulary for those infants comes from the other words spoken by the parents to the child about the books and about the topics of the books. Simply reading is good and reading that is linked to conversations with the child can be golden.

We need the care teams who care for children in each setting to figure out who on each team is doing the work of teaching brain development science, practices, processes, and opportunities to at least one parent for each child.

Learning by parents is never more focused and more child directed than it is during the pregnancy, birth, and first levels of care settings and direct care experiences for new mothers and fathers. That is a high opportunity time for teaching both new fathers and new mothers how to interact with their children in ways that will meet the brain support needs of their children.

We Need Both Direct Coaching and Support Materials That Continue the Teaching at Home

Every care site and every caregiver should have access to a useful set of support materials for their patients that can be shared at the care site and taken home by the parents for each child. Those kinds of materials exist in many settings and they can be made available to all care sites and care teams relatively easily.

But even when there are no support materials in a setting that are available to the caregiver, we need each caregiver to simply explain verbally to the parent of each very young child that having basic and consistent interactions with their child will build brain strength in their child.

That specific piece of information doesn't need to be supported by a tool kit to be conveyed in a meaningful and life-changing way to a parent. It can be simply said to each parent. Direct coaching on that key issue from the caregiver to the parent can have major impact all by itself.

It can be even better and more effective when there are tool kits to help teach that information, but simply making that point about the positive impact of exercising each child's brain directly to each parent in a face-to-face setting can have a major impact on a parent that can change a child's life.

We Need Reminders as Well

To help the most children, it is useful to have follow-up support tools and to have on-going communication approaches relative to those issues as well. Reminders to each parent with a very young child about useful interactions with the child can happen regularly in a systematic way using a number of easily available communication tools.

There are a small number of Internet tools in limited use now that send text messages to parents reminding the parents to interact directly in key ways with their children, for example. Chapter Twelve of this book lists some of those Internet supported reminders.

That connectivity package and that connectivity support tool kit will undoubtedly get continuously better in fairly short time frames because the tendency of computer and Internet supported connectivity tools is to continuously improve… particularly when those tools add real value to people's lives.

Those various connectivity tools actually can add great value — and we need to use them often and well.

The most effective and key influential teaching reminder for most parents, however, when mothers bring their infants into care sites for examinations, immunizations, periodic episodes, incidents, pieces of care, and when the caregiver team in each site adds brain development messages and teaching to each encounter.

There are few communications of any kind that have more impact than having caregivers reminding the mothers of very young children during those encounters about the very explicit and immediate brain development opportunity that exists right now for their children.

Evaluating Child Progress on Those Issues Can Also Be Useful

It can also be a good thing during those encounters with the parent and infant for the caregivers to check on the children in systematic ways to see how well each child is interacting in some basic ways relative to those encounters.

In some care settings, putting formal processes in place to do early childhood development evaluations can be a good thing to do — with parents told immediately about any issues and opportunities for their child that are detected in that education process.

The Pediatrician's Academy has shared a list of some very useful evaluation tools that caregivers can use and care sites should understand what those tools are.

Caregivers Should Encourage Parents to Talk, Read, Sing, and Interact

The key and most useful thing that needs to be done in those encounters is to have the caregivers teach each parent about the value of direct and personal focused interaction with their child — and to teach parents what kinds of interactions can have the most value and benefit for their children.

The tool kit of basic interactions that parents can learn to use to exercise their child's brain isn't complex or technical. Direct interactions are the key tools for each parent to use to make brains strong.

Parental interactions with children are the key tools and the most effective approaches that build brain strength in each child. Direct and focused interactions by an adult with each child are key steps for helping each child.

Children with zero adult interactions tend to end up with tiny vocabularies by the time they enter kindergarten. Those children with very low levels of adult interactions end up with fewer neuron connections — and the children with the lowest interaction levels too often can end up with the physical brain damage that is created by toxic stress syndrome.

Those children face very difficult lives.

Speak Constantly, Read, Interact, and Show Warmth to Each Child

By contrast, the children whose parents speak constantly to them, read regularly to them, interact frequently with them, and show consistent and real warmth to them end up with much larger vocabularies, stronger brains, better learning abilities, and those children avoid the life altering brain and physical damage that results from toxic stress syndrome.

Parents who don't know that science and who have not had those opportunities explained to them are less likely to do the useful and functional things in their own homes with each child that strengthen their child's brain.

The basic set of things that build a strong brain for a child can happen in each home for each child. Those beneficial activities are all anchored on basic direct adult interactions with each child.

Talk, Read, Interact, Ask Questions, and Sing to Build Strong Brains

Care teams need parents of each child to know that talking to the child is a very powerful and effective interaction that each parent can do for a child.

Care teams also need to encourage reading to each child. Caregivers should teach parents that reading to their child even half an hour a day can change the learning trajectory for their child.

Reading books and talking to the child about the books that are being read both teaches children the critical link between symbols and meaning and teaches basic thought processes that create linear thinking. Reading creates its own levels of value and that value is enhanced when the adult in each child's life also talks very directly to the child.

Asking questions can also add great value relative to creating both thought processes and verbal interactions.

Simply asking questions every day to each child is a highly effective interaction that also can build brain strength and neuron connections that last the child for life. Talking constantly to each child about the setting and the situations each child is in can cause millions of words to be spoken to each child in those key years.

Those spoken words by key adults help children learn to think, and those spoken words strengthen connections in each child's brain.

So for pediatric care teams, the approach of encouraging mothers and fathers to read, talk, and sing to their children can be an extremely important thing to do in every set of encounters with parents.

Caregivers Can Help Create Access to Books

Helping mothers with the reading, talking, and singing functions can add to the levels of success for each child. Care teams can often determine whether basic help in those areas is needed by the mother or family.

If, for example, a mother has no books or if mothers can't actually read, themselves, then caregivers can and should help mothers get access to books and should encourage mothers to find someone in their family, community, or setting who can do those reading functions with their child.

Mothers who understand the value of reading, but who can't read themselves, can often find someone else to read to their child. Also — everyone needs to realize that the mothers who can't read themselves can still give their infants high levels of very useful and effective brain development support by simply talking directly in caring ways to their child.

Reading is good and talking is essential as a brain-building tool. Talking all by itself builds the connections that children need — and the talking done to a child does not need to be connected to a book to have major value.

Caregivers can teach all of those realities to each parent for each child in the course of caring for each child.

Free Books and Text Messages Can Help

When reading is possible, reading can be a wonderful brain development tool. Several studies have linked reading levels in homes to income levels in homes.

Higher income homes do tend to have both more books and higher income homes tend to spend more time reading to children.

One study showed that the average well-to-do mother had over a dozen books in the home to read to each child — and that same research showed that almost 60 percent of the low-income homes did not have one single children's book in their home.

Another study showed that one-third of low-income mothers do read every day to their children — but over half of the low-income mothers did not read to their child at all.

We Can't Change Income Levels but We Can Change Reading Levels

The fact that one-third of the low-income mothers who were studied in that survey did read to their children every day is extremely important information because it tells us that it is entirely possible for children in low-income homes to have someone read to them and to directly benefit from reading.

Low-income homes that value reading can clearly make reading a reality for children. Low-income is not an absolute barrier or a functional barrier to reading. Low-income homes can and do read to their children now.

We need to make that percentage of low-income families who read daily to their child much higher in order to benefit more children.

The children from that one-third of the low-income homes who do have daily reading will clearly do much better in school then the children in the homes where reading does not happen at all.

The key factor that exists for each child relative to learning readiness isn't their family income — it is their family approach to reading and their family approach to interacting with their child.

We cannot change family income — but we can change family approaches to having books read to each child.

For the families who do not read today, we need our care teams who interact with each mother and family to teach the value of reading and we also need to create access to books. It is much harder to read to a child in any home if there is not a single book to read in the home.

"Reach Out and Read" Provides Books for Homes

Some of the best child-focused care sites now make children's books available to new mothers during early visits. Some care sites point mothers to various settings where reading support exists.

One of the programs that is often supported by pediatricians is called "Reach Out and Read." That program is described in Chapter Twelve of this book. It is focused on getting books into the homes that need books.

Any programs that provide books to the homes who do not have books is a good program for children. You can't read books that don't exist.

We need people in each community setting and in each care setting for low-income people to create access to books for all of the children who need books in those key years.

We are a nation of great resources. We need to channel some of those resources into those particular uses and we need to do that channeling now.

Reusing books can be part of the process. That often happens in family settings now. Families often reuse books inside of families. We need to extend that process of reusing books to have families helping other families by making books available for reuse.

Well-Used and Well-Loved Books Should Get Extended Lives

Well-to-do families who read extensively to their children often have shelves full of children's books that sit idle and gather dust as the children who used those books grow older. We need better mechanisms in place to get those much loved and well used children's books from those homes to a new set of children so those special books can change even more lives and can be loved and well used in new settings.

Various communities need to build ways of doing that distribution and those distribution approaches that are created in various settings need our targeted support. Linkages to care sites can be a very good way of creating that support.

Some child focused care sites today also pass out teaching materials like cups, blankets, caps, and t-shirts that contain printed reminders to the parents to read, talk, play, and sing to their children. Those care sites who distribute those materials want the parents to remember the messages about those interactions once the parents return to their homes.

Some care sites even send text message reminders to parents to interact in those ways with their new infants and toddlers.

All of those messages and support materials from care sites come with a high level of credibility with parents because of their trusted source.

Caregivers need to make this issue a priority because if we are going to succeed in getting all children school ready for school by the time each child enters school, then the care teams for each mother and each child need to be part of the education and support team in highly credible and functional ways.

Caregivers Need to Make Early Brain Development a Top Priority

No one has more credibility with mothers, fathers, and families than caregivers. That point is worth repeating. No one interacts with children and their parents more consistently and directly in those key years than caregivers. That fact creates a functional opportunity that we should not waste.

Using those direct caregiver encounters with each child as a mechanism for communicating key messages about brain development exercises and interactions to each parent has clear and obvious value for each child.

No aspect of biological development has a bigger impact on the entire lives of children than building strong brains for each child in those first key high opportunity years when our brains develop.

We need the caregivers who clearly understand that science and who recognize that biological opportunity to choose to use that knowledge with their patients to improve the lives of all of their early childhood patients by teaching that science to the parents of each child.

All Child Caregivers Want to Help Children

All caregivers for children became caregivers for children to help children. That is their career path and that is their personal motivating life objective. Helping children is their goal and it is their mission.

Building stronger brains very directly helps each child and helps achieve that mission for each caregiver. Sharing this information with parents in ways that help parents support their children in that key development area and key time frame is one of the best things that the caregivers can do to actually have a major positive lifetime impact on each child.

We know that for most children who go to their regular pediatric visits, there are multiple pediatric encounters with our children in those first key years.

There is no excuse for every parent who goes to those encounters not to know that key set of facts about their children in those key years when that information has its highest medical, biological, and functional value for each child.

We need our care teams to make strengthening each child's brain a care delivery priority and we need our care teams to help parents build intentional and consistent parenting practices that benefit each child.

Too many children fail today. We need our caregivers to reduce those failures — beginning now.

CHAPTER TEN

We Need the Internet, Arts, Sciences, and New Technology to Support Our Growth Agenda for Children

WE LIVE IN a highly connected world. People text one another and engage in social networking communities with one another in very high numbers and high volumes every day. People use the Internet for research, learning, connections, and commerce in ways that expand almost daily.

People use the Internet to learn things, support activities, make decisions, and make various kinds of purchases.

We need to use that set of linkages and connections in a variety of ways to help with the approaches and processes that support strengthening brains of children in those key years.

We need to use several Internet tools to support the learning process for kids directly and we need to use those tools at multiple levels to help parents and other caregivers in their child raising and child support activities.

At a base level, we need to explain the core science of early brain development biological realities in easily accessible ways through the Internet for use by any people who are concerned about the intellectual underpinnings for our early childhood child support activities and approaches.

The Internet is a great tool for communicating science. We need to use that tool to communicate this body of science to everyone who can make use of that learning.

There are actually a number of excellent Internet sites now that explain those issues. We need to do a better job of sharing those sites and those learning resources with more relevant people.

Legislators, community leaders, policy makers, parents, families, and various kinds of caregivers for children can all benefit from having easy to access descriptions of the best and most useful science about those issues.

Parents, in particular, need that core scientific information about why we need to help each child with the right interactions in those early years of life in order to be most effective in those interactions with their own child.

The Internet can explain why parents need to interact with each child and can also teach parents exactly what is possible to do for their child to strengthen their child's brain. Research data is good and direct coaching about the most effective parenting approaches can be even better.

The Internet is a good tool to use to get that set of "how to" information to parents and to all other people who care for our children in those key years. The Internet can also be a useful tool to connect parents with other parents for purposes of mutual teaching and mutual support.

We Need the Internet to Describe What Parents Can Do

The pure and basic science is good to know. The Internet can help people get access to the great research being done at Harvard, Davis, Stanford, Yale, the University of Washington, the University of Minnesota, and a number of other relevant research settings.

Each of those academic research based settings has information available on the Internet that describes their work and communicates their research findings.

Organizations like The Urban Child Institute, The Million Words Institute, and the First Three Years Institute also each have their own Internet supported teaching tools, reports, and graphic illustrations that help explain key science and key issues relating to those first key years of development for each child.

The Internet Can Help Parents Know How to Interact with Their Child

Parents can learn parenting skills on the Internet as well. Both written materials on the Internet and YouTube types of videos can help parents figure out good, effective, pleasant, and fun things to do with their child that strengthen their brains.

Various kinds of interactive sites for parents — and social media connectivity approaches for parents — can also make use of that tool kit in ways that help parents and other caregivers.

A highly useful use of the Internet that is even more beneficial than teaching that basic science to people is having the Internet explain in accessible formats and in clear and functional terms to new parents exactly what can be done by each parent to help their children grow and thrive.

Videos that show parents how other parents interact with their own child can be particularly useful.

It can also be extremely useful for parents who want to know how to interact with their children to see through various videos what other parents in settings like their own have done to help their own children.

Videos showing parents talking, reading, singing, and playing with their children can serve as teaching tools and as role models for new parents. The Internet can be a highly useful tool for communicating about those approaches and practices to parents and families of young children because videos can be a very effective way of demonstrating effective approaches rather than simply describing effective approaches.

We Need to Connect Parents with Parents Through the Internet

Many parents have figured out fun, useful, and effective ways to help their children grow their brain strength. The Internet gives us a great tool to use to help share that learning by parents about parents to parents and directly with parents.

We learn by example. We can learn a lot be seeing good examples in action and by seeing and hearing how those behavior examples directly worked for real children.

We need to do a better job of making that kind of information available to parents on the Internet. Watching a father ask fun questions to a 2-year-old child can give other fathers of 2-year-old children ideas and suggestions about those kinds of interactions far more effectively than having the new father reading about those interactions.

We need to create interaction tools and sites that let parents communicate directly with each other as well. A number of community-based parenting groups have created internal dialogues and communications between parents that are reinforcing and educational for the parents.

We need smart people to expand the use of those kinds of tools, and we need to create a culture and robust set of learning and teaching interactions through use of those tools. We need to teach ourselves collaboratively how to be better parents and we need to use the Internet more effectively as a tool to do that work and facilitate that sharing.

We Need the Science and the Practice

This is the right time for us to make both the science and the practice of helping develop children's brains easily available and accessible on the Internet.

YouTube videos can help that entire learning process for parents significantly. Having good YouTube videos that show other parents interacting with their children in ways that cause their children to both have fun and to grow more intelligent can be extremely useful to parents who are motivated to provide that support for their child, but who are trying to figure out specifically what to do with their own child and exactly when to do what is needed with their own child.

We Learn by Watching and We Learn by Doing

We learn by example and we learn by doing. Watching and doing are two of those most effective learning tools we have for major areas of our lives. Direct interactions with other parents can be a key part of the process. Videos that show best practices can also be very useful. Seeing how other parents do those growth-provoking interactions with their children in effective ways that are pleasant for both parents and children can be a golden way for parents to learn.

Then — after watching those examples — actually doing those kinds of interactions with a child creates a set of experiences that each parent can build on to figure out the very best and most pleasant ways of interacting with their own child.

We don't need perfection.

There isn't one right way to do those interactions. There is no perfect approach. There are many very good approaches that all work. There are a number of effective patterns and useful approaches that can be effective as brain exercise and as fun activities for both parents and children.

The Internet can help tee up and teach those approaches and can make lives better for the children whose parents learn those skills.

We Need Parental Chat Rooms and Interactive Dialogues

We need a rich and robust set of Internet support tools to have the best shared learning experience between parents. As part of that experience, we need parental chat rooms, interactive parental dialogues, and we need expert question and answer sessions from parents and other aspects on those topics available on the Internet.

Once people understand the importance of those interactions with their children, we need to use the Internet to help parents figure out fun and effective ways to interact with their own child.

We need education experts in various settings and from various groups to produce their own Internet tools and we need parental interactions — with "other parents like me" — to also be part of the learning tool kit.

We need all parents to understand those issues and we need all parents to know how to provide that direct interaction support to their own child. The Internet can be invaluable in that process.

We need to do a much better job of using that tool for those purposes. This is a call to action to people who have that skill set to create those kinds of tools and interactions.

Each community group should have its own group leaders on the Internet preaching and teaching the value of those early interactions. Each group who wants to help their own children do well can benefit as a group from having its own cultural specific and culturally aligned examples and teaching tools that are available through Internet links and various texting and social media connections.

We Need News Media to Understand Those Issues

To fully achieve a national culture and regional cultures of continuous learning for all of us from birth on, we also need our news media to understand and work with those issues.

Some media outlets have done great and useful stories and articles about those issues. Scientific American, National Geographic, Newsweek, and The New York Times have all done very useful and informative pieces on brain development in our youngest children. Multiple other media outlets have done good pieces on those sets of issues and opportunities as well.

But the truth is that far too many other media outlets have almost no sense that those are key issues for our children today. Even the media outlets that have done great pieces on those issues tend to drop the topic after those substantive pieces run their course and become old news.

To help every child in each setting and to create a culture of continuous learning for settings across America, we need constant media support and attention to those issues. We need our media to do stories that celebrate successes and describe best practices in early child development.

We also need media stories that expose failures, risks, setbacks, and shortcomings when we fall short of helping our children in any setting with those key areas.

Our news media can come up with major communication approaches and with reporting focus topic lists that are based on those activities and those outcomes.

We Need a Culture That Celebrates Continuous Learning – from Birth On

We need our arts, movies, and TV shows to also have those messages about that time of early childhood development embedded in them at the points where those messages make sense. That is actually beginning to happen in some scripts.

Having mothers in movies or in TV shows describing clearly the relevant child development science to someone else in the TV show or movie to explain why the mother in the show did something specific with their own child that was relevant to the plot of the movie or the TV show can be a good and long remembered teaching tool for us all.

Even rap songs could, in some cases, have some of those points about creating strong brains in children embedded in them. The best rappers, themselves, clearly had someone in their own lives who gave that gift of personal brain exercise to them in those key first three years.

Each of those rappers must have had someone in their own first years of life who was interacting directly with them at that point in time or those rappers would not have the dexterity of language needed now to rap.

A Debt Is Owed by Each Rapper to Whoever Stimulated Their Brain

A debt is owed by each rapper to whoever created that particular neuron linkage tool kit for each rapper in that key point in their life. There are probably ways that those factoids and insights could be relevant to a future rap — even if it is as indirect as a male rapper wanting to have children with a mother who will give his kids the right kinds of brain growth that will cause those kids to be able to succeed and to be winners going down whatever life paths they choose to follow.

If our various artists include points about those issues in their art — then that inclusion can be part of our education process about those issues for everyone.

Our Artists Should at Least Build Strong Brains in Their Own Children

If our artists don't go down that path of adding that wisdom and those insights to their art, our artists should at least be sure that as they raise their own children that those opportunities for early neuron connectivity exist for their own children.

It's pretty clear from looking at the families of talented people that some of the talented people have interacted well and effectively with their children in ways that helped their children in those early years become talented as well — and it is also highly likely that some talented people did not do what needed to be done to help neurons connect and grow strong in their own children's brains in those first key years.

Some families have multiple generations of obvious talent and some families fall short and have next generations who do not have the abilities and the capabilities of their parents.

Each child is on his or her own path — and each path has its own internal consequences. Each talented person who has children can have a major impact on the life paths for each child.

We Can't Guarantee Perfection – but We Can Build Imperfection

We can't guarantee perfection for children in those processes, but we can guarantee various levels of imperfection by having children whose connectivity needs are absolutely not met in that key time frame for biological brain growth.

We can absolutely guarantee that problems and significant challenges will happen for children by having children whose toxic stress neurochemicals are activated in damaging ways by the way they are raised in those early years.

Those children with that toxic stress syndrome need our help and those children with that set of problems and issues will probably need our help for their entire lives.

That is a tragedy — and that might inspire some level of artistic response because art often focuses on tragic occurrences.

We Need Electronic Tools That Support Needed Interactions

It could be a very good thing for us to actually have an electronic tool kit of some kind that could help us help each child in those key early years.

One of the biggest opportunities that we face today relative to those issues and to the basic early childhood connectivity agendas and strategies is to somehow figure out ways of creating the needed levels of neuron connectivity for our children in ways that are electronically supported.

Having some kinds of electronic tools to help us do that work of early brains development could be a major asset and benefit for the process.

Screens alone do not make brains grow.

TV Alone Does Not Strengthen Brains

We know from research that simply watching TV does not make the brain grow. Scans placed on infant brains show that watching TV can entertain a child, but it doesn't trigger the brain functions that create links and growth in an infant brain.

We know from good research that children can lose ground on their early learning status by watching too much TV. TV does not build the right learning process tool kit in the brain of a child.[73,74]

We know from good research that it takes a direct and personal interaction for the child with another person to make that part of the brain grow in a child.

There is a kind of an imprinting process that happens for our children that is only triggered by direct interaction with a person.

Baby kittens learn future cat behaviors by watching and interacting with mother cats. Baby kittens usually do not learn their future behaviors by watching ducks or butterflies. Kittens are programed to study and emulate cats.

Similarly, the parts of infant brains that light up electronically when growth is happening only light up when an infant or child is actually interacting with another person. That person is usually, in the life of children, the child's mother — but other adults can and do fill that need and other adults can also trigger that growth function in children.

We also know that television, alone, does not trigger any brain growth in those early years. Some studies show an actual loss of vocabulary in very young children who only get their visual input from television.

In later years — after the brain connections are safely in place for each child — then watching the right television shows can trigger great growth in knowledge and can create real insight for a child. In those first key years, however, television, alone, adds no value to the physical growth of the brain. That strengthening process that we need for each child's brain only happens when children directly interact with an adult.

We Don't Know Yet If a Combination Approach Adds Value

We now know that particular piece of science about the need for direct interaction with an adult. What we don't know yet is if a new set of interactive electronic tools — some kind of iPad-like tools and new generations of interactive cell phones — can also trigger brain growth if their use with each child is linked in some way to the child also interacting with another real person at that same time.

We need that research to be done. Some people are working on those issues. The questions are extremely important.

Can the needed brain growth that happens in a child's brain when mothers read to a child from a book also happen when a mother reads to a child from an iPad? Can the needed growth in a child's brain happen when a child interacts directly with an iPad while the child is also being held by the mother or held by another trusted adult?

Can we use electronic devices to help parents read books to their children — and could that be particularly helpful in some cases where the parents, themselves, do not read or do not read well?

Initial research appears to show that reading to a child from an iPad that is directly simulating the functions of a book does seem to help the child improve their reading skills — but if the reading is non-linear and if it involves making jumps from the words on the screen to other topics, those jumps seem to weaken the brain development a bit for the child at that point relative to both reading skills and linear thought.

In other words, it appears that when the iPad simply emulates a book, the tool seems to works well and functions much like a book. But if the iPad content has non-linear linkages, then the linear thinking skills in a child are not built as well as they are built by a more linear, pure, and traditional book reading process.

We Need Major Research into the Impact of Interactive Electronic Tools

This is an area where we need more research soon and we need to link that research quickly to helping our children in a very direct way.

We see major levels of use of those devices now by very small children. We need to be sure that those uses of those devices are building needed brain cells and not just entertaining small children or even causing those children to lose linear thinking skills.

In a best-case situation, if the right tools are built and if those new tools are both affordable and accessible, and if those tools are used by the children in ways that help brains grow, then that new interactive tool kit may have an extremely good set of consequences for children.

In worst case situations, if the children are isolated, insulated, and merely passively entertained by an electronic tool — but are not directly stimulated in ways that strengthen neuron connectivity — then the children whose brains develop under the impact of those more problematic tools could end up with new kinds of dysfunctional problems and might even have a whole new set of negative syndromes that we don't even suspect or have names for today.

Using electronic screens purely as a book read by a parent to a child apparently does not seem to raise those concerns at this point. Books work well to exercise the brain of a child. Electronic books also can exercise a child's brain.

Now we need to figure out what other ways we can use to engage the entire electronic tool kit as support for our children.

Improving Connectivity and Reducing Toxic Stress Would Be a Good Package

It would be a wonderful thing if we could figure out a set of electronic tools that involved parents and children interacting in ways that create brain growth and that also help with toxic stress avoidance for our children.

We need some very smart people to figure that set of functions out and to develop those tools.

Various kinds of electronic tools could obviously be particularly useful when mothers or fathers are illiterate, but those tools could possibly have great use for all families if they can be used in ways that meet the children's needs and can help the parents do their part of the growth functioning.

The truth is that a very high percentage of families have various electronic tools in their homes now. We need to figure out how to use those basic tools most effectively to help our children.

Texting Can Distract Mothers from Their Child

We also need to make very sure that mothers and other caregivers do not focus their attention too much on texting other people and then ignore their children while texting.

Children who are functionally ignored because of texting parents can go through multiple levels of difficulties for obvious reasons.

Texting can create its own kinds of isolation for a child. Isolation is isolation, regardless of the cause or the trigger, and we know how much damage isolation can do to a child. That science and that damage are both unquestioned.

This is not a call to end texting. That is both impossible and not necessary.

We do need the caregiver for each child to set aside time regularly that is text free and focused directly on each child. Text free time focused directly by the adult on the child should be a goal and a practice for every parent who texts.

That text free time frame for each child needs to be an intentional and deliberate process for each parent and caregiver or it is highly unlikely to happen.

We now know that we need direct and regular contact with each child and we need that contact between parent and child to be direct and interactive in order to trigger the results that we want and need for brain development and brain strengthening for a child.

It would be deeply unfortunate if we closed the learning gap between higher income children and lower income children by having the mothers of higher income children spending so much time with texting and other levels of electronic connectivity that they end up functionally isolating their children in those key months and years when direct interactions with a child exercise and build the child's brain.

We need the Internet to help parents understand all of those issues and we need to use the Internet so that parents can see models of other parents and caregivers showing how those interactions can achieve the best results.

The Internet Can Remind Us as Well

Using the Internet as a simple reminder tool to remind mothers/parents to interact directly with very small children can be useful all by itself.

One experiment used regular texts that were sent to each mother at pre-arranged times to remind the mothers to set aside their other interests — including texting — to interact with her child that experiment had a very high level of success.[59]

The study showed that the interaction time with children for some mothers who received those reminder texts significantly increased.

That approach and others like it can have obvious value as child support approaches.

Another study simply sent texts to each mother at regular intervals to remind the mothers about the advantages and the possibilities of brain development for their children. That study simply sent reminders of those basic facts to mothers on a regular basis with no other interventions.

At the end of two years, the learning levels for the child whose mothers received those basic and simple text reminders was more than two full months ahead of the learning levels for the children who did not receive those reminders.[56]

That study is cited in the final chapter of this book. Having a baby who is two full months ahead of other children at only 2 years old is a powerful and highly positive impact. The only tool that was used to create that benefit was a text sent to mothers telling the mothers that they could, in fact, strengthen their child's brain.

Mothers who received those texts spent more time interacting with their children than the mothers in the same study who did not receive the texts. Those additional interactions with each child had the impact that interactions tend to have — each child with that support had better learning abilities at age three as a result.

Mothers love their children. Mothers want their children to do well. The simple text reminder helped those mothers who received the reminder to actualize their love in a focused and effective way with their child.

We Need to Figure Out Creative Ways to Support Parents

We need to use the Internet as support tools that are part of an overall development plan and strategy for each child. Overall, we need to understand our key sets of goals for interactions with each of our children in those early years. We need to collectively figure out a wide variety of creative and functional ways of helping parents in each setting create those needed interactions.

The Internet and various electronic and social media tools can all help with that process.

We need to teach effective approaches to parents and other caregivers in effective ways that we can communicate electronically and support in our media and through our various Internet tools.

We Are Just Beginning to Benefit from That Set of Tools

The Internet needs to be a key part of our strategy to build strong brains in our children. We are just beginning to benefit from using that set of tools for those purposes. We need to make our use of the Internet to support our children an asset, a benefit, a workable set of processes, and we need to make those processes continuously better.

Very smart people who are Internet experts should be building applications now that can further and support all of those agendas. The goal is clear. The need is great. The tool sets are, at this point, largely unknown and only in their pilot and experimental stages. They are not robust and they are currently not widespread and easily available.

It's time to change that reality to make lives better for our children. Every life we save is a life we save. Every child whose life trajectory is enhanced benefits forever from having that better set of capabilities.

Creative people can help save lives and make lives significantly better by channeling their creativity into approaches that can achieve those goals.

CHAPTER ELEVEN

Saving All Kids and Lifting All Ships

Now THAT WE understand all of those issues about key brain development biological time frames for each and every child, it would be criminal for us to not use this information to save all of our children.

It would also be sad, tragic, and almost criminal for each of us to know this information and not share it directly with anyone in our lives who is about to have a baby or who now has a baby, infant, toddler, or a very young child in their lives and who needs to personally understand those processes right now for the sake of their child.

When the caregivers for any young child understand those issues, decisions can be made daily by the caregivers that can improve the life of the child.

We need everyone in America to understand those issues — and we particularly need every parent of every new child to understand those issues. The parents of newborn children all love their children and parents need this information to give their children the best pathway for their lives.

Those issues are not so complicated that they require significant support processes or extensive educational materials to teach the key points. Once we understand those issues, we can all explain the key points to relevant people in relatively few words.

Because it is easy to explain, there is no excuse for not explaining those points to people whose child will benefit directly and immediately from the parents having this knowledge.

We each should be personally accountable for having anyone in our lives who needs this information to have access to this information. We owe it to people

— to our societies' children — to make this knowledge part of the lives of the people who care for each child.

We should all make that commitment to share that information in relevant ways and we should make that commitment now.

We need everyone who has young children to know this information. We can achieve that goal if we each teach that information to anyone who has a young child.

The financial impact for each child — all by itself — makes that information with worth knowing. When children get the right levels of neuron connectivity support in those key early years, that support enables those children to graduate from school and it enables those children to not be school dropouts.

Collect a Million Dollars and Avoid Jail

The lifetime income difference between the average school dropout — doomed to a life of frequent unemployment combined with minimum wage employment — and the average income of an actual graduate, exceeds $1 million. That is a significant amount of money. The basic reality is that helping children build strong brains in those golden early years can be a million dollar gift given by parents to their children.

Not going to jail is another gift from parents of almost inestimable value. Prison is a bad and often damaging place to be. Prison life can be ugly. The other people who are also in prison can be bad, dangerous, angry, and damaging people. Convicted felons lose voting rights and have impoverished and weakened legal status even after they are released from prison.

Prison is bad. Jail is bad. Gang membership can also be damaging and bad for a child and for a prisoner.

We need to help children have the learning levels necessary to read in order to change those life paths for all children.

Eighty-five percent of the young people in our juvenile justice system either read poorly or don't read at all.[11] Children who can't read drop out of school.

The likelihood of a Black male high school dropout going to jail is nearly 80 percent.[65,67,69,70]

Those are horrible and horrific numbers and those are very ugly realities.

So we need parents to read, talk, and sing to their children. Reading, talking, and singing to infants and toddlers to keep them from being damaged later by dysfunctional and angry people in prison or being forced to be with dysfunctional and angry people in gang-related street and community situations is a gift of great merit and great love that a parent can give to a newborn child.

Society Will Collectively Benefit When We Do This Well

The challenge we face now is to figure out as a society how to give that gift to every child. We all benefit at multiple levels when that gift is actually given to a child.

Schools clearly will have immediate benefits from children being given that higher level of learning ability as a gift. Our schools will be able to focus their efforts on children who come to school ready to learn when the students who come to school are actually ready to learn.

Our prisons don't need to bear the expense of incarcerating any people who actually don't end up going there as prisoners.

The number of teen pregnancies can decrease significantly and the number of teen health problems can also diminish. Toxic stress syndrome children tend to have layers of other health problems that impede their progress and create expenses and care delivery challenges for our public care systems.[25,26,55]

Giving that gift of brain growth and emotional security to each child has multiple layers of benefits to us all.

Several highly reputable economists at the University of Chicago, the University of Minnesota, and Harvard University have projected that the return on investment for society of investing money in those initial years of each child's life is a multiple of every dollar spent. Read their work to see why those very capable people believe that to be true.

There are many upsides to getting this issue right for our children. There are no discernable downsides to helping those children in that key time of need and opportunity for each child.

We need to help the children in each community, each setting, and in each family who has newborn children get the support each child needs in those first key years.

We Need to Build on the Best Approaches

A number of research programs are doing great research on those child development topics and agendas. A number of really solid childcare programs in a number of settings are doing good things to help the children in their settings who need that support. We need to build on those best programs in each of those settings.

Most care for the very youngest children in those key months and years takes place in each child's home, so we need to do what needs to be done to make each home the focus for the effective support of each child.

A significant amount of care happens in day care settings — both formal group settings and family level-based day cares. We need each of those day care settings to support the learning process for each child.

The next chapter of this book describes some of the science that is relevant to those issues. That chapter also describes some of the programs that are working now across various communities to help our very young children today in a wide range of settings.

We Need More Than Pilots at This Point

There are some positive things happening for some of our youngest children today in a number of settings. But those positive things that are happening for children in those settings are just the tiny tip of what we need to be a massive public health iceberg that brings needed help to each child in that key period of time for each child.

Pilots are good and fine, but we need more than pilots in a number of settings to help large numbers of children at this point in our history.

We need a public health campaign that actually creates universal awareness of those issues and that creates broad opportunities for all children across all settings to get the support each child needs.

At this point in time — all of us need to be part of the solution. We can all help. We need everyone who understands those issues to be part of that campaign to help all children by helping other relevant people to understand those key issues.

Knowledge Is Power

Knowledge is power. Understanding those issues increases our power over them. When people understand those issues relative to their own children, then people can make better and more informed choices about the interactions that happen with each child.

The new science reinforces that set of interaction in ways that give us better tools and better insights than we have ever had.

This is the right time for that new science about brain development in children to exist and this is the right time for adults to be doing needed interactions for each and every child. This is a good time for us to support each other in those efforts and to make very sure that each child who is relevant to us gets the support that we now know each child needs.

We need a culture of continuing learning for America and we need that culture to begin its impact at birth for each child. We need the care systems and the care teams for each child — beginning with the obstetrician and the hospital and transitioning to the caregivers in our pediatric care settings — to be teaching and supporting those practices for each child.

We need all parents to know the potential to help their own child in those key areas during those key years.

That support and knowledge are clearly not happening far too often for many of our children now. Most families and most communities are not aware of those sets of issues and those key opportunities today.

Too many children are being damaged. That damage is happening right now far too often without anyone who cares for those children understanding or knowing that inadvertent damage is being done to their child by not interacting with their child or by not providing the right levels of support for their child.

We need awareness immediately on those issues for each person involved in the care of each child and we need that awareness in all relevant settings.

This is a job we can all do.

We all need to help create that awareness. The functional likelihood of that awareness existing across all of us and across all relevant settings will increase significantly if each person who does becomes aware does what can be done to share the awareness with other people in our lives.

We Need to Give Parents the Tools to Help Each Child Succeed

Parents love their children. Parents want their children to succeed. People in communities all want the children in their communities to succeed. Everyone wants children to do well and everyone wants the children in their life to have the best chance in life.

We now need to understand collectively and as parents how we can achieve those goals and then we need to act together in various ways to make that success for each child happen.

The children who do well now do well because that support exists for each child. We know that this support process works for a child because it is working today for millions of children.

We need to use what works and we need to use what works for each child.

Success for children can be enhanced in all settings when the people who are relevant to each child very intentionally help each child succeed.

That needs to be our goal. Each child needs our support.

Each child who is helped will be on a different life path because that child has been helped.

This is a very personal agenda for each child, and it needs to be a shared cultural agenda for all adults.

We Can Help All Children to Do Better

The need for helping children extends beyond the currently disadvantaged children who have low vocabularies in kindergarten and who can't read at all today. We need all children to benefit. If all parents from all groups understand those biological truths and developmental opportunities, then all children in America from all groups can have their developmental experiences enhanced.

That knowledge and insight about those developmental issues can help every single child.

If we do this right and if we do this well and if we create a national agenda of continuous learning for all children — starting with birth — we can actually help all children do better.

That strategy can be a rising tide that lifts all ships. The children of affluent people and the children of impoverished people will all benefit from having their parents understanding and utilizing those opportunities for each child in those golden, high opportunity years when the biology of the brain makes those interactions relevant and effective for each child.

We can become brighter as a nation if all of our children get excellent levels of support in those earliest years. We can have the best work force in the world and we can continue to lead the world in innovation and in creativity because we will have even more people being creative and innovative.

Other Cultures Stifle Creativity and Suppress Intellectual Growth

Too many other cultures in the world stifle creativity and practice various kinds of intellectual suppression, repression, and oppression. We, by contrast, have led the world in many ways for many years by utilizing our creativity and by recognizing, supporting, and even rewarding innovation at multiple levels.

We need to stay on that path and we need to do our most creative and innovative work at even higher and more inclusive levels so that we have more people able to contribute to the greater good.

Being more inclusive in our creativity approaches is a cultural manifestation and an economic blessing that we will be able to build on collectively if we have all of our children becoming all that they can be with the right level of early childhood support.

We All Need to Be Accountable to Make That Growth Real

We need all of us to support that childhood support agenda and we need each of us to be accountable for helping make that agenda real for the children in our lives.

If we do this badly, the greatness of America will fade into a sad morass of intergroup anger, intergroup division, and even intergroup conflict. We could become just another sad and divided country at war with itself.

If we do this well, and if we very intentionally and very effectively help all of our children from all of our groups do well, then the greatness of America will be enhanced by a future of intergroup success.

Success is the better choice.

Let's win.

We know how to make that happen.

CHAPTER TWELVE

Science, Public Policy, and Early Childhood Development Programs Are All Making Progress – We Now Need to Accelerate the Pace and Expand the Process to Save Every Child

WE ARE AT the cusp of a golden age for research into the development and functioning of our children.

Great research has been done and more is underway. Talented and dedicated researchers in a number of very important care settings and highly competent academic settings are learning more every day about how our brains develop, and about how our interactions with the world around us in those very first years of our life shape who we are and what we do in major ways for the rest of our lives.

As that body of research is building its scope and momentum, we are also seeing some changes in approaches to helping children in those first months and years of life in a number of settings that are moving in the right direction.

A number of innovative and badly needed efforts to help children in those key time frames are being put in place in a number of pilots and programs. Inspired and guided by that research and those insights, targeted programs to help children in the first months and years of life are being built, tested, and implemented in a number of communities by people who very much want to close the learning gaps that exist in their settings.

The public policy focused and privately funded charitable foundations that support much of the innovation and public policy progress that we see as a nation are also increasingly adding support for early childhood development to their priorities and to their direct financial support programs and strategies.

After a long history as a country of not focusing at all in any systematic or structured ways on children in those golden months and years, we are beginning to see new awareness of those opportunities and we are seeing a range of new efforts that are intended to make a functional difference in the lives of those children.

The tide is swinging toward awareness and toward enlightenment on those early child development opportunities, problems, and issues in a number of settings. That is an extremely positive development that we need to encourage and support.

It makes sense to briefly recap both that learning process and that progress, and to describe some of the programs and approaches that are now helping with these highly important efforts in this final chapter of this book.

The science is increasingly visible.

Go to the Internet and pull up the growing body of information about the science of brain development in those first years of life. That body of science is growing at a lovely rate. There are multiple pieces on the Internet on that topic that are worth reading and watching today. The number of available resources available on the Internet to both teach us and support us relative to those programs is growing at an accelerating pace.

The new TED talk by Dr. Nadine Burke Harris on the lifelong impact on children of damaging events that happen in their first years of life, for example, is worth watching by everyone in policy positions and caregiver settings who cares about young children and who wants to understand the impact of early stress on children that continues to affect children in important ways for their entire lives. More than a million people have watched that Ted Talk by Dr. Harris.

Some of the most significant research has been done by Professor Patricia Kuhl and her team at the University of Washington, into the brain functioning of very small children. Dr. Kuhl also has a TED talk on those issues that people should see.

Dr. Kuhl and her team have amazingly sensitive, powerful and capable electronic scanning devices that can actually track activity levels in infant brains at a very early age. She has used those devices to do some extremely meaningful and capable research about the early childhood brain development processes that the world should know about.

Dr. Kuhl has a couple of lectures available on the Internet that are worth watching by anyone who is interested in the first years of life for each child.

National Geographic magazine just wrote a very powerful and clear report on brain development in the first years of life that uses examples from Dr. Kuhl's work.

Several major magazines are beginning to look at those issues. *The Economist* has done several articles on early childhood brain stimulation and *Newsweek* magazine just released a special issue dealing exclusively with childhood development into the first years of life that also focuses on the importance of those first months and years for each child.

Another very important set of powerful research into the impact of stress situations on children and on the damage that happens to children facing stressful situations who develop toxic stress syndrome problems has been done by Dr. Ross Thompson and his team at U.C. Davis in California.

Anyone wanting to get a sense of that set of problems for children and a wide range of other related child development issues would be well served by reading the papers written by Dr. Thompson and his team.[1]

Jack Schonkoff and his team at the Harvard Center for the Developing Child has done some similar work that deserves our respect and review.

Dr. Beatrice Beebe at Columbia University and her research team of analytical psychologists have done some technology-assisted research on "The Origins of Twelve Month Attachment" that offers us incredible insight into the impact of very specific parent/child interactions at the very beginning of life.

The Journal of the American Academy of Pediatrics has joined the effort and they are now focused as well on helping children in those first years of life. The

Academy has done some very powerful work on Early Childhood Adversity, Toxic Stress, and the Role of the Pediatrician that are also helping pediatricians across the country understand some of those key issues.[2]

The work of the Academy will encourage many American pediatric caregivers to encourage reading and support targeted early development for their patients. They deserve our recognition and our gratitude for taking those issues on as a public health agenda and initiative.

The Institute of Medicine did a seminal piece on early brain development in children that has shaped thinking in medical science circles on those topics ever since that report was written.[3] Their piece — "From Neurons To Neighborhoods: The Science of Early Childhood Development," laid the groundwork for both the science and the context for those issues with the skill and the clarity that we expect from the Institute of Medicine.

Their well reasoned and well researched work on that extremely important subject has been inexplicably overlooked as an influential policy guidance document for our country for many years, and that report is now beginning to re-emerge as a high value piece of research and policy thinking that we can all use to help build some basic grounding of our thoughts about children in those first years.

The long-term impact of early childhood stress on people has also been studied over a very long period of time by Dr. Vince Feliti and other innovative and dedicated researchers for Kaiser Permanente of San Diego. The amazing and powerful research done in their "Adverse Childhood Experiences (ACE)" study clearly shows the lifelong impact of early year negative experiences at levels that give us great insight into the need to help our children minimize early levels of adverse experiences.[55]

Dr. Feliti's ACE study should be required reading for anyone doing public policy work or health care planning work relative to children. The ACE study has data so powerful that it changes paradigms about public health issues for both adults and children for many readers.

270

The Telegraph of London recently featured an article on a related set of issues in Great Britain, and they accompanied their article with brain scans showing significant differences in physical brain size for a normal 3-year-old brain and for the brain of a neglected 3-year-old. That visual statement made by those scans was clear enough to be painful to see.[46]

Work done by researchers at UCLA about stimulation for children in the first months of life have recently echoed those findings.

So there is a growing body of science that supports and has inspired the recommendations in this *Three Key Years* book. It has not been widely shared information but that entire array of learning clearly points in the directions that are outlined in this book.

We are beginning to share that information that is being developed by all of those research programs about early brain development more effectively, but that sharing has been a very recent effort. We are doing a weak job of getting that information to educators and caregivers, and we have done an even weaker job of getting that information to parents, families or communities in this country.

We need to do that work of sharing that vital and life changing information well and we need to do that information sharing now. The quality of the available information about the science and the processes involved in early childhood brain development is improving rapidly and we need to learn better ways of sharing that knowledge with all members of our community — from parents, to caregivers, to educators, and to policy makers and government officials who are relevant to these efforts and issues.

As a very useful example of the kinds of things that we need to do with consistency and volume, The American Academy of Pediatrics and the "Zero To Three National Center For Infants, Toddlers, and Families" jointly produced a wonderful and very readable publication in September of 2013 called, "Early Brain and Child Development."[1]

That piece should be read by everyone interested in those issues for both care delivery and policy development perspectives. It is clear, persuasive, comprehensive, and that extremely useful document has been read by far too few relevant people.

Multiple Academic Centers Are Studying Those Issues

We are approaching the point where our policy makers should have no excuse for not including that new learning and new wisdom about early child development into basic policy level and functional program level decision-making and leadership priorities.

We are now in a world where multiple highly regarded and highly competent academic centers are very directly and very explicitly studying those issues, and creating a growing body of clear and persuasive science about the extreme importance of early childhood development and early childhood support that we need to use to guide what we actually do with and for the children of our country.

The institutions doing that work are in the front rank of our academic centers. Both Stanford University and Harvard University have done remarkable work on early brain development issues. The University of Minnesota has done some very good work on those issues as well.

Columbia, Yale, Berkley, The University of Washington, The University of Chicago, and several University of California sites are all doing important research on those issues.

The academic centers that are doing that work are generally not doing a very good job of explaining the significance of their findings to either caregivers or policy makers in relevant settings. That failure to explain those key findings to the most relevant non-academic parties seems to be true in part because those centers tend to see their role as doing research, and they tend to leave dealing with the consequences of their learnings and their insights to other segments of our society.

As a leader at one of the sites doing some of that important research said very clearly — "We do the research. Someone else needs to figure out how to use what we learn in some useful way. That isn't our job. We are academic researchers, not research utilizers."

Some of the academic centers and their leaders — like Dr. James Heckman, Dr. Patricia Kuhl, Dr. Ross Thompson, and Dr. Beatrice Beebe — do make very clear and very accessible public presentations about their findings, but even those presentations tend to be to smaller audiences, and they are too often not being heard by either our educators, our policy makers, or the current administrators for our various public programs who really need that information to do the very best job of running their programs.

The information about these opportunities and about these needs for our children is not secret, but that information is not effectively shared with the people who most need to know it a very high percentage of the time. We need to do a much better job in that regard.

We need legislative and congressional committees who are asking well-informed questions about these issues. We need the people who run education programs and welfare programs in all communities to know this information. We need mayors and governors to know what they can do to close the learning gaps in their communities that are dooming far too many of their citizens to lives in prison and to futures of economic deprivation and educational failure.

Failure is not too harsh a word. The vast majority of high school dropouts from many of our communities end up in prison. If we do the right things in those first years for each child, most of those dropouts would be able to read and they would not drop out of their schools.

The new levels of research explain the opportunities we have to help our children, and they very clearly guide us to ways that can give us better futures for large percentages of our children.

Anyone who wants to get a good sense of what those various academic research programs are learning can go to each of their websites for more information on those issues.

Stanford Research Showed Differences at 18 Months

The implications of that research to the real world of children today are extremely powerful. They are also immediate. That immediacy surprises people who think of this as a long-term set of issues. In reality, the research teaches us that the direct implications of those processes for each child don't take decades to play themselves out.

The implications and the consequences of those learning processes for each child happen in time frames that can be measured for many children in months.

Research done at Stanford by Anne Fernald, for example, showed that there were significant differences at only 18 months of age between the children who had more reading and talking interactions from adults and the children who had very low adult linked interaction levels.[3]

The gap in learning for those children was already measurable and significant at that early age. Eighteen months is not a long time.

That information about those actual highly immediate time frames clearly should cause policy makers, caregivers, and program administrators to think about how they can help the children for whom they are accountable in some useful ways that will make a difference for those children in those first 18 months.

The helping process that changes the future for each child doesn't involve rocket science and it does not involve complex interactions. Very simple interactions add great value.

Speaking adds value.

Very good research that is described extensively earlier in this book has now shown that simply speaking to children in supportive ways at that point in their lives can make a major difference in the size of early vocabularies and in the reading ability and reading readiness levels for children.

One influential study that our caregivers and educators should all know showed a set of low-income children who had fewer than 200 words spoken to them by adults each day. That compared to more affluent families in the same study who spoke thousands of words each day to their children — ranging up to 12,000 words per day, per child.[4]

Not surprisingly, the children who heard many more words spoken each day understood many more words by the time they got to kindergarten. That linkage between the words heard by each child and the vocabulary levels that were understood by a child was true for children of all races and all economic statuses. The children from all groups who heard more words knew more words.

Far too often, the learning gaps we see in too many of our schools are attributed in public policy settings and in our news media to race and ethnicity. That is a dangerously wrong and functionally misleading attribution. That linkage belief is entirely inaccurate.

We now know from all of that research that is being done that each child goes through the same biological brain building processes and the same brain building time frames, and that the differences we see between children and the intergroup learning gaps that we see now that are troubling to so many Americans, are based on the level of early brain exercise received in the first months and years of life by each child from each group.

Those learning differences that we see in so many settings today are not actually based on race or ethnicity. They are based on differences in brain exercise levels for individual children.

There are, unfortunately, clear patterns for those interaction levels with children that do reflect back to other economic issues and to some group linked behavior patterns and beliefs about parenting approaches that we can and should address — but those differences do not reflect back to biological issues that are linked to any group at an inherent or functional racial or ethnic level. That thinking was wrong. It is easy to see why people might look at some of the macro-data we see in some of those settings and reach that assumption, but that assumption is wrong.

We know that the key differentiation factor and the functional issue that creates the range of learning ability levels for our children is clearly neither race nor ethnicity. It also isn't any actual functional, direct, or inherent link to the specific economic status for any child.

The difference that exists between the groups of children is actually the very child specific brain exercise levels that happen for each child in those first key months and years when our brains develop.

The Key Differentiation Issues Are Early Year Brain Exercise Levels

The layers of new research that have been done by all of those programs about the brain development processes and the array of new programs that help children from all groups do well in those first months and years free us from believing that the learning difference issues that we see in far too many settings today are either ethnic or racial. The key and foundational differentiation issue between individual children that changes the life paths for each child is the actual brain exercise levels that are directly experienced by each child in those first key months and years of life, because that is the time frame for the biological development process that happens in the brain of each child.[1]

We probably did not need academic research to prove that point about race and ethnicity — but the good news is that we now do have very good research on those issues, and that research does prove those points about the functional biological impact of brain exercise on each child in those first key years to be true.

All children from all groups go through the same biological brain development process and all children go through that same biological process in the same time frames.

Each and every child goes through the same set of physiological brain development processes and each brain either benefits from the interactions that happen in that time frame, or is damaged and under developed by the lack of interactions that happen for each child in that specific and important time frame.

The current body of research into child development and the various pilot-programs that are being implemented in various sites to help children are also improving our understanding of the functional things we can do to exercise the brains of children in those biologically critical time frames. As a result of those programs and that research, we now understand more clearly and explicitly the value that is created for each child by various direct interactions with each child.

We need to have everyone who is relevant to those issues to understand those specific interactions and their impact on children. We need educators and caregivers to understand those issues and we need community leaders from all groups who understand those processes and those biological realities, and who then use that understanding to help the people in their groups and their communities.

Group leaders who want to close learning gaps for their groups can use this information to reach out to all parents and to all families in their group to teach that basic biological science and to encourage the specific behaviors that transform lives for their children.

We need group leaders and trusted messengers in each group to encourage the direct interactions with each child that will help all children in each group build the brain strength that will support life long learning and close those gaps forever.

Groups who want to end learning gaps now have new tools that can keep those gaps from forming. That information needs to be communicated in multiple ways to the parents and the families of each group.

We also need to figure out various ways of helping all parents with the support for their children that will give their child the best set of resources and the right level of interactions that will create success for each child. As part of that process, we need all parents in all groups to know exactly what can be done to build the highest levels of learning ability for each child.

We need all parents to know the value and the benefit of talking, reading, singing, and playing directly and consistently with each child.

Interactions Build Brains – Talk, Read, Play, Sing Are Powerful Interactions

Again, we are being very well served by recent research and recent program development efforts in building that knowledge base and sets of insights. Very useful research and successful care and education support programs have shown us what kinds of interactions with a child in that key and high opportunity time frame directly provide functional benefit to each child.

This book has discussed those processes and those tools at length in several sections. They bear repeating here in this final chapter because they are so important and so useful and because they anchor our efforts to keep learning gaps from having the kinds of impacts in our future that they have had in our past.

The basic set of interactions that create functional brain exercise benefits for each child include talking to a child, interacting with a child, reading to a child, and singing to a child. Each of those interactions adds clear value to brain development in very young children.

Several important studies have looked at the impact, prevalence, and function of reading as a tool for interacting with our children.

The American Academy of Pediatrics has recently been sharing that information with the community and with their member physicians.

Reading to children has clearly been shown to have a very positive impact on children's vocabularies and thought processes.[5] Studies show that the children who have higher levels of personal reading time tend to have larger vocabularies and higher levels of learning skills when they arrive in school.

Children who have had fewer books read to them in those first key years tend to have lower vocabulary levels and the children who had few book hours and few direct interaction hours with adults tend to have more difficulty learning to read and more challenges in doing well in school.

Those linkages have been studied and the patterns are clear. The implications of those patterns are also increasingly clear.

One of the problems that we face as a country is that not all children are getting sufficient interactions with adults and not all children are having books read to them in those key biological windows of opportunity.

Low-Income Children Tend to Have Fewer Books Read to Them

There are clear patterns that tie the number of interaction hours with adults and the number of reading hours and books read to children to the income levels of the adults in their family.

It is important for us all to understand the science. Income levels, all by themselves, have no direct impact on any brain. There is no direct functional connection between cash levels in any situation or setting, and the actual neuron connection levels that exist for any child.

However, what is true is that low-income children tend to have fewer books read to them. And it is also true as a pattern that low-income children tend to have fewer words spoken to them.

Studies have shown both of those behavior patterns to exist in this country in ways that link indirectly to income levels in the homes.

Economic differences between families have been linked in a number of useful and credible studies to the average amount of reading time given to each child and to the extent of the direct adult interaction times that happen for each child.

One study showed that higher income children in a community were read to more than 1,000 hours on average between birth and kindergarten. A set of lower income children in that same study in that same time frame received fewer than 30 hours of reading time between their birth and kindergarten.[17]

The children who had more reading hours and who had more adult interaction time did better on their kindergarten vocabularies and the children who had more reading and talking hours before kindergarten also had better reading skills in the third grade.

Income Does Not Build Brain Cells

The differences in performance that we see for each child are not a functional and inherent link to the economic status of each child. High-income children who do not get significant brain exercise support in those first key years end up with reading problems. The low-income children who do have more books read to them and who do have more direct interactions with adults in those key years also have higher reading levels and better school performance.

The differences that are most relevant to each individual child are the differences in reading times given to the child and the differences in direct adult interactions and in the number of words spoken to each child — and not the actual family income levels for any child.

Income does not build brain cells. Or erase them. Brain cells and neuron connections are built and reinforced separately in the brain of each child based on the impact and the level of adult interactions that happen in those key years of biological development for each child.

That fact completely explodes stereotypes and erroneous beliefs about learning ability levels for children that were anchored in race, ethnicity, or even economic status. Our new science has liberated us from that racist thinking and points us to the real issues, the real opportunities, and the real problems that exist at a child specific level for each child.

Half an Hour of Reading Time Has a Positive Impact

The new science is clearly pointing us in wonderful and timely ways to functional paths we can follow to help each child improve their brain connectivity levels.

One very encouraging aspect that we are learning from the collective set of research is that children don't need the most extreme support levels from adults and parents to do well. Basic levels of reading and interacting with children can have a major positive impact on each child.

The difference between a child having no reading time and no interacting time at all, and a child having at least a moderate amount of reading time and interacting time with adults is large and can change lives.

It can be life damaging for each child who is deprived of those interactions with adults in that key period of time and it can be life enhancing for a child to have those interactions. We need all parents and all communities to understand that risk and those consequences.

Having absolutely no reading time and no interacting time with adults can create very negative outcomes for a child. By contrast, even moderate reading times with a child can create very positive results.[3]

There is a growing sense that half an hour of reading time per day for a child combined with direct interaction with an adult for another half hour or more each day can literally be life changing for children — in comparison to the children who experience only a very low level of interactions each day in those key development months and years.

Parenting approaches as basic as having 20 questions a day asked to each child combined with half an hour of direct parental interaction time for each child — time without texting or similar distractions — with regular adult interactions happening for each child each day — can clearly change children's lives significantly.

Thirty, Thirty, and Twenty Can Make a Difference

We now know that we can do positive things for children in relative moderation that can make a major difference in the life trajectories of our children.

Thirty minutes of direct time, 30 minutes of reading time, and 20 questions asked and answered can be a powerful support strategy for a child. Those activity levels lend themselves to target setting by parents.

Basic research and applied learning both support parents and families setting up daily interaction goals for each child. A number of functional programs that have been set up to help children are showing us that children can benefit significantly when help in those key areas is given to the child daily.

All of that research is coming up with the same sets of functional conclusions and insights that tell us all how critically important it is for us to help support each of our babies, infants, and very young children in the basic levels of brain development support from birth on.

Even though income levels do not have a direct link to brain development, it is obviously very true that low-income mothers and fathers often have a much more difficult time getting access to both resources and time to do that reading to their children.

If a mother is working two low income jobs to put food on the table, pay the rent, and buy clothing for her child — and if the mother has difficult transportation issues getting to and from either the work place, or the day care resource that is being used for the child, then it can be extremely difficult to find the time or the energy to read and interact every day with the child.

Life can be harder at many easily understandable levels for low-income families.

Higher income families have more resources. Higher income families average a dozen books per child. Many low-income homes do not have a single book.

So the point being made here in explaining the learning gap from the perspective of individual brain development is not that income levels are irrelevant. They are extremely relevant. The point being made here is that the income levels alone, and income levels by themselves, do not have a direct and functional impact on any brain.

The consequences of having low income create a number of problems and challenges, and those problems can have clear impacts on learning skills. We need to understand the real problem and the actual situation for each child, so we can fix the real problem for each child.

We need to figure out how to help each child from each income level have the support needed in those key months and years.

We now need creative people in every setting — creative and innovative people from every family and every community — to figure out what can be done to help every child.

That should be a challenge for America that we collectively take on. We have not put our collective creativity and our focused and directed energy to the task of figuring that set of functional issues out, and it is time now to do that thinking because we now actually know and understand the real issues and we now clearly need those solutions.

Learning Does Not Begin at Kindergarten

All of that extensive body of research being done in all of those settings also completely, thoroughly, and irrevocably dispels the old beliefs that learning, education, and intellectual development in children start for each child at kindergarten or at some equivalent age.

Many people still believe that learning begins at kindergarten. Some people believe that learning begins at pre-kindergarten programs that happen for 4-year-olds.

Those people with those very well intentioned, very good hearted, and very traditional beliefs about when learning begins are dangerously wrong. Learning does not start at kindergarten and learning also does not begin with the prekindergarten efforts.

We do want our children to have great kindergarten and great pre-kindergarten support and settings, but the real learning for each child starts well before that time and it starts well before those programs.

All of the new science tells us that learning at very important and life-altering levels begins at birth. The very first months of life literally give us some great opportunities to be teachers for our children.

The technology assisted research done by Dr. Beebe and her team at Columbia and the equally innovative technology supported work done by

Dr. Kuhl and her team at the University of Washington, both teach us that learning for each child literally begins at birth.

The first years of life are critically important as teaching and learning years. The children who only have a few hundred words in their vocabulary by age three generally have a very hard time learning to read and it is very difficult to close that gap for those children after that age.

We need to help the children who are behind at that point in their lives in every way we can, and we need to know and remember that it is not hopeless for each of those children after that point. Real progress can be made.

But it is much more difficult to get the best results for each child after those first three years for the biological reasons that are outlined in the research cited above in this book.

Going back to the importance and impact of the time frames that happen for each child far before kindergarten, some very interesting and very recent, unexpected research that was done in Brazil showed a positive link between breastfeeding infants and the intelligence level and economic success levels of the people who were breastfed. That particular study of the lifetime impact of breastfeeding was done in Brazil over a three decade long time period.

The children in that particular study who were breastfed longest had higher IQs at age 30, and also had income levels that were significantly higher than the children who were breastfed less than a month or not at all.[96]

That income difference for the people in the study at age 30 was not affected by the income levels of the families for each child.

Spending individual and personal time as adults interacting very directly, several times a day, with infants who were in nursing situations seemed to help both the overall brain capability levels, and the interpersonal skill sets for the children in that particular Brazilian study.

It is entirely possible that the children who developed higher levels of personal security in those early months of being nursed then had personality traits that led them to be paid more money in their jobs three decades later.

Those different outcomes for those children might have been anticipated or predicted by people who understood the brain exercise value that results from direct and trusted adult interaction with each child in those early time frames, and who also understood the emotional security that results from having direct child/mother physical interactions in those first weeks and months of life.

James P. Grant, former Executive Director of UNICEF had a quote at the 1994 International Conference on Development that fits the findings from that particular research — "Breastfeeding is a natural safety net against the worst effects of poverty. If the child survives the first month of life (the most dangerous period of childhood) then for the next four months or so, exclusive breastfeeding goes a long way toward canceling out the health difference between being born into poverty and being born into affluence," Grant said. "It is almost as if breastfeeding takes the infant out of poverty for those first few months in order to give the child a fairer start in life and compensate for the injustice of the world into which it was born."

That is a powerful set of thoughts and concepts.

All of the new brain development research tells us that we need to help each child immediately if we want to achieve the highest benefit level for each child — and that learning for each child begins at birth — maybe even a little before birth.

All of that research tells us that we need major learning to happen for each child well before kindergarten if we want our children to do really well in kindergarten and in the school years that follow kindergarten.[1-4]

That growing set of insights is guiding a number of people in creating various ways of helping children.

A Growing Number of Programs Are Providing Significant Benefit to Children in Those Key Years

Partly due to the growing body of research that is being done into the pure science of brain development for children in these age categories, a growing number of operational programs are doing good and useful things to support the process of development and early learning for actual children in actual settings.

A number of programs in a number of settings are helping children in those key time frames and some of those approaches are having significant success with children that we also need to understand.

The famous Abecedarian study done back in the 1970s in Chapel Hill, NC was a brilliant piece of work that pointed the way to child-focused interactions that changed life trajectories for children. That truly wonderful study is still bearing fruit in its follow-up versions decades later. The positive consequences for the children in that study have clearly continued through their adult years.[13,19,20,73,74]

A number of other early childhood interaction programs have also had significant successes that deserve celebration. In-home counseling — often nurse-based programs — have done very useful in-home coaching for parents in a number of settings. The Nurse-Family Partnership program, for example, has provided real value for a very large number of families.

Early Head Start has had a positive life long impact for some children.

The Center for Youth Wellness program in San Francisco ran by Dr. Nadine Burke Harris works directly with disadvantaged children with toxic stress problems in that city. That program has had significant success with the children they serve and some aspects of that work are described in Dr. Harris's TED talk.

The Thirty Million Words program in Chicago run by Dr. Dana Suskind has worked very directly with disadvantaged children under the age of three in that city, and her program has had remarkable successes with the children she is helping there. She writes well and persuasively about her findings and her work.

Her website is also worth viewing. The videos are very powerful. The pride shown by the mothers in her program whose children have larger vocabularies and who are good learners makes the point about parental support and parental love for each child obvious and clear.

The Harlem Children's Zone program run by Dr. Geoffrey Canada was set up to begin in the earliest part in each child's life. They have also extended their impact target for children's education and development back to the first months of life for the children who are admitted into that program.

Each of those programs has had great success in their communities and each of those programs deserves to be understood and emulated in other settings.

Cities Can Be Catalysts for Improving Learning Affiliates

Other programs that have also achieved levels of success and deserve attention include The Providence Talks project in Providence, Rhode Island. That program is coaching low-income families about the value of verbal interactions with the very young children and making electronic tools available to help parents with those efforts.

Cities can be excellent catalysts and anchor organizations for those kinds of effects, because all children are local and each city can benefit by having learning gaps disappear. Leadership at the National League of Municipalities is looking at those issues for those reasons.

In each of those settings, people have focused on very young children in ways that have helped change the neuron strengthening process in those very youngest children. The consequences in each setting have been uniformly positive — as we might expect once we recognize that those early years are, in fact, the most intense biological activity opportunity time frame for each child.

We are beginning to see a number of public policy related programs that are focused on those issues and we see a growing number of people who are working to both create coalitions to support children and to enhance governmental approaches that are aimed at helping our youngest children.

Several Focused Programs Are Now Supporting Early Childhood Issues

A growing number of advocacy programs are now helping people in communities and policy environments better understand those issues and those opportunities for our youngest children. The Zero To Three Institute has been a well-respected national leader for those efforts and has published some materials that set a gold standard for work in those areas.

The national Too Small to Fail Campaign and the very local San Francisco Bay centered Bay Area Council Talk, Read, Sing Campaign have both created positive momentum toward early childhood learning support and community education. Those campaigns are currently working with each other in Oakland, CA, in coordination with the KR Foundation and First 5 California, to help infants and toddlers in that city get a better start in life.

Too Small To Fail is also doing good work to bring people together on those issues at a national level. That specific initiative is working to create both awareness of the key opportunities in multiple settings and is helping to set up and manage programs that can make a difference for groups of children in several focused communities.

Reading Support Programs Add Real Value

There are a number of programs — like "Reading Is Fundamental" — that help children by making books available to children. One study showed that more than half of the low-income homes had no books and that low-income mothers were literally eight times more likely to read to their children if someone makes books available. Programs like "First Book" can help correct that problem.

The Billion eBook free eBook program is just launching and promises to make some of the most popular children's books available as free books for all connectivity approaches with the goal of getting books to families with young children.

Far too many low-income homes have no children's books today. A glaring need that will be increasingly met by some local programs is the fact that up to 80 percent of the pre-school and after school programs for low-income children also have absolutely no books.

We clearly need better programs and better processes to get good and useful real books and accessible and low cost eBooks for children into those situations and settings.

First 5 Commission Is Teaching Parents About Early Year Opportunities

The First 5 Commission for Children and Families that was created by the State of California has focused in the last few years on helping children get needed support for brain development in those first key years of life. The Commission has done several targeted television and radio campaigns, and has implemented related educational efforts to educate new parents and other people in California communities about their opportunities to support their children in those first months and years of life.

The results of those first communication efforts and the initial media campaigns about early interactions with children will be studied again this year to see if the awareness levels have changed for those issues with both policy makers and parents. Initial studies done by the University of Chicago indicated that more than 70 percent of the California mothers who heard and remembered the First 5 ads that taught the value of those interactions consciously and deliberately changed behavior to read and talk more to their children after hearing those messages.

All mothers and fathers love their children and all parents and families want their children to do well. When parents and families learn basic and achievable ways of helping their children to do well, then the natural tendency is to do what can be done to help their child.

The author of this book is the current chair of that Commission.

The First 5 Commission uses tobacco tax money to help children and families from birth through year five for children. First 5 has been running both television and radio ads to inform new parents of those brain development opportunities for their children, and to make that information part of the public health agenda for all Californians.

Those issues will also be explained clearly in both printed materials and video pieces that will be given to all new mothers in California by the end of 2015.

The website for First 5 currently gives parents support at multiple levels with Internet-based tools to help with their early childhood interaction approaches and activities. The work of that website will be continuously improved and enhanced to be a direct tool for parents and caregivers.

A major part of the messaging efforts for the next campaign will rely on using "trusted messengers" to take that information in multiple ways and through multiple communication channels and approaches to parents and families.

The Superintendent of Schools for the State of California and the head of the California Health and Human Services Agency have both pledged in a joint public setting to work with First 5 to make sure every new mother in California a year from now understands the opportunity to exercise her baby's brain.

County level First 5 programs in a number of California counties are also working directly with caregivers who go into homes to support parents directly in those efforts in the places where the children actually live.

WIC Offers a Great Interaction Opportunity

The First 5 Commission of Los Angeles County currently has a very innovative $20 million pilot program that was set up to work with the California WIC program for Los Angeles City and County. That WIC program was described in Chapter Eight of this book.

WIC is a national program that was set up decades ago by the Federal Government that provides coaching and support about nutrition and health issues to mothers across the country who are on Medicaid. First 5 of Los Angeles is working with WIC in that very large county to bring needed information about early childhood brain nutrition on a direct contact basis to more than 100,000 WIC beneficiaries who are currently served in Los Angeles County.

WIC may turn out to be an almost perfect tool for helping parents initially understand those issues in useful ways. That pilot in Los Angeles may lead and inspire WIC programs in other parts of the country to set up similar approaches.

If the pediatric caregivers offer direct counseling to the parents of those children during their normal pediatric visits, and if that counseling is reinforced by WIC counselors who can also channel the low-income WIC supported mothers to various available support resources and to supplies of children's books, there is a high potential for making a positive change in the lives of many children.

Preliminary data about the impact of that coaching by the WIC team in that setting showed a 37 percent reduction in the learning gap for dual language children.

A Growing Number of Important and Influential Foundations Are Also Now Supporting and Guiding This Work

Some of the most influential, most prestigious, and very well funded private foundations in this country are supporting this work at various levels. That is a very good thing and that role by those key foundations needs to be recognized and supported. We need very smart and highly influential people with a well-grounded public policy perspective to help tee up and lead various levels of early childhood education work across a wide range of communities.

Public policy foundations and charitable foundations that do that kind of work for multiple other issues are increasingly coming to take on the role of helping to figure out what to do for this set of children's issues in various settings. Some of our most influential and most effective foundations are now doing meaningful work in those areas.

Those foundations can help create overall community strategies and they can also help fund pilot programs, and fund and manage operational programs that are doing that work in various settings.

Some of the most important foundations in America are now providing both financial resources and intellectual guidance for both research into early childhood development, and to support operational pilots and programs that focus on those issues.

Those important foundations that are now helping with those efforts increasingly recognize that we can't eliminate the major performance gaps that exist today between groups of people in this country by simply focusing on retrospective remediation of the current problems, and by addressing the functional challenges that are faced now by the older children who already have major difficulties with their reading abilities and their learning levels.

We Need to Prevent the Gaps Rather Than Just Closing Them

There is a growing awareness in the foundation world of the indisputable biological reality that we need to eliminate those gaps between groups of children by keeping those gaps from occurring in the first place.

Foundations and their brain trusts can give us a great resource to support that thinking and to help guide that body of work so that we can make better first years experiences a reality for all of our children.

The Buffet Early Childhood Fund, The David and Lucille Packard Foundation, The Annie E. Casey Foundation, The Gates Foundation, The W.K. Kellogg Foundation, The California Foundation, and a number of other local foundations are all currently focusing energy and resources on those extremely important issues. The Minneapolis Foundation and The George Family Foundation, for example, are both working with the Mayor of Minneapolis and her team to help figure out ways of reducing the extremely high learning gaps that exist for the minority populations in that city.

Sesame Street Leadership is also now helping to create those early childhood support agendas, acknowledging that the primary answer for child development in those first years is parents, not programs.

Children who do get the right support in those first key years of life can benefit later from Sesame Street and from similar education programs and resources.

A growing number of Washington D.C. policy organizations are beginning to look at those issues as well. The New American Foundation and Families USA are both looking at those sets of issues. New America is making this issue a policy priority.

The American Enterprise Institute is beginning to look at those issues and is sharing some information about those problems and opportunities.

The National Governor's Association and The League of Municipalities are also both considering those issues as areas of focus, and those highly influential organizations will have great leverage points to make a difference in a wide range of settings as they get further involved in those processes.

There Is Growing Awareness and Support

So there is growing awareness in this country at multiple levels about those sets of issues and opportunities. A growing number of organizations and communities are beginning to recognize the fact that we need to do key work to help all of our children and we need to do it now.

Lives are being derailed and lives are being damaged and impaired every single day when that early development and brain strengthening work isn't done for a child. Lives are being enhanced, lives are being changed and lives are being directly improved in very significant and positive ways that change the trajectories of entire lives when that work actually is done for a given child.

The choice is clear. Each life we save is a life we save.

It's time to save the lives of all children in this country, beginning at birth. We need to make a collective and shared commitment to save our children, and we need to do the right things in each setting to make that commitment a reality and a success.

We need our school systems, our legislators, our Medicaid programs, our public safety programs, our pediatricians, our parent/child related caregivers, and our leaders for each of our ethnic, racial, cultural, religious, and community groups to all support our children in those key years.

We need parents and families who understand both the extremely important opportunities and the dire risks that are faced by each child in those key years.

We need parents and families to also know how to save each child. We also each need to take this knowledge, now that we have it, and figure out ways that we can each help change the future for at least one child.

Because the process happens one child at a time, we can each have a very real, meaningful, and positive impact by teaching this information to the parents of at least one child. Personal accountability requires each of us to share that information now that we have it.

We are failing far too many children today. It's time for that failure to end.

We know how to end it.

Three key years.

Let's use them well for each child.

Endnotes

The endnotes listed below in this section were used in the book to simplify reference. Each has a small note included explaining some of the key and relevant points. The notes do not represent at any level, a synopsis of each cited piece — but basically provide a simple pointer explaining some of the key information elements from each reference piece that influenced the book.

1. *Zero To Three Journal* — September 2013
   "Early Brain and Child Development"
   Done in collaboration with the American Academy of Pediatrics.

   (Comprehensive set of articles that cover brain science, early brain development, reading, safe environments, early childhood home visiting programs, and Toxic Stress — Encourages caregivers and parents to exercise brains of young children and discusses the importance of early literacy.)

2. Office of the Assistant Secretary for Planning and Education research brief — March 2014
   "The Early Achievement and Development Gap"

   (Learning gaps are detectable as early as nine months — widen by 24 months. Children from families with low contact are six months behind at two years. Children from lower SES families know 30 percent fewer words at 18 months. Major gap in cognitive skills exist between children whose mothers have a college degree and mothers who have less than a high school degree. At nine months, major gaps exist between White children and minority children. Biggest gap is with Native American children. Black and Hispanic children were also behind at that age.)

3. *Stanford Report* — September 25, 2013
   "Major Learning Gaps Exist Before Two Years Old," Anne Fernald, Ph.D.

   (Major learning gap between children exist at 18 months old — some children are six months behind by age 2. Learning levels are linked to words spoken to children in each group. Lower income children are likely to have fallen behind in learning skills before they are two years old.)

4. Rice University
   The Early Catastrophe: The 30 Million Word Gap By Age 3, Betty Hart and Todd R. Risley
   (Significant differences exist between children on learning levels that are triggered in part by the words spoken to children in the first months and years of life. Children from families on welfare heard an average of 616 words per hour. Working families, on average, spoke 1,251 words per hour to their children. Children from professional families heard 2,153 words per hour. There were also differences in the level of negative and positive messages to children. Children from professional families heard 6 positive words for every negative word. Working class families used 2 positive words for every negative word. Children from families on welfare heard 2 negative words for every positive word.)

5. *New York Times* — June 24, 2014
   "Pediatrics Group to Recommend Reading Aloud to Children from Birth," Motoko Rich
   (American Academy of Pediatrics strongly recommends that pediatricians encourage all parents to read to their children. The ADA encourages all families to read daily. Only one-third of the families below the poverty line currently read to their children daily.)

6. Urban Child Institute website — December 27, 2014

   "Baby's Brain Begins Now: Conception to Age 3"

   (Brain anatomy and early development science — major elements of each child's brain are developed and structured in the first years of life.)

7. Ounce of Prevention Fund website — March 2015

   (Children with learning problems are 25 percent more likely to drop out of school, 40 percent more likely to become a teen parent, 50 percent more likely to be in special education, 70 percent more likely to be arrested for a violent crime.)

8. Wikipedia "Incarceration" search

   "List of Countries by Incarceration Rate — Prisoners per 100,000 Population in 225 Countries"

   (The United States clearly has the highest incarceration rates in the world by a wide margin. We imprison far more people than any country on the planet.)

9. Live Science website

   "Fourteen Percent of U.S. Adults Can't Read"

   (Sixty-three percent of prison inmates have reading problems. A disproportionately high number of prisoners read poorly or do not read at all.)

10. U.S. Department of Justice and U.S. Department of Commerce Study — 2007

    (Thirty percent of federal inmates, 40 percent of state prison inmates, and 50 percent of persons on death row are high school dropouts.)

11. *Forbes Magazine* — December 25, 2010

    "A $5 Children's Book vs. a $47,000 Jail Cell — Choose One," Steve Cohen

    (Sixty percent of Prison Inmates are illiterate — 85 percent of juvenile offenders have reading problems. Early reading to children can change life paths in positive ways and should be a preferred strategy.)

12. Center for the Developing Child, Harvard University — March 2015

    "A Science-Based Framework for Early Childhood Policy — Using Evidence to Improve Outcomes in Learning, Behavior, and Health for Vulnerable Children"

    (Early brain architecture, positive learning environments for children. Early years effectiveness factors. Intervention strategies. "Serve and return" effectiveness. Parental leave policies.)

13. The Carolina Abecedarian Project website — December 29, 2014

    "The Abecedarian Project"

    (Children who receive direct and individual brain exercise support from adults who work directly with each child in the first years of life do significantly better in school in later years.)

14. First 5 Commission website — updated regularly

    (The First 5 website explains and describes the basic "Read, Talk, Sing" interactions with children that build strong brains for each child. The website has advice to parents about how to achieve those goals.)

15. *Exchange Magazine* — November/December 2010
    "Early Brain Development Research Review and Update," Pam Schiller, Ph.D.

    (Brain growth in early years — interplay of genes and environment. Experience wires the brain — repetition strengthens the wiring. Early relationships affect wiring. Music and language function overlap. Set higher expectations for all children. Touch is critical to learning. New technology is clearly creating new neuron connectivity pathways in our brains — "We learn to react more quickly to visual stimuli, improve some forms of focus and attention, and become more adept at noticing images in our peripheral vision." Possible creating alienation from direct people contact.)

16. *New York Times* — January 18, 2015
    "The Power of Talking to Your Baby," Tina Rosenberg

    (Children on welfare heard 600 words per hour — working mother children heard 1,200 words per hour. Meredith Rowe — professor at University of Maryland said — "Poor young women do not know that it is important to talk to their babies.")

17. Packard and MacArthur Foundation report — 2009
    "America's Early Childhood Literacy Gap"

    (Middle income families had 1,000 to 1,700 hours of book reading with an adult — for children in low income families, that number was only 25 hours.)

18. The Annie E. Casey Foundation report — January 29, 2014
    "Learning Groups Exist For Some Groups"

    (There are major learning gaps between groups of people in many communities. Eighty-three percent of Black students, 81 percent of Latino students, 78 percent of American Indian students, 55 percent of White students and 49 percent of Asian students are not proficient at reading by the end of the third grade — dual language learners in those communities were 93 percent non-proficient. Those issues need to be addressed in each setting.)

19. Coalition for Evidence Based Policy website — 2014
    "Perry Preschool Project"

    (Shows positive impacts on children of early coaching and support).

20. Abecedarian Study website
    "Early Education Intervention"
    Frank Porter Graham, Child Development Institute, Chapel Hill, North Carolina

    (Infants supported with early interactions and interventions had higher IQ's at age three and higher math and reading achievement by age 15.)

21. University of Chicago Harris School of Public Policy Studies
    "Invest in the Very Young"
    James J. Heckman, Ph.D., Nobel Laureate in Economic Sciences

    (Efficiency of the country would be enhanced if human capital investment were reallocated to the very young. Interventions with children in early years have high return on investment. Interventions in later years have lower economic returns. "Cognitive Ability is formed relatively early in life and becomes less malleable as children age." Reported reductions in criminal offenses were as much as 70 percent for the children who benefited from early interventions.)

22. NBC News, Annie E. Casey Foundation report — January 28, 2014
    "Learning Gap Has Grown,"Allessandra Malito

    (The learning gap has grown in a decade between high income and low income children. Eighty percent of low-income fourth graders do not read at their grade level compared to 49 percent of wealthier counterparts.)

23. "The Knowledge Gap: Implications for Early Education" — 2001
    Susan B. Neuman

    (Middle income neighborhoods averaged 13 books per child — low-income children in day cares only had one book for every 300 children. Low-income children rarely receive cognitively stimulating content in reading interactions. Poor readers in grade one have a high probability of being a poor reader in grade four.)

24. Economic Policy Institute website — 2002
    "Inequality at the Starting Gate — Social Background Differences in Achievement as Children Begin School," David T. Burkam and Valerie E. Lee

    (Lower income children have a disadvantage. Achievement scores also low for Black and Hispanic children. Parenting — 15 percent of White children have a single parent — 54 percent of Black children and 27 percent of Hispanic children live in single parent homes.)

25. The Future of Children publication
    It Takes Two Generations: Strengthening the Mechanisms of Child Development
    "Stress and Child Development," Ross A. Thompson, University of California, Davis

    (Impact of stress on children — beginning with prenatal stress — and includes biological reactions to perceived threat or danger. Explains the damaging impact on children of chronic activation of stress. Stress undermines physical health and biological health. The plasticity of biological and behavioral systems is a resource for remedial interactions. Investment in the very young has a higher rate of return than investment in later years.)

26. The Future of Children report — 2005
    "Stress and Child Development," Ross A. Thompson

    (In-depth research into the kinds of stress faced by young children and the impact of that stress in biological and emotional ways for each child. Explains the physiological impact of stress relative to toxic stress syndrome and explains how interactions from caring adults can buffer the levels of stress.)

27. *Pediatrics Journal* — Supplement 2, S65-S73
    "Home Visiting and the Biology of Toxic Stress: Opportunities to Address Early Childhood Adversity"

    (Toxic stress can be reduced in children with the right level of support.)

28. *New York Times* — June 24, 2014
    "Pediatrics Group to Recommend Reading Aloud to Children from Birth," Motoko Rich

    (American Academy of Pediatrics strongly recommends that pediatricians encourage all parents to read to their children. The ADA encourages all families to read daily. Only one-third of the families below the poverty line read to their children daily.)

29. *Minnesota Post* — January 20, 2014
"New study: High-quality preschool for poor kids under 3 would eliminate achievement gap"
Beth Hawkins

(Economic data about the benefits of intervening with children in those first key years shows that the economic return for intervention has been proven to be extremely positive.)

30. Minnesota Federal Reserve Bank website — March 2003
"Early Childhood Development — Economic Development with a High Public Return"
Art Rolnick and Rob Grunewald

(Economic return on investment from early childhood.)

31. *National Geographic* — March 2015
"Baby Brains — The First Year," Yudhijit Bhattacharjee

(Science of brain development in the first year of life — with the long-term impact of brain exercise for very young children described and explained. Children raised with more attention and more interactions had greater learning ability and children raised with more warmth had better memory skills. Brain sizes differed as well for the children who had less stimulation. Children master the grammatical rules of their own language at a very early age. Children with more words spoken to them had better vocabularies and better learning skills. Television did not improve language skills. Parents who receive help in early parenting skills had lower stress in their parenting and better skills.)

32. Proceedings of the National Academy of Sciences of the United States of America — 2000; 97 (22): 11850-11857
"A new view of language acquisition," Patricia Kuhl

(The relationship between brain development and language acquisition is now more clearly understood — and points to the need for early intervention with each child.)

33. *Exchange Magazine* — 2001
"Brain Research and Its Implications for Early Childhood Programs — Applying Research to Our Work," Pam Schiller

(Significant new brain research should become the basis for early childhood support programs.)

34. Urban Child Institute publication — November 2014
"Baby's Brain Begins Now: Conception to Age 3"

(Neuroscience of early brain development — illustrations and neuron data. Explains the pruning processes that happen for neuron connections that do not get used.)

35. Brain and Language — 2009
"Language or music, mother or Mozart? Structural and environmental influences on infants' language networks," Dehaene-Lambertz, G., Montavont, A., Jobert, A., et al.

36. The National Institute of Mental Health website — March 21, 2015
"The Teen Brain: Still Under Construction,"

(Teenagers are close to a lifetime peak in physical heath, strength, and mental capacity — but often have issues and problems relative to judgment, risk taking, and interpersonal behavior. Brain growth in some parts of the brain peaks at adolescence. The brain circuitry involved in emotional responses is changing during the teen years. Reproductive hormones affect thinking as well. Sleep deprivation can also be a problem for mental functioning for teenagers. The change process continues through the teen years.)

37. *Harvard Magazine* — September-October 2008
"The Teen Brain — A Work In Progress," Debra Bradley Ruder

(The teen brain is not a less experienced adult brain — it is a brain going through a paradoxical time of development. The brain motivation process extends into the mid-twenties. Female brains peak two years before male brains. Teen brains are more vulnerable to external stressors.)

38. Ted Talk
Patricia Kuhl, co-director, Center for Mind, Brain, and Learning, University of Washington
(The Ted Talk by Dr. Kuhl explains with extremely clear examples and current science why the first months and years are so important for each child.)

39. Acta Paediatrica — 2008
"Television Viewing Associated with Delayed Language Development"
W. Chonchaiya and C. Pruksananonda

(Study links television watching to delays in language development.)

40. Colorado Early Learning Summit paper — May 21, 2003
"Born To Learn: Language, Reading, and the Brain of the Child"
Patricia Kuhl, co-director, Center for Mind, Brain, and Learning, University of Washington

(Learning starts for children before birth. Very young children have incredible learning skills. Language skills also begin immediately after birth — and then wane. Children can hear sounds from all languages at six months old and cannot hear sounds not used in their own language after a year. The language heard by the child shapes their language learning and vocabulary. The brain has a trillion or so neurons at birth, but they are not well connected. Up to age three, children build neuron connections furiously. Then the brain "prunes" unused connections and strengthens connections that were used. The first years are extremely important for brain development.)

41. *London Telegraph* — January 2013
"Babies Listen to Their Mothers Voice in the Womb, Research Suggests," reporting staff
(Newborn babies are able to tell the difference between their mother's language and another language. Fetuses listen to what their mothers are saying in the last 10 weeks of pregnancy. Professor Christine Moon of Pacific Lutheran University and Professor Patricia Kuhl of the Institute of Learning and Brain Sciences at the University of Washington showed that babies who were only 30 hours old could already distinguish between languages.)

42. Harvard University Press — 2002

"Neural Plasticity: The Effects of the Environment on the Development of the Cerebral Cortex," P. Huttenlocher

(The brain does not develop in a vacuum or based on pre-programmed pathways. Environment is important).

43. *Seattle Post-Intelligencer* — September 21, 2001

"Babies Help Uncover the Secrets of the Human Brain," Gregory Roberts

(Babies can hear sounds from all languages at birth and lose the ability to hear sounds that they haven't heard by 2 years old. Japanese children cannot hear the sounds "r" or "l" after they are one.)

44. Harvard University website — 2015

"Key Concepts for Child Development," Center for the Developing Child

(Early experiences affect the development of brain architecture in each child. Adverse experiences early in life can impair brain architecture — with life-long impact. "Serve and Return" interactions with children strengthen the child's mental capacity and social skills. Toxic stress can result from negative experiences for young children and can have a life-long negative impact. Children need to learn self-regulation and decision-making and those skills can be impaired by adverse experiences.)

45. *Medical Daily,* study by Joan Luby, Washington University — October 29, 2012

"Chilling Brain Scans Show the Impact of a Mother's Love on a Child's Brain Size" Christine Hsu

(Shocking graphic image of brain scans for a nourished and supported child and a neglected child.)

46. *London Telegraph* — November 29, 2014

"What's The Difference Between Those Two Brains?," Alasdair Palmer

(Powerful images of differences in brain sizes based on brain exercise levels for children in the first years of life.)

47. American Academy of Pediatrics website — June 24, 2014

"Business, Medical, and Non-Profit Partners Launch New National Effort at CGI America to Help Close the Word Gap"

(The Academy strongly encourages all pediatricians to encourage reading and to support basic parenting skills for very young children. Reach Out and Read will pass out 500,000 books through 62,000 pediatricians. Text 4 Baby is part of that effort).

48. *New York Times* — January 18, 2015

"A Book In Every Home — And Then Some," David Bornstein

(Eighty percent of preschool and after school programs for low-income children do not have any children's books. Programs are trying to get more books into low-income homes. Forty-two percent of families cannot afford to buy books. A study in Germany found that the number of books in the home strongly predicted reading achievement — even after correcting for parents income and education. Another study of 70,000 students from 27 countries found that having multiple books in a home was as good a predictor of children's academic success as the families education level or income levels.)

49. *City Journal* — Autumn 2014
    "Culture and Achievement — Families Shape Their Children's Prospects More Profoundly Than Anything Government Can Do," Kay Hymowitz
    (Immigrants in multiple countries have lower reading skills and learning levels than the original populations — Finland, Norway, etc. Finland has 29 percent illiteracy with immigrants.)

50. *Pediatrics* — 2011
    J.P. Shonkoff, A.A. Garner, and the American Academy of Pediatrics Committee on Psychosocial Aspects of Child and Family Health
    (Toxic stress, brain development, and the early childhood foundations of lifelong health.)

51. Center for Disease Control website
    "The Health and Social Impact of Growing Up with Adverse Childhood Experiences" Robert Andra, M.D., M.S.
    (Adult impact of Adverse Childhood Experiences in early childhood — shows a lifelong negative impact on people's health for people who had multiple Adverse Childhood Experiences — or ACE's).

52. *Pediatrics Journal* — December 26, 2011
    "Early Childhood Adversity, Toxic Stress and the Role of the Pediatrician — Translating Developmental Science Into Lifelong Health"
    Andrew S. Garner, Jack P. Shonkoff, and Benjamin S. Siegal
    (Reasons for having pediatricians involved in preventing toxic stress.)

53. *Excessive Stress Disrupts the Architecture of the Developing Brain: Working Paper #3*
    Cambridge, MA: National Scientific Council on the Developing Child, Center on the Developing Child at Harvard University, 2005
    (Early stress in children can harm early brain development for each child.)

54. *Development and Psychopathology* — 2001
    "Early adverse experience as a developmental risk factor for later psychopathology: Evidence from rodent and primate models," M.M. Sanchez, C.O. Ladd, and P.M. Plotsky

55. *The American Journal of Preventive Medicine* — 1998
    "The Adverse Childhood Experiences Study," Dr. Vincent Felitti, Kaiser Permanente
    (Adverse childhood experiences have a huge impact on later life health care. The researchers measured Ten Adverse Childhood Experiences — or ACE — for thousands of people and identified a direct link from multiple ACE's for patients to mental illness, prison time, and chronic disease onset. People with four ACE's were at 240 percent higher risk for hepatitis and were 390 percent more likely to have COPD. The team has done multiple studies since that time with the data and is showing very powerful linkages from those early experiences and later levels of health).

56. *New York Times* — November 14, 2014
"To Help Language Skills of Children, a Study Finds, Text Their Parents with Tips"
Motoko Rich

(Children whose parents received text messages about reading to their children performed better on literacy test than children whose parents did not receive such messages — very low cost — two to three months ahead of the children whose parents did not get texts).

57. Text 4 Baby website

(Mobile service that has enrolled more than 700,000 pregnant women and new mothers to do text related baby care tips. Significant positive behavior changes have resulted from the text support.)

58. *Journal of Educational Psychology* 94 (1), 145-155 — 2002
"Quality of book-reading matters for emergent readers: An experiment with the same book in regular or electronic format," M.T. De Jong and A.G. Bus

59. NBER Working Paper Series (National Bureau of Economic Research) — November 2014
"One Step at a Time: The Effects of an Early Literacy Text Messaging Program for Parents of Preschoolers," Benjamin N. York and Susanna Loeb

(Children of parents who received text messages about interacting with children made significant learning skills improvements in the first years of life.)

60. Proceedings of the National Academy of Sciences — Febuary 21, 2012
"Maternal Support in Early Childhood Predicts Larger Hippocampal Volumes at School Age," Joan L. Luby, Deanna M. Barch, Andy Belden, et al.

(Larger hippocampal volume was seen in brains of babies who were nurtured and who were not depressed.)

61. American Promise Alliance website — 2009
"Consequence of Dropping Out of High School," Dr. Andrew Sum, Northeastern University

(Young people who drop out of high school are 63 percent more likely to be incarcerated or otherwise institutionalized than their peers with four-year college degrees.)

62. Write Express Corporation website
"Two-thirds of Students Who Cannot Read Proficiently by the End of the Fourth Grade Will End Up in Jail or on Welfare,"

(Eighty-five percent of all juveniles who interact with the juvenile court system are functionally illiterate. Prison inmates who learn to read in prison have only a 16 percent chance of returning to prison vs. a 70 percent likelihood of returning to prison for people in prison who do not learn to read.)

63. *Reznet News* — December 26, 2014
"Math, Reading Gap Among Native American Students," Christine Armario

(Students on reservation schools scored 25 points lower than Native American students in public schools. No progress since 2005. Dropout rates as high as 65 percent.)

64. National Literacy Trust, a Great Britain website — November 2008
"Literacy Changes Lives — The Role of Literacy in Offending Behavior"
Christina Clark and George Dugdale Trust

(Sixty percent of British prisoners have difficulties in basic literacy skills — 60 percent had literacy problems and 40 percent had severe literacy problems. Eighty percent of prisoners read below the level expected of an 11 year-old child.)

65. *New York Times* — October 8, 2009
"Study Finds High Rate of Imprisonment Among Dropouts," Sam Dillon

(People who drop out of school are more likely to be imprisoned — and the risk is even higher for minority dropouts. One in four Black, male dropouts is currently incarcerated. One in 10 White male dropouts is in jail — and only one in 35 high school graduates are in jail.)

66. Procedures of the National Academy of Science — 2007
"The economics, technology, and neuroscience of human capability formation"
J.J. Heckmen, University of Chicago Nobel Laureate

(Sound economic policy based on biological realities calls for this country to support our children in the early years of life for each child when we can achieve the most improvements based on direct interactions with each child.)

67. Correctional Population in the United States website — December 31, 2010
"Incarceration Rates by Race and Ethnicity — 2010"

(The U.S. has more prisoners than any nation in the world and minority Americans are significantly more likely to be imprisoned than White Americans. Hispanic Americans are four times as likely to be imprisoned and Black Americans are roughly six times more likely to be in jail.)

68. National Adult Literacy Survey — 2007
"Literacy Behind Bars"

(Percentage of prisoners in U.S. jails who read at the lowest two literacy levels is 70 percent.)

69. *Christian Science Monitor* — August 18, 2003
"US notches world's highest incarceration rate"

(The United States imprisons more people than any other country.)

70. U.S. Department of Justice and U.S. Department of Commerce Study — 2007

(Thirty percent of federal inmates, 40 percent of state prison inmates, and 50 percent of persons on death row are high school dropouts.)

71. Literacy Resource Office website — 2014
"Inmates Have the Lowest Academic Skills and Lowest Literacy Rates of Any Segment of Society," U.S. Department of Education

(Nationwide, three-fourths of state prison inmates are dropouts, as are 59 percent of Federal inmates. Dropouts are 3.5 times more likely to be incarcerated. Of all African American dropouts in their 30s, 52 percent have been imprisoned.)

72. The Sentencing Project website — August 2013
   "Report Done to the United Nations Human Rights Committee"
   (Racial minorities are more likely to be arrested the White Americans, more likely to be convicted if arrested, and have longer sentences imposed when convicted. African American males are six times more likely to be incarcerated than White males and 2.5 times more likely to be arrested than Hispanic males. At current trends, one of three African American males will go to prison over a lifetime. One of six Hispanic males and one of 17 White males will be imprisoned.)

73. *Racial Disparities*
   "Racial Disparities in the American Criminal Justice System"
   Ronald Weich and Carlos Angulo
   (In Maryland, 70 percent of the drivers stopped and searched by police were Black — and Blacks made up 17.5 percent of the drivers. In Volusia County, Florida, 70 percent of the drivers stopped by police on the Interstate Highway were Hispanic or Black — and only 5 percent of the drivers were Hispanic or Black.)

74. *Huffington Post* — October 4, 2013
   "One in 3 Black Males Will Go To Prison in Their Lifetime," Saki Knafo
   (Wrote that Black youths were arrested at twice the rate of White youths while White youths were slightly more likely to have abused drugs in the prior month.)

75. *The Economist* — October 2013
   "Why Does America Have Such a Big Prison Population?"
   (America has 5 percent of the world's population and 25 percent of its prisoners. The percentage of people behind bars is five times higher than Great Britain, seven times higher than France, and 24 times higher than India.)

76. Melissa Institute for Violence Prevention Teach Safe Schools website — March 2015
   "Link Between Students Reading Ability and Behavior Problems"
   (Below grade reading levels are linked in some children to aggressive, anti-social, and delinquent behaviors — with 85 percent of youth who get in trouble with the law experiencing reading difficulties. Fifty percent of youths with a history of substance abuse and 70 percent of adolescents and adults in prison have reading difficulties.)

77. *RT USA* — December 29, 2014
   "Incarceration Rate for African Americans now six times the National Average"
   (Black young men without a high school diploma are more likely to go to jail than to find a job.)

78. *Applied Developmental Science* — 2002
   "Early childhood education: Young adult outcomes from the Abecedarian Project"
   F.A. Campbell, C. Ramey, E. Pungello, J. Sparling, and S. Miller-Johnson
   (There clearly were long-term positive consequences that resulted from the early childhood interventions that were done with the children in the Abecedarian study that indicate that investing in children at that early age is a very good investment.)

79. High/Scope Press — 1993
"Significant Benefits: The High/Scope Perry Preschool Study Through Age 27"
L.J. Schweinhart, H.V. Barnes, and D.P. Welkart

(The advantages that resulted in early school years from helping exercise children's brains in the first years of life continue to show significant positive impact over two decades later.)

80. *The Human Brain Book* — 2009
R. Carter, S. Aldridge, M. Page, and S. Parker

(The basic design and functioning of the brain is becoming more clearly understood — and has very consistent patterns and structures for all people.)

81. High/Scope Press — 2004
"The High/Scope Perry Preschool Study Through Age 40: Summary, Conclusions, and Frequently Asked Questions"

(The advantages of the early brain development continue to occur.)

82. *Scientific American Mind* — September/October 2010
"The World at Our Fingertips," D. Cabreer and L. Cotosi

(Good basic description of key brain science issues.)

83. *Archives of Pediatric and Adolescent Medicine* — 2007
"Extensive television viewing and the development of attention and learning difficulties during adolescence," 161(5), 480-486, J. Johnson, J. Brook, P. Cohe, and S. Kasen

(Adolescent children with extensive television viewing shared negative consequences for learning skills during adolescence.)

84. *New York Times* — April 10, 2013
"The Power of Talking To Your Baby," Tina Rosenberg

(The Lena Research foundation invented technology that allows study and treatment of child language delay. More than 200 countries and research hospitals are now using the technology. One site — in Providence, Rhode Island — had a 55 percent increase in the number of words spoken to children.)

85. *Irish Times* — July 8, 2014
Motoko Rich

(Sixty percent of higher income families read to their children daily — only one third of low-income families read to their children daily.)

86. Goddard parenting guides — 1999
"Right from birth: Building our child's foundation for life: Birth to 18 months"

87. U.S. Department of Education website — July 1999
"Start Early, Finish Strong: How to Help Every Child Become a Reader"

(Robert Needlman quote: Mothers receiving welfare are eight times more likely to read to their children when provided with both books and direct encouragement.)

88. *New York Times* — December 26, 2014
"U.S. Prison Population Dwarfs That of Other Nations"
(The United States has far more people in prison per capita than any nation in the world.)

89. *The American Prospect*
"How mass incarceration turns people of color into permanent second-class citizens"
Michelle Alexander

90. *Journal of Education Psychology* — 1990
"Growth of reading vocabulary in diverse elementary schools"
T.G. White, M.F. Graves, and W.H. Slater
(Low-income first graders have vocabulary of 2,900 words. First graders from professional homes have 5,800 word vocabularies.)

91. *Developmental Science* — September 2013
"Stanford Study," Anne Fernald, Ph.D.
(Measured learning skills development and impact of early mothers of parental interactions — richer language leads to better learning skills.)

92. Center on the Developing Child at Harvard University — 2007
"A Science-based Framework for Early Childhood Policy: Using Evidence to Improve Outcomes in Learning, Behavior, and Health for Vulnerable Children"
(The Center on the Developing Child at Harvard is doing a wide array of important research on early brain development and the impact on the life of each child.)

93. New York: Collins Living (subsidiary of Harper Collins) — 2009
"iBrain: Surviving the technological alteration of the modern mind," G. Small and G. Vorgan

94. *Zero to Three Journal* — March 2015
"Screen Sense: Setting the Record Straight — Research Based Guidelines for Screen Use for Children Under 3 Years Old," Claire Lerner and Rachel Barr
(Extensive new research tells us that some levels of interaction with various passive and interactive screens can be damaging for very young children and some forms of interaction — particularly interaction that also involves a parent — can have value and can create benefits for very young children. The article cites more than a dozen useful research studies on those topics.)

95. Institute of Education Sciences — National Center For Education Statistics — 1996
"Reading Literacy in the United States"
(Low-income homes had very low literacy levels. Sixty-one percent of low-income children owned no books at all.)

96. Committee on Integrating the Science of Early Childhood Development, Institute of Medicine — 2000
"From Neurons to Neighborhoods: The Science of Early Childhood Development"
J.P. Shonkoff and D. Phillips

(Important report explains the importance of helping children's brains develop well in the first years of life and describes the underlying biological science and functional consequences that makes that strategy a good one for society.)

97. Reading Is Fundamental website — January 18, 2015

(Two-thirds of America's children living in poverty have no books at home.)

98. Procedures of the National Academy of Science — 2006
"Economic, Neurobiological, and Behavioral Perspectives on Building America's Future Workforce," E.L. Knudsen, J.J. Heckman, J.L. Cameron, and J.P. Shonkoff

(The pure economic advantages to be derived for the economy from focused investments in our youngest children are increasingly clear and beyond challenge as an economic model.)

99. PsycARTICLES
"Preschoolers Learning From Video After a Dialogic Questioning Interaction"

(Children who watched videos and who had dialogic interaction with adults about the videos in the process had better learning scores after four weeks than children who just watched the videos.)

100. Water Cooler Conference website — multiple conference years
"Expert speakers making presentations at an annual conference on early childhood development," Mollie Munger, co-chairwoman

101. *The Lancet* (British medical journal) — March 17, 2015
"Longer Duration of Breastfeeding Linked With Higher Adult IQ and Earning Ability,"

(Dr. Bernardo Lessa Horta — Federal University of Pelotas in Brazil looked at 3,500 Brazilians over 30 years and tracked differences in IQ and in personal income levels for people who had been breastfed for over a year and people who had been breastfed briefly or not at all. The people who had been breastfed the longest — regardless of the income levels of their parents — had higher IQ's and made significantly more money at age 30.)

102. First 5 Commission for Children and Families website

(The website contains extensive information about early brain development and early childhood health issues. It identifies resources and makes information available to support parenting approaches and skills.)

103. Recommended YouTube pieces

(Dr. Patricia Kuhl and Dr. Nadine Burke Harris both did Ted Talks that are very much worth watching. The talks are brief, succinct, and point to key biological science, medical science, and the lifetime impact of early support for each child.)

104. UT San Diego — March 30, 2015

"With Higher Incomes, Child Brains Expand in Areas Linked To Education — Researchers Say," Bradley J. Fikes

(The brains of higher income children who received more direct interactions from their parents or families were larger in several areas than the brains of lower income parents — with the study controlled for age, sex, and genetic ancestry.)

105. Columbia University Media Center — March 30, 2015

"How Poverty Shapes the Brain — A Study Co-Authored by Kimberly Noble Offers Powerful New Evidence"

(Increases in parent education and parent income are associated with increases in the surface areas for numerous brain regions in children. Relatively small differences in income levels for the lowest income children made the biggest relative difference in brain size.)

Three Key Months Are Also Times of Great and Early Opportunity for Each Child

BOTH BRAIN DEVELOPMENT and important emotional processes that are supported by the brain begin as soon as each baby is born. Those processes functionally begin immediately after birth.

There is no period of time when babies are not both affected and influenced by the world they have been born into. Direct experiences and the direct interactions that each child has with the world in the days and months immediately after each child is born can all have significant and relevant impact on both initial brain growth and on going emotional stability and security levels for each child.

Each child is born with the ability to discern very quickly whether the world around him or her is safe or unsafe. Immediately after being born, children cry. They are also hungry. They each discern very quickly and very directly how the world around them responds to their crying and to their hunger.

Each child reaches mental conclusions about the world they live in from the nature of the response to their crying. If the response they receive to their expressed concerns and to their perceived needs in those first days and weeks of life is to be picked up, cuddled, and comforted, and when they are hungry, if the response they experience is to be fed, then the child's brain tends to make the assumption that he or she has been born into a safe world.

However, if the child tends not to be picked up and if the child is not cuddled or fed when those needs are expressed, then the assumption is made from that information that this world might not be a safe and supportive place.

We now know from some fascinating research that those first days and weeks of life for each child actually are a time of great opportunity relative to giving a sense of security to our children. A number of studies have shown that the children who have a sense of security, and who perceive and experience responsive, comforting, and supportive interactions with their care givers at 3 months old, tend to have more positive interactions with other people at one year old, and even more positive interactions at 3 and 5 years old.

The key patterns of experience and reaction for each child can develop quickly. The assessment of the world happens immediately and it can have significant longer-range impact. Baby Rhesus monkeys who are given immediate support right after birth tend to be more secure and have better interactions with their peers at older points in their life than the less fortunate Rhesus infants who are isolated and not responded to at that point in their lives.

We have an increasing awareness of the fact that a significant opportunity exists at that point in time to create and build security levels for each infant by responding in positive ways to the needs of each infant in those very early days.

People used to believe that nothing external affected the personalities and the individual security levels of infants until the children were much older. Some theorists believed that it made sense to very deliberately and intentionally let babies cry without directly responding during those early points for fear of spoiling the baby, and encouraging more crying.

Actual research shows that those theories were incorrect. Spoiling a baby is not the result of responding to those needs in those early months of life.

In fact, the babies who have their needs met in those first weeks and months and who have positive interactions in those time periods with their mother or principal caregiver tend to cry less later, and often have more secure relationships with their caregivers at 1 and 3 years old. Spoiling the baby in some way by meeting their needs quickly and responsively in those first weeks and months does not seem to happen or be a problem.

Some remarkable research has video taped infant/mother interactions at 1 and 3 months old, and has shown that the positive interactions that can be seen between mothers and children at that point tend to have beneficial long-term impacts. Dr. Beatrice Beebe and her teams of researchers and therapists at New York State Psychiatric Institute and Columbia University have done some extremely useful research into those issues.

Their research has extended for years, and has been a great learning opportunity for us all. It has been echoed by research done at The University of Minnesota and at the University in Berkeley in California. The researchers in each of those settings looked at the impact of initial experiences on later capabilities and emotions of children.

Opportunities to Create Emotional Security Begin in the First Weeks and Months for Each Child

We now know that there are some extremely positive opportunities for helping the emotional stability levels of children that happen in those first weeks and months of life.

The observations are that the children who feel responded to when they express needs in those first weeks and months tend to do well as a result and often have a better sense of direct bonding with the adults in their lives.

Children who don't feel responded to — or who feel that they are triggering either invasive or negative responses from the adults in their world when they cry — tend to do less well in those areas.

That situation and process isn't complicated. It makes both logistical and logical sense. Immediately after being born, children send signals that they need adult responses. Their security levels tend to be higher when adults respond in positive ways, and their security levels tend to be lower when the signals sent by the babies are either ignored or generate negative responses.

Those patterns of response and reactions would seem to meet the expectations of both parenting instincts and common sense. As one child care leader often says, "It is very nicely affirming that the new science that we are building about child care so often reinforces common sense, and so often simply tells us intellectually to do what our hearts already told us to do in more direct ways."

Science, instincts, and our hearts in this case all say, listen to the baby in those early weeks and months and respond when the baby needs a response. Keep responding in comforting ways when the baby is unhappy, and give the baby space to orient him or herself to the world when the baby does not need us as adults to directly respond and interact.

The children at that very early age often do not respond with dependable and clearly positive patterns to the attempts of their parents to comfort them, and that set of seemingly unhappy responses by the child can be confusing and even frustrating for some parents. It is sometimes difficult or even impossible in the moment and in the situation for a parent to comfort a concerned and unhappy child — and that continuing unhappy reaction by the child can make the comforting process more difficult for the parents of the child.

We now know that the comforting process itself offers benefits to the child even though the benefits might not be apparent in that moment and in each specific interaction.

Parents need to know and understand that it is the right thing to do to continue to respond in comforting and loving ways to the needs of the child even when the child doesn't seem to be comforted by the response. We need to teach those interaction realities to all parents and build those responses and that understanding into both the practice and culture of parenting.

Each child is learning about the world they live in through the nature and context of those responses and continuing to comfort an angry or unhappy child tells that child that a key part of the world is on his or her side. That is a good message for all very young children in every setting to receive.

So we now know that the first three months of life can be key and useful times for creating emotional security in a child. They clearly are not the only times for parents to create that sense of both emotional and physical security for a child, but we now know that those first weeks and months can be high opportunity times for giving that support.

We Need Each Child to Get That Support in Those Key Weeks and Months from Someone

Usually, in the world and the society we are in, that opportunity to respond directly to the child in those first weeks and months comes from a parent — most often the mother of the child. The functional reality is that mothers tend to provide the overwhelming majority of direct contacts with children in those first weeks and months in almost all settings.

All mothers want their children to do well and to thrive. We have not done a consistently good job of supporting that process and explicitly helping mothers understand the full set of approaches that can be used by each mom in those first key months and years to help their children.

Very few mothers have been shown and taught the science about the opportunities to help thriving and success levels for their children that occur in the first weeks, months, and years of life.

That information about the importance of those direct interventions and interactions in those first weeks, months, and years of life for each child should be widely known by all relevant parties, and it should be used to help guide both parenting decisions and public policy thinking. We need every mother and every father to understand those processes and those opportunities even before their child is born.

As we look at various parenting leave options and at parental leave strategies for the mothers in our own society and communities, there clearly is solid evidence that having a parent who is able to be with a child in those first three months can have disproportionately useful and positive long term effects, and that those levels of direct and highly focused parenting in those time frames can trigger highly beneficial long term consequences for each child.

Those first weeks and months can actually have a functionally disproportionate impact on those particular levels of development for many children. Looking at mothers as the usual first level of parenting support, we now know that it can be very good and can create significant benefit and value for each child to have his or her mother able to be there to care for her child during those special parenting opportunities.

Nursing a baby creates its own set of related health and security benefits for the child and should also be encouraged and supported by us all.

That research about the importance of those first weeks and months also tells us that when the mother has work obligations or other functional or situational realities that keep her from those sets of interactions with her child in that period of time, then we should figure out other ways of having those direct interaction needs met by each child.

We need to figure out how to help each child. That opportunity exists one child at a time and how we deal with that opportunity has a direct impact on each child.

There are other options beyond mothers that can work to meet those needs for individual children. Fathers can fill that role. Other family members and friends can have those interactions with the infants as well.

Childcare support people can also do those interactions with a child.

Having fathers or other family members or any level of caregivers fill that role and fill that role well is more likely to be successful when we clearly define exactly what that actual function and role is for the caregiver in that high opportunity time frame.

Success by both mothers and fathers can be enhanced to at least some degree if the parents of a child have an explicit awareness of those issues and understand their relevance to their child and either provide that support themselves or arrange for someone else to do it for their child.

As with so many other areas of child-raising, knowledge is power. Knowledge is both enabling and empowering. Fathers, various other family members, and designated caregivers for the child are all more likely to meet those needs well in that time of high opportunity and high need for the child when the needs are understood and when the relevant support processes are clearly defined.

Whatever strategies we chose and whatever caregivers we use, we do need to help each child. We should be sure to have a plan in place for each child that has someone meeting those response needs in that important and very immediate time frame for each child.

Three key months creates a set of child support opportunities that deserve the same kinds of support we all need to give in the first three key years of life relative to the approaches that strengthen children's brains.

The *Three Key Years* book that this addendum is attached to explains the consequences of not exercising brains in those high-impact first three years, and also explains the massive opportunities that exist when we do provide that support for neuron connectivity in our children in those key years.

We need to support that three-year process of building stronger brains, and it would be a good thing to help make those first three year's activities and efforts even more successful by creating the right set of direct interaction-responses for each child in the first three months of life for each child.

The key for us as a nation today is to meet the needs for each child. We need families, parents, friends, caregivers, educators, and communities to be collectively and individually committed to meeting those needs for each individual child.

We want to build strong brains and have emotionally secure children, and we very much want to avoid having children suffer from toxic stress syndrome. We can do that by having the right sets of interactions with our children and by helping all children avoid both isolation and stress.

There is extensive research that shows very young children who feel constant isolation or stress are much more likely to suffer from toxic stress syndrome. Toxic stress syndrome damages brains and can create negative and dysfunctional patterns of behavior. Dr. Ross Thompson and his team of researchers at the University of California at Davis have shown us how we can keep that toxic stress syndrome from happening by providing positive direct support to every child.

We very much want to give each child the kinds of positive daily experiences that buffer each child against the toxic and damaging neurochemicals that create that syndrome.

We have a range of positive opportunities to help each child.

Every child we help has a different life as the result of being helped. Every child we save from a more difficult life is a child whose world is different in very positive ways because we provided that support.

That is extremely important and highly beneficial work to do. Both emotional security and stronger brains are worthwhile sets of benefits to create for our children. Both learning gaps and insecurity levels do not need to happen.

Let's save every child.

Let's save every child beginning with the time immediately after each child is born, and then continuing to support the education and learning processes for each child through all of the years when we can make life better for each child.

Three key months.

Three key years.

Let's not waste either one for any child.

Addendum Resources

The resources for this addendum include links and references to some of the relevant research that supports the sense of urgency and opportunity in those very early times of life for each child. The research into the very first months and years of life is robust and growing and teaches us increasingly important and useful information about the impacts of interventions and interactions with infants in those initial time frames for each child. People making public policy decisions about support for child raising, parenting, public health, and even public education should be aware that this research exists, and should be aware of the directions that it points.

Beebe, Beatrice, Ph.D. "My Journey in Infant Research and Psychoanalysis: Microanalysis, a Social Microscope." New York City, Routledge, 2014. Print.

Chehrazi, Shahla, M.D. Book Review of "The Origins of Attachment: Infant Research and Adult Treatment" by Beatrice Beebe, Ph.D. and Frank M. Lachmann, Ph.D." San Francisco Center for Psychoanalysis, December 30, 2014.

Romano, Judith T. "Early Brain and Child Development: Connections to Early Education and Child Care." ZERO TO THREE: National Center for Infants, Toddlers, and Families, September 2013.

"A Science-Based Framework for Early Childhood Policy; Using Evidence to Improve Outcomes in Learning, Behavior, and Health for Vulnerable Children." Center on the Developing Child, Harvard University, August 2007.

Thompson, Ross A. "Development in the First Years of Life." The Future of Children. Spring/Summer 2001.

Thompson, Ross A. "Stress and Child Development." The Future of Children. April 2014.

Made in the USA
Middletown, DE
13 April 2016